Dedicated to my beloved father, Ita Stephen.

I wish you were here to hold this book in your hands. I miss you more than words can express. Thank you for believing in me with unwavering faith and for always encouraging me to embrace my God-given purpose. Your love, wisdom, and support continue to guide me, even in your absence. You will forever be cherished in my heart and memories, Ete.

With all my love,

Your daughter

CONTENTS

INTRODUCTION

I was first introduced to emotional intelligence during what I thought was just another casual conversation with my father. Looking back now, I realize that moment was far from random. It was a pivotal, divinely orchestrated encounter designed by God to set me on a path toward growth, healing, and purpose.

We were sitting in the living room of our home in Nigeria, and my father was in his usual spot. Like in most Nigerian households, there was that one spot in the living room that was "Daddy's favorite." It wasn't a strict rule or anything; he just liked sitting there, and over time, everyone came to think of it as "Daddy's seat."

During our conversation, my father shared a story about two people he knew well from his childhood who ended up with very different paths in life. One attended a public university in Nigeria, while the other had the opportunity to study abroad at a prestigious Ivy League school. The one who stayed in Nigeria wasn't necessarily the smartest in his class, but he was known for his wisdom, strong character, and exceptional social skills. On the other hand, the one who studied abroad was highly intelligent, but he lacked self-awareness and empathy and struggled with interpersonal relationships.

After graduating, both began their careers. The one from Nigeria thrived, building strong relationships and excelling in his role. His success eventually led to a high-ranking promotion that required him to relocate abroad and pursue his master's at a prestigious institution in the U.S. Meanwhile, the one who had studied at the prestigious Ivy League school struggled to keep a job. His poor character and lack of people skills led to him being fired from several positions, ultimately forcing him to move back to his hometown and start over.

"Two people. One had better opportunities and what seemed to be a brighter future to many. Yet, the other ended up with a more favorable outcome. Why do you think that is?" my father asked me.

I sat there, pondering his question, eager to hear his profound insight. Then he simply said, "Emotional intelligence." It was the first time I had encountered the term "emotional intelligence."

"Emotional intelligence, or EQ," my father explained. "While the world often emphasizes IQ, there will be times in your life when your EQ will carry you further than your IQ ever could."

I reflected deeply on my father's words. I was already very familiar with Intelligence Quotient (IQ). In fact, my sisters and I would often test our IQs just to see how we measured up to the likes of Albert Einstein. I've always enjoyed being perceived as intelligent, but I had never given much thought to emotional intelligence (EQ), nor had I considered my own level of it.

At the time, I was struggling to build and maintain healthy relationships, both at school and church, because I was ruled by my emotions. I would say and do things purely based on how I felt in the moment, with little patience to untangle those feelings and understand what was really going on inside me. On top of that, I was entangled in a very unhealthy friendship that left me emotionally drained. I found myself becoming more insecure, anxious, and easily irritated. My boundaries were as non-existent as the plot in a bad Nollywood movie.

I was a serial people-pleaser with little control over my emotions. The more I reflected, the clearer it became—I had very little emotional intelligence. I'm naturally a sensitive person, and God created me with the ability to feel things deeply. I tend to dig to the root of situations and address issues head-on, but I didn't know how to steward this gift of emotions in a way that would yield positive results. Instead of building up, my emotions often caused damage and tore things down. I realized I needed to develop my emotional intelligence.

With a desire to become a healthier person, I committed myself to learning everything I could about emotional intelligence. I watched countless YouTube videos and TED Talks. It became a daily routine, almost like an after-school program or night job I had created for myself. There was one YouTuber I followed religiously, and I considered him my personal development coach. I would even send him emails, and he would respond. I read Daniel Goleman's "Emotional Intelligence" and devoured other self-help books.

I became fixated on the idea of self-actualization. I wanted to unlock my fullest potential. Determined to master emotional intelligence, I was done being bullied by my own mind and emotions. I was eager to step into 'Ekemini 2.0' and see who I could become.

As I continued my journey toward mastering emotional intelligence, something unexpected happened. Despite all the effort I put into learning, growing, and self-reflecting, I still didn't feel fulfilled in my relationships or my personal growth. No matter how much I learned, it always felt like there was more to uncover, more to perfect. It was exhausting. The pressure I placed on myself to become this "better" person—compassionate yet firm, kind but not a people-pleaser, loving but with boundaries—started to weigh heavily on me.

At times, it felt like I was running in circles, chasing an ideal version of myself that I could never quite reach. And the harder I worked, the further behind I felt. Slowly, what had once been a genuine desire to grow became something toxic. It was as if the more I tried to "improve" myself, the more self-absorbed I became. Without realizing it, I had placed myself at the center of everything, becoming almost selfish with who I was becoming.

That's when it hit me: the missing piece in my emotional intelligence journey was Jesus. I couldn't become a better person on my own, no matter how hard I tried. I needed His help, His guidance. Emotional intelligence was important, but I realized that true growth and healing required more than just self-awareness—it required surrender. Only through Jesus could I learn to love deeply, set healthy boundaries, and live in community rather than isolation. I realized that as much as we lean on self-help, what we truly need is 'God-help.' After all, how can the self truly help itself when it's the very thing in need of help?

When I invited Jesus into my personal development journey, everything began to change. I stopped striving to do better and be better on my own. Instead, I turned to scripture, and through the Holy Spirit, I began to see emotional intelligence and personal development through a biblical lens. I discovered that emotional intelligence is not just a modern concept but one deeply reflected in biblical principles. Slowly but surely, I began to see the fruit of aligning my growth with His guidance.

My relationships transformed as I learned to communicate with intentionality, navigate conflict with grace, and forgive more freely. I began to set healthy boundaries—not out of fear or guilt, but from a place of emotional balance and stability. I was no longer ruled by my emotions but started stewarding them in ways that honored God and reflected His heart.

I discovered that when emotional intelligence is rooted in faith, it has the power to reshape every aspect of life. As I surrendered to God, the relentless pressure to 'fix myself' began to fade, replaced by a deep sense of peace and purpose. I found freedom in knowing I didn't have to navigate this journey alone.

But here's the thing: Jesus is still the missing piece in so many people's emotional intelligence journeys. Looking around, I noticed how our world has become obsessed with self-help. We devour countless books, binge motivational talks, and relentlessly pursue the elusive goal of "unlocking our full potential." Yet, despite all this, we're experiencing record levels of loneliness, broken relationships, depression, and selfishness. Why? Because too many are still trying to navigate personal growth on their own. They're striving for transformation while neglecting the gift of God's grace, turning self-improvement into a burden of perfectionism rather than a journey of sanctification.

Many have dismissed the Bible, treating it as merely a historical text instead of the living, active, and illuminating Word of God—a manual for life that guides us, makes our paths straight, and grants us the wisdom to navigate every facet of our lives. We live in a culture that celebrates expressive individualism, where the self is exalted above all else. We've become so focused on personal growth that we've lost sight of the beauty of community and human connection. Self-help has become solely focused on self, creating a culture of isolated growth that denies the truth: real transformation is as much communal as it is personal.

The more I observed, the more I saw how we've misused powerful concepts. We've normalized "cutting people off" the moment they no longer serve us, mistaking personal discomfort for toxicity. The word "toxic" itself has become overused, slapped onto anything or anyone that triggers or challenges us. Even the idea of boundaries, which should protect and preserve relationships, has sometimes been twisted into a tool for isolation. It's as if we've been given the tools for growth but refuse to read the Creator's manual, fumbling through life without the instructions we so desperately need.

In our pursuit of self-actualization, we've overlooked a fundamental truth: we need God for true personal growth. No amount of self-help can replace the transformative power of His guidance. We strive to become better versions of ourselves, yet without Him, all our efforts leave us empty, exhausted, and unfulfilled. It is only through God that we can achieve the wholeness we seek, not only in our personal development but also in our relationships. He helps us cultivate deeper, healthier connections with others because it's His help—not self-help—that brings lasting growth, fulfillment, and the ability to love others well.

This is where my inspiration for writing this book came from. The purpose of this book is to bridge the gap between faith—our relationship with God—and personal development. When our spiritual growth aligns with our personal development journey, it becomes a powerful reflection of our sanctification process. Your growth in emotional intelligence is more connected to your sanctification than you may realize.

In this book, we'll explore the concept of emotional intelligence through the lens of faith, examining our emotions in a way that aligns with God's Word. We'll discuss the role emotions play in our lives and how growing in self-awareness and emotional maturity can help us become a clearer reflection of Jesus Christ. Some people subtly deny their own emotions—and the emotions of others—becoming detached from them. On the other end, some are so consumed by their emotions that their entire world and life decisions are driven by them. This book is designed to help you find balance: to steward your emotions in a way that honors God, using them for all He intended while learning to manage them rather than being controlled by them.

You'll learn how to grow in emotional intelligence, strengthen your relationships, and ultimately improve the quality of your life. But this is not just another self-help book. I've included exercises, activities, and reflection questions throughout, each carefully designed to help you integrate what you're learning into your daily life and personal growth journey. I encourage you to pair this book with a designated journal—a space where you can reflect, jot down your observations, and engage deeply with the exercises. Let it become your personal roadmap for growth, a tangible record of your progress and transformation.

Before diving in, I encourage you to pause and pray. Ask the Lord to open your eyes and give you deeper insight into how this book applies to your daily walk with Him and your relationships. Invite Him to refine your understanding of emotions and reveal how they reflect His image. Ask Him to prepare your heart for the work He desires to do in you as you journey through this book.

Don't just skim through these pages—immerse yourself in them. Sit with each chapter. Engage with the questions. This book will challenge you to confront difficult emotions and face hard truths. It will likely require a deeper level of vulnerability, pushing you to rethink how you approach situations and relationships in your life. At times, you might feel like it's reading you more than you're reading it. You'll laugh, you might cry, and you'll definitely find yourself thinking profoundly.

Are you ready to live a transformed life? Let's begin!

PART I

01

WHAT IS EMOTIONAL INTELLIGENCE?

Imagine you're in the middle of a heated conversation. Tensions are rising. Your emotions are swirling. It feels like there's an anvil lodged in your throat, tightening it and making it hard to speak. Your eyes sting with unshed tears, and your heart is racing. You feel that familiar urge to either explode or shut down. It's the response you tend to fall back on in moments like these.

Many of us give in to that temptation, letting the wave of emotion dictate our response. But now, imagine something different happens: you pause. You take a deep breath, feeling the tension release, even if just a little. You reflect on how you're feeling and choose your next words carefully. In that moment, instead of reacting, you choose to respond. That moment of self-awareness—that pause before action—that's emotional intelligence at work.

Now, picture another scenario: you do react, and the situation escalates. Later, during personal reflection, you realize you overreacted—you let your emotions take control, and the conversation spiraled out of hand. But instead of burying the frustration or pointing fingers, you dig deeper to understand what truly triggered you, why you reacted the way you did, and how you could have communicated better. You then make the intentional decision to reach out, take responsibility for your part, and revisit the conversation. This, too, is emotional intelligence: the ability to own your actions, seek reconciliation, and resist the urge to hold grudges or assign blame.

So, what exactly is emotional intelligence? According to Google AI, "emotional intelligence (EI) is the ability to recognize, understand, and manage your own emotions, as well as the emotions of others." It's also known as emotional quotient (EQ), and I'll be using these terms interchangeably throughout this book. Emotional intelligence is a set of skills critical for successful relationships, effective communication, and overall well-being.

The concept of emotional intelligence was popularized by psychologist Daniel Goleman, who emphasized its importance in both personal and professional success. Goleman's research helped frame emotional intelligence around key skills that can be organized into four fundamental pillars, which provide a comprehensive understanding of how we navigate both our inner emotions and our external relationships.

Now, let's dive deeper into each of these pillars to explore how they shape the core of emotional intelligence and impact our lives.

The Four Pillars of Emotional Intelligence

The four pillars of emotional intelligence, as outlined in emotional intelligence theory and particularly in the work of Daniel Goleman, are:

1. Self-awareness

2. Self-management

3. Social Awareness

4. Relationship Management

These pillars provide a comprehensive understanding of emotional intelligence. The first two pillars, self-awareness and self-management, relate to the first half of emotional intelligence: the ability to recognize, understand, and manage your own emotions. The remaining two pillars—social awareness and relationship management—focus on the second half of the equation: the ability to recognize, understand, and effectively navigate the emotions of others, ultimately fostering healthy and meaningful relationships.

Self-Awareness

Self-awareness is the ability to recognize and understand your own emotions, moods, and drives and how they influence your thoughts and behavior. It also involves being aware of your strengths, weaknesses, values, and the impact your emotions have on others. This awareness allows for accurate self-assessment—you become more attuned to your abilities and limitations. By understanding your emotional tendencies, defense mechanisms, and personal patterns, you can make more informed decisions about how to navigate challenges.

Self-awareness also boosts self-confidence because confidence stems from having an honest understanding of what you're good at and where you need improvement. It requires a willingness to be truthful with yourself about your behavior and actions. This honesty is essential for growth and development.

Self-awareness is crucial because it sets the foundation for how we process emotions and respond to challenges. It gives us the ability to pause and reflect before reacting. Instead of making emotional, knee-jerk reactions, self-awareness allows you to assess situations with greater clarity and make conscious, intentional decisions.

For example, I know that when I'm stressed, I tend to become overly critical and negative. If I've had a long, stressful day, I may come home and start nitpicking, pointing out everything that's wrong or out of place, and directing that frustration toward my husband. Because I'm self-aware, I can recognize this emotional tendency. I'm able to realize that my irritation isn't actually about my husband—it's about my own tiredness and stress. Instead of falling into a critical mode, I might say something like, "I realize I'm being overly critical. I'm sorry, babe, you don't deserve that. It's not you—I've just had a stressful day. I think I need some rest, and we can spend time together later."

Being self-aware helps prevent emotional outbursts, misunderstandings, and misdirected frustration in relationships. It ensures that you respond to situations with clarity rather than reacting impulsively based on how you feel in the moment.

Self-Management

Self-management is the ability to regulate and control your emotions, especially in stressful or challenging situations. It's about maintaining control over your impulses, thinking before acting, and managing your emotional reactions in a constructive way. Self-management involves delaying gratification and staying focused, even when emotions are running high. It enables you to adjust your emotional responses when things don't go as planned, ensuring that your actions align with your values.

One key aspect of self-management is trustworthiness—not just in terms of how others can trust you, but how you can trust yourself. We often think about trust in relation to others, but it's equally important that we can rely on ourselves. Can you trust yourself to respond to a situation in a way that aligns with your moral values and principles rather than acting impulsively in a way that shows a lack of self-control? Self-management ensures that you can handle your emotions in a way that upholds your integrity.

Managing your emotions also helps protect your relationships. It allows you to handle feelings like anger, frustration, or anxiety in a way that prevents unnecessary damage. When you manage your emotions, you're better equipped to resolve conflicts, maintain harmony, and stop small disagreements from turning into major conflicts. Self-management ensures a peaceful and respectful atmosphere, even under emotional pressure.

Sometimes, managing your emotions means knowing when to walk away from a situation, take a break, or simply remain quiet to avoid saying something you might regret. For example, let's say you're in a heated argument with your sibling. The conversation is escalating, and you feel yourself getting angry. Instead of shouting or saying something hurtful that you can't take back, you pause, take a deep breath, and suggest, "Let's take a break and come back to this when we're calmer." By managing your anger, you prevent the argument from escalating and avoid saying something you might later regret.

As Christians, we're also called to cultivate self-control, which Galatians 5:22-23 identifies as one of the fruits of the Spirit. God has given us the ability to grow in this area, and He calls us to steward our emotions wisely. Self-management isn't just a skill; it's a spiritual practice. Learning to control our emotions and align our actions with God's Word allows us to reflect His character in our relationships and daily interactions.

Social Awareness

Social awareness is the ability to recognize and understand the emotions of others, as well as the dynamics within a group or environment. It includes empathy—the ability to sense what others are feeling—and organizational awareness, which involves understanding social and relational dynamics. Social awareness helps you be emotionally attuned to the people around you, allowing you to respond with kindness, support, and love when needed, thus deepening your relationships.

At its core, social awareness is about putting yourself in someone else's shoes and understanding their emotional experience without judgment. It's about intentionally considering the feelings of others, just as you'd want them to consider yours. One key aspect of social awareness is service orientation—caring for others and being attentive to their emotional and practical needs.

For example, as an extrovert, I naturally enjoy socializing in large gatherings, but I'm also mindful of those who seem withdrawn or uncomfortable. I often notice that one person sticking to the wall or feeling out of place, and I make an effort to engage them in conversation. It's not about interrupting their quiet but about making them feel seen and cared for, recognizing that they may be anxious or shy. This is social awareness in action—helping someone feel included by recognizing their emotional state.

Social awareness also involves recognizing subtle emotional changes in your relationships. Let's say you're visiting your parents, and you notice your mom is unusually quiet and withdrawn. Instead of ignoring it, you ask, "You seem a bit off today. Is everything okay?" She might reveal she's feeling lonely because you haven't visited as much. By showing empathy and offering reassurance, such as planning more frequent visits, you strengthen your bond and foster a deeper emotional connection.

Social awareness challenges us to love others as ourselves. It allows us to look beyond the surface and engage with others' emotional experiences in a compassionate and meaningful way.

Relationship Management

Relationship management is the fourth pillar of emotional intelligence. It's the ability to build and maintain healthy, positive relationships with others. This involves clear communication, effective conflict resolution, collaboration, and the ability to inspire and influence others. A key aspect of relationship management is using emotional awareness to motivate people and connect with them on a deeper level.

Every relationship—whether personal or professional—will encounter disagreements or friction at some point. This is natural, as we all come from different backgrounds, have unique experiences, and hold varying values. Learning how to resolve conflicts and manage relationships is essential to sustaining meaningful connections.

For example, imagine a couple, Paul and Valerie, who often argue about how to spend their free time. Paul enjoys socializing with friends, while Valerie prefers quiet nights at home. Instead of letting the conflict fester, Paul decides to use relationship management skills to address the issue. He listens to Valerie's concerns and shares his own feelings. Together, they come up with a compromise—setting aside certain nights for socializing and others for quality time at home. By remaining calm, empathetic, and solution-focused, Paul is able to strengthen their relationship rather than letting disagreements drive them apart.

Managing relationships also means being attuned to emotional dynamics and recognizing when emotional support is needed. A great example of how *not* to offer emotional support can be found in the story of Job from the Bible. After Job lost his children, his wealth, and his health, his friends came to comfort him. At first, they did something wise—they sat with him in silence for seven days, which was a great start. But then, they couldn't help themselves; they started talking, and that's where things went wrong. One of his friends, Eliphaz, even suggested that Job must have done something wrong to deserve his suffering (Job 4:7-8). Talk about missing the mark! Instead of offering comfort, they ended up blaming him and completely failed to recognize his emotional needs.

Job's friends had good intentions but lacked the emotional and spiritual awareness that effective relationship management requires. They thought they were helping by offering explanations and advice, but what Job really needed was empathy, not judgment. The lesson here is that relationship management involves knowing when to offer a listening ear and when to simply be present. In other words, don't be an Eliphaz—when someone's hurting, sometimes silence is the best support.

Relationship management is the culmination of the other three pillars—self-awareness, self-management, and social awareness—because it relies on understanding both your own emotions and the emotions of others. It's key to ensuring that relationships remain healthy, respectful, and balanced, even in the face of conflict.

Understanding Your EQ Level

Now that we've explored emotional intelligence and the four pillars in detail, it's time to reflect on where you stand in your own EQ journey. Understanding these pillars is just the first step; the next is assessing your strengths and identifying areas for growth. Emotional intelligence isn't about being perfect in every pillar. Some people naturally excel in certain areas while needing to develop in others. For instance, you might be highly self-aware, easily recognizing your emotional triggers, but struggle with self-management when it comes to controlling impulses in stressful situations. It's also possible that you may be empathetic and socially aware, yet you find it challenging to manage conflict and maintain relationships.

Taking the time to assess where you fall on the spectrum of high EQ versus low EQ is crucial for personal growth. Below are some key signs that can help you determine whether you exhibit low or high emotional intelligence and guide you toward improving your EQ:

1. **Empathy:**

   Do you find it difficult to understand or share the feelings of others? Struggling to empathize and coming across as indifferent is a sign of low EQ. High EQ individuals, on the other hand, can easily put themselves in someone else's shoes, offering genuine support and care.

2. **Managing Anger and Emotional Outbursts:**

   Do you struggle to control your anger or often have emotional outbursts? Difficulty managing these emotions is a sign of low

EQ. High EQ individuals recognize their triggers, stay composed, and respond thoughtfully, even in challenging situations.

3. **Taking Responsibility:**

Do you tend to blame others for your problems instead of taking accountability? Shifting blame suggests low EQ. High EQ individuals take ownership of their actions and work toward solutions rather than avoiding responsibility.

4. **Expressing Emotions Clearly:**

Do you have trouble expressing your emotions, leading to confusion in your relationships? Low EQ individuals often struggle to articulate their feelings, while those with high EQ communicate their emotions clearly and appropriately, fostering better understanding.

5. **Forgiving and Letting Go:**

Do you find it hard to forgive yourself for past mistakes or let go of resentment toward others? Holding onto grudges is a sign of low EQ. High EQ individuals practice forgiveness and let go of bitterness to maintain healthy, positive relationships.

6. **Asserting Yourself Effectively:**

Do you have trouble standing up for yourself, leading to resentment or being taken advantage of? Low EQ individuals may struggle with assertiveness, while those with high EQ express their needs respectfully and confidently without causing unnecessary conflict.

7. **Recognizing Emotional Triggers:**

Are you unaware of what triggers your emotions, leading to unpredictable reactions? Low EQ individuals often don't recognize their triggers, whereas high EQ individuals have a keen awareness of their emotional responses and manage them proactively.

8. **Balancing Emotions with Reason:**

Do you let your emotions dictate your actions without reflection? Acting impulsively based on emotions indicates low EQ. High EQ individuals balance their emotional responses with rational thought, resulting in more measured and thoughtful decisions.

9. **Resilience to Offense:**

Do you get offended easily and find it hard to move past minor slights? Being easily offended is a sign of low EQ. High EQ individuals are more resilient and capable of processing and moving past minor offenses without holding onto negativity.

10. **Toxic Relationships:**

Do you often find yourself in unhealthy or damaging relationships? If so, this could be a sign of low EQ. High EQ individuals are more adept at recognizing red flags and setting boundaries, ensuring healthier connections.

11. **Engaging in Bullying or Aggressive Behavior:**

Are you a bully, or do you engage in aggressive behavior to get what you want? This is a sign of low EQ. High EQ individuals foster positive relationships through empathy and understanding rather than intimidation or control.

12. **Feeling Needy or Insecure in Relationships:**

Do you frequently feel needy or insecure or find yourself gossiping to feel connected? If so, this could indicate low EQ. High EQ individuals are secure in themselves and their relationships, communicating openly without the constant need for validation.

These are some of the key signs that can help you determine whether you or someone else may have high or low emotional intelligence. By recognizing these patterns, you can begin to assess where you stand and identify areas for growth. Take time to reflect on your behaviors and emotional responses in various situations to get a clearer picture of your current EQ level.

Remember, emotional intelligence is not a fixed trait; it's something that can be developed and strengthened over time with intentional practice and self-awareness. The more you invest in understanding and improving your EQ, the more equipped you'll be to handle your emotions, build healthier relationships, and navigate life's challenges with grace and wisdom.

How to Improve Your EQ

While this entire book explores many ways to enhance your emotional intelligence, this section focuses on some specific, practical steps you can take to consciously and intentionally work on improving your EQ. Here are some actionable strategies to help you further develop your emotional intelligence:

1. **Spending Time in God's Word:**

   The most crucial way to grow in emotional intelligence as a Christian is by spending time in God's Word and in His presence. Scripture provides the foundation for understanding and managing your emotions, while prayer allows the Holy Spirit to guide and refine you. As you immerse yourself in His truth, God renews your heart and mind, enabling you to align your emotions with His will. Let His Word wash over you, transforming your reactions and responses to reflect Christ's character in all areas of life.

2. **Practice Active Listening:**

   Focus fully on the speaker, avoid interrupting, and show that you're listening by reflecting back what you've heard. Active listening deepens your connection with others and helps you better understand their emotions.

3. **Pause Before Reacting:**

   In emotionally charged situations, take a moment to breathe and reflect before responding. This allows you to manage your impulses and respond thoughtfully rather than react out of emotion.

4. **Journal Your Emotions:**

   Writing down what you're feeling and why helps you reflect on emotional patterns and triggers. Journaling can also help you expand your emotional vocabulary, which is crucial for understanding and expressing your emotions more accurately. This will allow you to better manage your emotional responses in different situations. We'll dive deeper into expanding your emotional vocabulary in Chapter 2.

5. **Acknowledge Your Emotional Triggers:**

   Identify situations or interactions that often lead to strong emotional reactions. By recognizing these triggers, you can work on managing your responses and preventing emotional outbursts.

6. **Practice Empathy:**

   Put yourself in someone else's shoes to better understand their perspective and emotions. Empathy helps you connect with others on a deeper level and builds stronger, more meaningful relationships.

7. **Communicate Clearly and Assertively:**

   Express your feelings and needs openly while remaining respectful and considerate of others. Clear communication helps avoid misunderstandings and fosters healthier relationships.

8. **Improve Conflict Resolution Skills:**

   Approach disagreements with a problem-solving mindset, focusing on finding solutions rather than winning arguments. Healthy conflict resolution strengthens relationships and prevents unnecessary strife.

9. **Take Responsibility for Your Emotions:**

   Own your feelings and reactions instead of blaming others for how you feel. Taking responsibility fosters emotional maturity and helps you grow in self-management.

10. **Set Healthy Boundaries:**

    Learn to establish and communicate healthy boundaries to protect your emotional well-being. Boundaries are not just about keeping people out; they're about creating a space where you can show up authentically as yourself, giving others the opportunity to know you better. This helps develop deeper connections in relationships and fosters mutual respect.

11. **Educate Yourself on EQ:**

    One effective way to improve your emotional intelligence is by immersing yourself in learning. Read books (like this one), attend workshops, seminars, and conferences, or listen to podcasts that focus on emotional intelligence. The more you educate yourself, the better equipped you'll be to grow in your understanding and application of EQ.

12. **Consider Personal Development Coaching:**

Another practical step is to invest in a personal development coach. A coach can provide tailored guidance and feedback, helping you identify areas of growth and offering personalized strategies for improving your emotional intelligence. This one-on-one support can be a powerful tool in accelerating your EQ development.

Remember, it's not about striving for perfection or getting everything right all the time—it's about growth. And growth takes time. It's not always a straight path. Some days, you'll get it right, and other days, you might slip back into old patterns. But don't forget—you're not doing this alone. God is with you, refining you from the inside out. All you need to do is surrender and trust Him to bring emotional healing and fulfillment into your life.

By reading this book, you've already taken an important step toward improving your emotional intelligence. The fact that you're here shows that the desire to grow is alive in you, and that means you're already on the journey. Keep going, knowing that God is walking alongside you as you grow and transform.

REFLECTION QUESTIONS

1. What are your top 3 strengths and top 3 weaknesses? Now, ask someone who knows you well what they think your top strengths and weaknesses are. Reflect on the similarities or differences.

2. How would you rank the four pillars of emotional intelligence from your strongest to weakest? Why did you rank them that way?

3. Which pillar of emotional intelligence would you like to improve, and what practical steps can you take this week to work on it?

4. Who is someone you think has high emotional intelligence? Why do they come to mind?

5. Where do you think you stand based on the signs of high and low emotional intelligence? Why do you think you're at that level?

6. Think of a recent situation where you let your emotions dictate your actions. How could self-awareness or self-management have changed the outcome?

7. How do you typically handle conflict in your relationships? Reflect on whether you tend to avoid it, confront it directly, or try to resolve it. How can you improve your approach using what you've learned about emotional intelligence?

8. Consider a time when someone hurt or offended you. Did you hold a grudge, or were you able to forgive? What could relationship management look like in that situation moving forward?

9. How do you usually offer emotional support to others? Do you listen actively, or do you tend to offer advice and solutions? Based on the example of Job, how can you improve your ability to be present for others emotionally?

10. What is one area in your life where you struggle with self-management? How can you start practicing more self-control in that specific area?

02

UNDERSTANDING EMOTIONS

magine this: You've recently started a new job, and though you're doing your best to fight off imposter syndrome, the doubts keep creeping in. You tell yourself, "I'm here because I'm qualified. I deserve to be here." But the uncertainty lingers. Then, out of the blue, you get an email from your supervisor with a subject line that reads, "Quick one-on-one? Need to go over some things." Your heart skips a beat. Immediately, your stomach twists into knots, and you get that familiar sensation like you might need to make a quick trip to the bathroom. Your mind begins to race: "Am I in trouble? Did I make a mistake? Are they going to fire me?"

Pause for a moment. What emotions started to surface? Did your heart race? Did your stomach drop? Could you feel the anxiety rising? Were you able to properly identify the emotion that rushed through your body?

Now, let's switch gears. Picture this: You and your girls—your closest friends—have finally managed to coordinate a much-needed girls' night. It's been forever since you've all come together because, let's face it, adulting is hard, and matching schedules feels like solving a Rubik's cube blindfolded. But here you are, all gathered in your cozy living room. The air smells like your favorite snacks from DoorDash, there's a stack of face masks on the coffee table, and everyone's laughing— loudly, unapologetically, not caring what they sound like because it's *you guys*. It feels like no time has passed, even though it's been months. You're catching up on everything, from who's been dating who to embarrassing work stories. Between the laughter and the snacks, someone says, "I've missed this. I've missed *us*," and you feel a wave of warmth wash over you.

Now, pause again. As you imagine sitting in the middle of the love and laughter, taking it all in, what emotions rise up? Joy? Gratitude? Contentment? Did you feel your heart swell just thinking about it? What does this moment of reconnection make you feel?

Lastly, picture this: You're at your friend's engagement. Her boyfriend is down on one knee, and she's beaming with joy. Everyone's clapping and cheering, and you're right there in the middle of it, clapping along and smiling, genuinely happy for her. But as you watch, a small thought creeps in: *"This is the 10th engagement I've been to, and I'm still just trying to make it past a successful first date."* You try to brush it off, reminding yourself that your time will come, but the emotions are complicated. Joy for your friend and a longing for yourself—all tangled together. You try to stay present, celebrating her big moment, but you can't help but feel that little tug inside. You're truly happy for her, but you also wonder, *"When will it be my turn?"*

Pause one last time. What emotions are surfacing here? Can you feel the blend of feelings—joy for your friend alongside a pang of longing and perhaps a touch of yearning for yourself? How does it feel to hold both emotions at once, intertwined like this?

Now, take a moment and reflect: How did these scenarios make you feel as you read them? Did you notice a shift in your emotions with each one? Were you able to put a name to the emotions that surfaced—was it frustration, joy, envy, or hurt? Could you clearly identify what you were feeling, or was it a jumble of sensations that were difficult to label?

This is the journey of emotions. Every day, we are met with countless scenarios that stir up a wide range of feelings—some clear, some confusing. Emotions are complex, layered, and deeply woven into the fabric of our lives. But how often do we take the time to truly understand what we're feeling? How often do we pause to accurately label those emotions and explore what's happening inside us?

Emotions are not only a fundamental part of being human, but they are also powerful indicators of what's happening beneath the surface. In this chapter, we'll begin to unpack the nature of emotions, explore what they mean, and dive deeper into understanding how they shape our lives. We'll also take a closer look at how to expand your emotional vocabulary, giving you the tools to better identify, express, and process the full range of emotions you experience. But before we go any further, let's start with a simple question: *What exactly are emotions?*

Emotions are complex internal experiences that arise in response to the situations, interactions, and thoughts we encounter in daily life. They're not just fleeting feelings—they're signals from our mind and body, guiding us toward deeper understanding, meaningful connections, and purposeful action. Philosopher and YouTuber Leo Gura describes emotions as a "matrix of feelings in your body, a rich, complex matrix." For example, take anger. What is anger? It's more than just a word. It's a label we assign to a collection of sensations in our body and mind—a rush of heat, a racing heart, tension, frustration. Emotions, in their complexity, give language to what we feel deep within.

Think of your emotions like a compass. Just as a compass points you toward your true north, your emotions guide you toward areas in your life that need attention. They aren't just random waves of feelings; they're intentional signals pointing to places that need to be addressed, processed, or understood. Whether it's joy, frustration, sorrow, or excitement, each emotion is a guidepost directing you toward deeper insight and healing. Emotions are the language of the mind and body. They're always telling you something. Ignoring them or avoiding them is like ignoring a compass in the wilderness—you lose your way.

I remember once having a casual conversation with one of my good friends. She was talking about her week when, almost offhandedly, she mentioned that one of our mutual friends had forgotten to wish her a happy birthday. She brushed it off quickly, shifting the conversation back to whatever we'd been discussing before, but I could feel the weight of her words linger. I knew she was hurt, even though she was trying to downplay it.

I stopped her. "How did that make you feel?" I asked gently. She shrugged it off, insisting it didn't matter. But I could tell it did. "It does matter," I said. "Otherwise, you wouldn't have brought it up." I could see the hesitation in her eyes, as though she felt silly for even caring. To her, it was a 'small issue,' something not worth getting upset over. But I explained that it wasn't a small issue if it was affecting her and if it was starting to impact how she showed up in that relationship.

She had been avoiding that friend ever since because interacting with them reminded her of the hurt she felt. But here's the thing—her emotion was acting like a compass, signaling that something needed attention. She was hurt by not being celebrated by someone she cared about, and rather than dealing with it, she was running from it. Eventually, she talked to her friend about it, and it turned out that the friend had genuinely forgotten. Her friend apologized and made it up to her, and their relationship returned to being strong and healthy.

Now, if my friend hadn't processed that feeling, it would have eventually morphed into something bigger and deeper over time. And here's where it gets dangerous: the more we run from our emotions, the bigger and more uncontrollable they become. When left unaddressed, they take the wheel, influencing our behavior in ways we can't always control. This can lead to tension, misunderstandings, and distance in our relationships, creating rifts that wouldn't have existed if we had just taken the time to confront and process those emotions. It's a dangerous cycle because when our emotions are in control, we lose the ability to respond with clarity and grace, and the relationships we value most suffer as a result.

Some of us don't just avoid our emotions—we go to great lengths to distract ourselves from feeling them altogether. And while it might seem easier in the moment, it's incredibly unhealthy. I've been there. I remember vividly a time in my life when I did everything to escape my emotions—everything to avoid the weight of confronting them.

When my father passed away, something strange happened inside me. I felt a flood of emotions—overwhelming, heavy feelings I had never experienced before. The weight of grief, loss, and heartbreak was so intense, and truthfully, I was scared to confront it. I was terrified of what might burst out of me if I even tried to open that emotional door.

So, I distracted myself. But here's the shocking part: my distraction wasn't something "typical" like binge-watching Netflix or shopping. No. I threw myself into ministry. I poured myself into serving on the prayer team, leading small groups, offering encouragement through my podcast, and counseling people in the inner healing and deliverance ministry. I was doing all these good things, almost as if my good works were what would heal me or make me whole. I was doing things *for* God, but I was running *from* God Himself—running from the one thing I truly needed to do: feel.

Every night after a long day of ministry, I would return to my room, and there it was—this undeniable, tangible weight of God's presence. I could feel Him there, waiting for me, silently asking me to bring my pain to Him. But I ignored it. It felt like the proverbial "elephant in the room"—me, God, and this enormous weight of unprocessed grief between us. And I chose, every night, to avoid it. I would go straight to bed, pushing the emotions down as far as I could, convincing myself that sleeping would make them disappear.

One night, after repeating this cycle, I heard God speak to me in the quiet of my room. "You're disappointed in me," He said.

I was stunned. Disappointed? Me? I immediately denied it. "No, Lord! I could never be disappointed in You. You're a good God! How could I even think such a thing?"

But God wasn't fooled. He pressed again, gently but firmly: "You're disappointed in me. It's okay. I can handle it. Bring your disappointment to me, and let me heal you."

In that moment, my heart broke wide open. The words sank into me, and all the emotions I had been pushing down came rushing to the surface. I started shaking, and before I knew it, I was crying uncontrollably, pouring out everything I had been holding in:

"Yes, Lord. I am disappointed. I don't understand. Why did You take my dad away? I'm heartbroken. Why now? Why him? I didn't even get to make it up to him for all the ways he loved, supported, and provided for me. I wanted him to see me succeed. I wanted him to walk me down the aisle. I wanted him to meet my future husband and hold my children. This feels so unfair, Lord. Why?"

This was the first time I had truly let those feelings come to the surface, and it was in God's presence that I found the courage to do so. In that moment, God reminded me of something so important: He's not afraid of my emotions. He's not overwhelmed by my grief. He cares for me deeply. He wired me to feel, to go through life with emotions, and He can heal and redeem every single one of them.

How merciful is our God? He named the very emotion I couldn't put into words—disappointment. In acknowledging it and pouring it out before Him, I was finally able to start healing. It didn't happen overnight, but day by day, I felt lighter. I experienced God as "Jehovah Nacham," my Comforter, in a way I never had before. If I hadn't gone through that grief, I never would have known God in this deeper dimension.

If I had kept distracting myself and dodging my emotions, avoiding them at all costs, that disappointment would have grown, becoming heavier and harder to bear. It would have seeped into every area of my life, shaping how I interacted with God, my family, my relationships, and even how I viewed myself.

As John Green once wrote in *The Fault in Our Stars*, "That's the thing about pain. It demands to be felt." If we ignore it, it doesn't fade away. It only grows louder, taking root in places it was never meant to be. Can you imagine if I had never confronted those emotions? I wouldn't be here writing this book today. There is purpose in our emotional journey. There is strength in vulnerability, in the rawness of our complex emotions. But we must face them. We must feel them. And we must bring them to God.

Here's the truth: while running away from your emotions is unhealthy, running to them for everything, as if they're the ones in control, can be just as dangerous. Emotions are valuable guides, but they're not supposed to be your ultimate decision-makers. They help you navigate situations and relationships, but they're not meant to be in the driver's seat. They're signals, not masters. The key is balance—allowing yourself to feel and process your emotions but always bringing them before God for His direction and guidance. In His presence, you find the wisdom to navigate through those emotions in ways that lead to healing and clarity. Emotions aren't meant to have the final say; they're meant to guide you, to point out what needs your attention. Don't let your emotions drive the car, but don't leave them stranded on the side of the road, either. Let them serve their purpose, but always bring them to God for counsel. It's through His Word that we learn to respond rightly and align our actions with His will.

Just because your emotions can influence your behavior doesn't mean you should always act on them. In fact, your actions don't have to follow what you're feeling, especially when your emotions are pushing you in a direction that contradicts God's Word. God has given you the gift of free will—the ability to choose—and even your emotions don't override that. You have the choice to follow God's truth, even when your emotions are leading you elsewhere. They're not your god. They're not meant to rule over you.

Take Psalm 23:4, for example: *"Even though I walk through the valley of the shadow of death, I will fear no evil, for you are with me; your rod and your staff, they comfort me."* Now, let's be honest: walking through the "valley of the shadow of death" doesn't sound like a peaceful stroll in the park! Imagine the fear David, the author of this Psalm, could have felt walking through that dark, terrifying valley. Fear is a natural response—it tells us to run, to hide. But David made a deliberate choice to move past his fear. He chose to walk with God, even in the face of something terrifying. He chose not to let fear control or paralyze him. Instead, he surrendered it to the Lord. It's like he stared fear straight in the face and said, "You're not the boss of me."

This is what it means to face your emotions with God's guidance. It's not just about becoming emotionally intelligent or having healthier relationships—it's about spiritual strength. It's about not letting your emotions bully you into making decisions but instead turning to God. When you choose to trust God in the middle of your emotional mess, you become more than just emotionally wise—you become a serious threat to the kingdom of darkness.

Emotions aren't meant to rule us, nor are they meant to be ignored—they're meant to be processed, understood, and stewarded well.

Our emotions don't just affect us mentally, spiritually, and relationally—they impact us physically, too. Emotions aren't confined to the mind; they resonate throughout the body, triggering physiological responses such as changes in heart rate, blood pressure, and hormone levels. For instance, joy can make your heart race or leave you feeling light and carefree. Fear, on the other hand, can flood your system with adrenaline, preparing you for a "fight or flight" response, leaving you sweating and on edge. These physical reactions are your body's way of responding to the mind's signals, creating a bridge between your mental and physical states.

But here's something crucial: When we store our emotions or leave them unprocessed, they take up residence in the body, manifesting in ways you might not expect—like chronic tension, fatigue, or persistent physical ailments. The knot in your stomach, the heaviness in your chest, the headaches that linger? Sometimes, they aren't just physical health issues but emotional ones. Emotions will find a way to express themselves, even if we try to suppress them. If left unchecked, unprocessed emotions seep into our behavior, our relationships, and, yes, even our bodies.

Research shows that certain emotions are tied to specific physical symptoms or areas of the body. Let's explore a few:

1. **Anxiety, Stress, and Digestion**: We've all heard about having "butterflies in your stomach," usually when someone's caught up in romance or crushing on somebody. But let's be honest—those flutters aren't reserved for candlelit dinners and romantic walks. Anxiety can trigger those same tummy twirls when you're stressed about work, life, or anything else. And it's not always cute. Those flutters are actually a real physiological response driven by the gut-brain connection. This connection, through the vagus nerve, directly links your brain to your digestive system. When we experience emotions like anxiety or excitement, our bodies release stress hormones like cortisol and adrenaline, which can throw digestion off track. That's what gives you the fluttery feeling, but it can also

lead to symptoms like indigestion, nausea, or even heartburn. And it's not just about momentary flutters—chronic emotional stress, whether from anxiety or long-term worry, can have more serious consequences. Research shows that ongoing stress can disrupt your digestive system to the point of causing conditions like irritable bowel syndrome (IBS) or colitis. So, whether it's romance or stress, your emotions can literally cause "tummy flutters," showing that what's happening in your mind often plays out in your gut, too!

2. **Stored Emotions and Back Pain**: Unresolved emotions, particularly stress or trauma, can lead to chronic back pain. Tension from emotional stress often lodges in your neck, shoulders, or lower back. Psychosomatic research, like that of Dr. John Sarno, suggests that repressed anger or anxiety can restrict blood flow to muscles, creating persistent pain.

3. **Trauma and Gut Health**: Unresolved trauma, especially when it triggers the body's fight-or-flight response, can lead to gastrointestinal problems over time. Trauma dysregulates the gut-brain axis, making it harder for the body to process stress, leading to inflammation and digestive disorders.

Processing your emotions is crucial for your overall well-being. By working through them, you not only free yourself emotionally but also alleviate the physical toll they can take on your body.

I remember a powerful experience a few years ago while interning at a Christian program in North Carolina. One day, we prayed for a woman who had been suffering from chronic stomach pain. Despite visiting several doctors, no one could pinpoint the cause. As we prayed, one of the ministry leaders received insight from the Holy Spirit: her pain wasn't a physical issue but the result of a deep-rooted anxiety. The moment she was delivered from the spirit of anxiety, her stomach pain disappeared. It was a reminder that emotions—especially anxiety—can manifest physically, and only by addressing the root cause can healing take place.

Now, here's the thing—her deep-rooted anxiety didn't just appear overnight. It wasn't a random feeling that took control of her body out of nowhere. Anxiety, like many emotions, often begins as a series of thoughts—small seeds of fear, doubt, or uncertainty that take root in the mind. Over time, these thoughts accumulate, layer by layer, until the anxiety becomes overwhelming and eventually manifests in the body. What started as anxious or fearful thoughts had grown into a heavy emotional, spiritual, and physical burden.

This brings us to an important truth: Emotions are windows into our thoughts. They are deeply intertwined, influencing each other in profound ways. When you feel anxious, it's often because your mind is flooded with fears, uncertainties, or perceived threats. Your emotions reflect what's going on in your mind, giving you a glimpse into those underlying thoughts and allowing you to address their roots.

For Christians, this is especially crucial because the enemy often uses our thoughts to manipulate us. If he can plant seeds of fear, doubt, or insecurity in your mind, those seeds can quickly grow into overwhelming emotions that cloud your perception and create distance between you and God. This is why Scripture places so much emphasis on what we think about. Philippians 4:8 reminds us, "Finally, brothers, whatever is true, whatever is honorable, whatever is just, whatever is pure, whatever is lovely, whatever is commendable, if there is any excellence, if there is anything worthy of praise, think about these things." What we allow into our minds matters because it influences how we feel and how we act.

Unchecked emotions can easily become the enemy's playground. If the enemy can manipulate your thoughts, he can lead your emotions into dark, destructive places, entangling you in a web of negativity. This is why it's vital to confront your emotions head-on, allowing God to shine His light on them, revealing their source, and offering healing. Don't let the devil bully you! As you journey through your emotions, remember that you're not alone. God meets you in your emotional experiences, guiding you toward healing, peace, and deeper intimacy with Him.

So, now we understand what emotions are and how crucial they are to every aspect of our lives. We've also learned the importance of feeling and facing them head-on rather than running from them or distracting ourselves. At the same time, we know that emotions shouldn't control us—they aren't meant to rule our decisions or dictate our behaviors.

Yet, there's still one foundational issue standing in the way of fully understanding our emotions—a missing piece of the puzzle. We're facing an emotional pandemic today: so many people struggle to identify and label their emotions. They don't know what to call what they're feeling, and that's a huge problem. How can you process or communicate your emotions to others if you can't name them?

Think about it. How can you unpack what's going on inside if you don't even know what it is you're feeling? The reality is that most of us don't have a wide emotional vocabulary. Day after day, we experience a spectrum of emotions, yet we rely on the same few words to describe them all. We know something is stirring within—perhaps annoyance, nostalgia, or defensiveness—but when asked how we feel, we often default to vague phrases like 'I'm fine' or 'I'm good.' But here's the thing: 'Fine' isn't an emotion, and neither is 'good.' So the next time someone asks how you're feeling, remember that!

This is where many people get stuck—resorting to broad terms like 'happy,' 'sad,' or 'angry' when emotions are far more nuanced. Our emotional vocabulary is often too limited for the complexity of what's really going on inside. We need more than just basic words to capture the depth of what we experience every day. We also need the patience to sit with our feelings long enough to untangle and accurately identify them.

For example, earlier in the chapter, when I shared about my grief during my dad's passing, I described the flood of emotions stirring within me. The only word I could think of to capture everything I felt was 'grief,' but grief was just an umbrella emotion. When I finally sat with those feelings and processed them in the presence of God, the Holy Spirit helped me identify one specific emotion beneath the surface—disappointment. Yes, I was grieving, but underneath that grief was a layer of disappointment I hadn't acknowledged.

As an emotional wellness coach, I've often had clients struggle to articulate their emotions. They might start to explain what they're feeling but eventually shrug and say, 'I don't know how to describe it.' It's hard to help someone process their emotions when they can't assign basic labels to what they're experiencing. Many people are unconscious of what's happening to them emotionally, unaware that their emotions are running their lives. This lack of emotional awareness and vocabulary is a significant issue. To grow in emotional intelligence, we need to expand our emotional vocabulary—building a richer understanding of the emotions we feel and learning how to name them more precisely.

A widely accepted theory developed by psychologist Paul Ekman suggests that we have six basic emotions: sadness, happiness, fear, anger, surprise, and disgust. Most people are familiar with these foundational emotions and often use them as umbrella terms to describe a wide range of feelings. But the reality is there are *hundreds* of emotions, each with its own subtleties and nuances. Emotions are far more complex than we give them credit for, existing on a spectrum and varying greatly in intensity.

Let's take anger as an example. Anger is a basic emotion, but within that category, many shades of intensity exist. Emotions can range from mild annoyance to full-blown fury, each with a different weight. Here's a spectrum of anger-related emotions, arranged from least to most intense. As you read through, think about how each feels and how the intensity builds:

1. **Annoyance**: A mild and temporary feeling of discomfort or displeasure.
2. **Mild Irritation**: A slight bother that doesn't provoke a strong reaction but still disrupts your peace.
3. **Frustration**: A more pronounced response to feeling blocked or thwarted, often resulting in agitation.
4. **Aggravation**: An escalation from irritation; harder to ignore, more disruptive.
5. **Resentment**: A lingering anger toward something or someone you perceive as unfair.
6. **Bitterness**: A deeper, unresolved anger that often leads to cynicism or negativity.
7. **Rage**: An overwhelming, uncontrollable form of anger that clouds judgment.
8. **Fury**: An extreme form of rage, often explosive and volatile.

9. **Vengeance**: A desire for revenge stemming from feelings of betrayal or injustice.

Can you recall a time when you felt each of these? Did the intensity increase as you moved down the list? This spectrum shows that anger isn't one-size-fits-all—it evolves. Being able to identify where you are on the spectrum is not just crucial for expanding your emotional vocabulary; it's essential for managing and regulating your emotions.

For example, have you ever found yourself in a conversation where you started out mildly irritated, but as the discussion continued, frustration built up, and before you knew it, you were angry? Recognizing the degrees of your emotions helps you pinpoint when things are escalating. If you can acknowledge the shift from irritation to frustration, you're better equipped to de-escalate before you reach a boiling point.

Now, let's explore another category: happiness. Happiness, like anger, exists on a spectrum. Here's how it breaks down:

1. **Contentment**: A calm satisfaction with what you have.

2. **Pleasure**: A momentary feeling of enjoyment from a specific experience.

3. **Cheerfulness**: A lighthearted happiness, often marked by smiles or laughter.

4. **Optimism**: A hopeful, positive outlook toward the future.

5. **Excitement**: A heightened state of happiness tied to anticipation.

6. **Elation**: Intense happiness, often linked to achievement or success.

7. **Euphoria**: A strong, overwhelming joy that makes everything feel lighter.

8. **Ecstasy**: The highest form of happiness, an intense, almost transcendent joy.

9. **Joy**: A deeper, more lasting sense of happiness that often comes from within, especially through one's relationship with God.

As you read through this list, did you feel the shift in intensity? The pleasure you feel during a fun night out is not the same as the excitement you feel when anticipating a life-changing event, and certainly not the same as the deep joy found in your relationship with God. Just as there are degrees of anger, there are also degrees of happiness.

Let's explore one more category: sadness. Just like anger or happiness, sadness comes in varying degrees and intensities. Here are some layers within the category of sadness:

1. **Disappointment**: The sadness or dissatisfaction that arises when something doesn't go as expected or hoped for.

2. **Loneliness**: A deep emotional ache stemming from a perceived lack of connection or companionship, which can intensify feelings of isolation.

3. **Melancholy**: A reflective, gentle sadness often connected to nostalgia or longing for the past.

4. **Sorrow**: A deeper sadness, usually triggered by loss or disappointment, often leading to emotional pain.

5. **Grief**: A profound sadness in response to loss, particularly after the death of a loved one, accompanied by intense mourning.

6. **Despair**: A state of hopelessness and profound sadness, often accompanied by feelings of helplessness.

7. **Desolation**: An overwhelming sense of loneliness and emptiness, often following significant loss or isolation.

8. **Wretchedness**: A state of deep misery and emotional distress.

9. **Devastation**: A crushing sadness that feels all-consuming, usually following traumatic events or profound losses.

As you can see, there are various degrees of sadness—some more intense than others. Can you recall times in your life when you've felt each of these emotions? It's important to recognize that not all sadness is the same. The disappointment you feel when a job opportunity falls through isn't the same as the devastation you might experience after a life-altering event like the loss of a loved one.

Emotions aren't static. They evolve, flow, and shift over time. They grow, reach their peak, and can even morph into entirely different feelings. For example, frustration might evolve into anger, and anger can eventually melt into sadness. It's a fluid, dynamic process. Unfortunately, many people lack the emotional vocabulary to understand the nuances of their emotions fully. They might just say, "I'm sad," when in reality, they're feeling more alone or disappointed.

It's when we take the time to reflect on the root causes of our emotions that we begin to identify them more accurately. By expanding our emotional vocabulary, we become better equipped to understand, manage, and express our emotions. The more specific we can be when naming our emotions, the more attuned we become to our emotional landscape. Identifying specific emotions allows us to recognize their evolution—whether it's anger intensifying from frustration to rage or happiness growing from contentment to elation. This recognition helps us manage emotions before they get out of hand or become overwhelming.

NAME IT TO FRAME IT:
THE EMOTIONAL AWARENESS EXERCISE

This simple but powerful exercise is designed to help you expand your emotional vocabulary.

Instructions

1. **Get a dedicated emotions journal or notebook.** This will be your space to reflect on your feelings and become more aware of the wide range of emotions you experience daily.

2. **Set a daily alarm.** Choose a consistent time each day to pause and check in with yourself. When your alarm goes off, take a moment to stop whatever you're doing and ask yourself, *How am I feeling right now?* Be honest—don't rush or dismiss what comes to mind.

3. **Write down the emotion(s) you're experiencing.** In your journal, describe the emotion you're feeling in as much detail as possible. Don't settle for broad terms like "happy" or "sad." Dig deeper. Is it contentment? Regret? Joy? Write down the specific emotion that best captures your current state.

4. **Reflect on why you're feeling that way.** Once you've named the emotion, reflect on what might be causing it. Did something trigger it? Is it a lingering feeling from earlier in the day?

5. **Do this every day for one week.** Repeat this exercise at the same time each day for one week. By the end of the week, you'll have a clearer picture of your emotional pat-

terns and a richer understanding of the emotions you experience.

Remember, not every emotion will be intense or complex. Sometimes, you might feel an emotion as simple as being at ease or slightly bored. The important thing is to be honest with yourself and stretch your ability to name what you're truly feeling.

Bonus Tips for Maximizing the Emotional Awareness Exercise

1. **Embrace all emotions.** As you do this exercise, don't judge or dismiss any emotions that come up. Every emotion has value, offering insight into your inner world.

2. **Use an emotion wheel.** If you're struggling to identify your emotions, look up an *emotion wheel* online. These tools break emotions down into categories and levels of intensity, helping you pinpoint exactly what you're feeling.

3. **Create a personalized emotional vocabulary list.** In your journal, dedicate a page to listing new emotions you discover throughout this exercise. Categorize them into different emotional families—anger, joy, sadness—and add notes on what triggers them for you. This personalized list will serve as a guide, deepening your understanding of your emotions.

4. **Use metaphors and imagery.** Don't just name your emotions—describe them. Use metaphors or imagery to capture how you feel. For example, if you're overwhelmed, you might write, "It feels like a storm brewing inside me." Describing your emotions in this way helps you connect more deeply with them and expands your emotional vocabulary.

By committing to this exercise, you will expand your emotional vocabulary and improve your emotional intelligence. You'll become more self-aware, enhance the quality of your relationships by communicating your feelings more effectively, and develop better emotional regulation skills. Ultimately, understanding your emotions is key to your personal growth and healing journey.

REFLECTION QUESTIONS

1. Do you find yourself avoiding or distracting yourself from your emotions? What are some ways you do this, and is there a specific feeling you're currently trying to avoid?

2. Can you recall a recent situation where your emotions intensified, like moving from mild frustration to anger? How did this shift impact your behavior?

3. What was your reaction to exploring the degrees of emotions like anxiety, gratitude, or confidence? Did it help you see your emotions in a new light?

4. Is there a biblical figure whose story inspires you by showing how they pushed past their emotions, trusted God during intense feelings, or didn't let emotions hinder their calling? How does this example encourage you to navigate your own emotional challenges?

5. On a scale of 1-10, how would you rate your emotional vocabulary, with 1 being limited and 10 being expansive? Do you often use broad terms like "happy," "sad," or "angry" for complex feelings? How has this impacted your relationships or emotional management, and how might expanding your vocabulary help you express yourself more accurately?

6. How comfortable are you with experiencing mixed emotions, such as feeling joy and sadness simultaneously? What does this reveal to you about the layered nature of your emotional experiences?

7. Think of a time when your initial emotion shifted into a different feeling. What did this evolution teach you about the complexity of emotions?

8. Which emotion would you say you experience most frequently? Why do you think this particular emotion tends to surface often?

9. How often do you pause to ask, "What am I truly feeling right now?" What insights have you gained by identifying your emotions more specifically?

10. How has your understanding of emotions evolved since starting this chapter? Are there any new concepts or perspectives on emotions that now feel meaningful to you?

03

DEBUNKING THE MYTHS

One of the most crucial aspects of improving your emotional intelligence and your overall personal growth is recognizing that you don't just have learning to do but unlearning as well! When it comes to emotions, many of us have picked up ideas that shape how we think, feel, and react. These ideas often stem from a variety of influences: personal experiences, cultural conditioning, family dynamics, and the social environments we grew up in. Whether we realize it or not, these factors have shaped how we view and engage with our emotions.

From the time we're born, we're bombarded with countless messages about emotions—how we should feel, how we should express (or not express) those feelings, and how to respond to the emotions of others. Over time, these messages shape our emotional beliefs, many of which are based on myths that have led us astray in our emotional lives.

Emotions are complex, and all too often, they're misunderstood. As a result, a lot of common myths have sprung up around them. These myths become ingrained in our thinking, subtly influencing how we handle our own emotions and how we respond to the emotions of others. If we want to grow emotionally and boost our emotional intelligence, we must be willing to acknowledge that some of what we've been taught and what we've absorbed about emotions is simply untrue. It means confronting the fact that our early experiences, social surroundings, and cultural backgrounds may have conditioned us to approach emotions in unhealthy ways.

In this chapter, we're going to take a close look at some of the most common myths surrounding emotions. We'll debunk each myth and replace it with the truth, helping you break free from old patterns and embrace a healthier, more empowered way of navigating your emotional world. It's time to unlearn what's been holding you back and relearn the truths that will help you thrive emotionally.

Myth #1: "Emotions Are Either Good or Bad"

This is a big one. Most of us have grown up labeling emotions as either good or bad. We categorize feelings like happiness, contentment, and excitement as "good," while we lump sadness, disappointment, or rejection into the "bad" bin. And because these emotions are seen as negative, we often suppress, avoid, or even feel guilty about experiencing them. Many of us hold a subconscious belief that there's a "right" way to feel in any situation. Society expects us to be sad at funerals, joyful at weddings, and confident when stepping into a new role. If our feelings don't line up with these expectations, we may feel pressured to hide them or even pretend to feel something else.

This urge to label emotions and judge ourselves for feeling a certain way can create an unhealthy pattern. We even judge others for expressing emotions we're uncomfortable with. And why? The human mind loves labeling things—it gives us a sense of control and security. Emotions, however, aren't so simple. They're complex, layered experiences that can feel overwhelming, so to avoid the discomfort, we quickly label them as "bad" to regain that sense of stability.

But here's the truth: emotions aren't inherently good or bad. They're simply *emotions*. They are signals, neutral indicators that show us what's happening within. Emotions are meant to guide us, to serve as a compass pointing us toward areas that need attention rather than being stamped with judgment. Each emotion, whether comfortable or uncomfortable, carries a unique message. Anger, for instance, might indicate a crossed boundary or an injustice that needs addressing. Sadness could signal a loss, inviting us to grieve and reflect. Even jealousy might highlight unmet needs or desires, revealing insights into what we truly value.

Our role isn't to judge emotions but to understand them. When we stop trying to categorize emotions as "good" or "bad" and start viewing them as valuable information, we open ourselves to deeper understanding. Emotions are valid; they guide us in responding to our inner world and external situations. By labeling some emotions as "bad," we only avoid processing them and, in doing so, miss out on what they're trying to tell us. We must remind ourselves that there is no "right" way to feel in any situation. Emotions are deeply personal, and they vary from person to person.

It's also important to know that different emotions can coexist. For example, when I got married, my roommate was thrilled for me but also sad. She was happy I was starting a new chapter but felt a bittersweet grief over me moving out after we'd shared an apartment and built such a close bond. So yes, even amid the excitement, there was a sense of loss—and that's okay! It's okay to feel multiple emotions at once; there's no single "right" way to feel.

Remember, emotions are natural responses, not moral judgments. While they are neither good nor bad, how we respond to them can be constructive or destructive. Our actions are what matters. In Ephesians 4:26-27, we read, "Be angry and do not sin; do not let the sun go down on your anger, and give no opportunity to the devil." Notice it doesn't say it's sinful to feel anger; it simply guides us on how to handle it. Anger itself isn't wrong, but it can lead to sin if we act impulsively or hold onto grudges. That's why it's so essential to bring our emotions to God, who can help us process them and give us wisdom on how to respond in alignment with His Word.

So, when an emotion feels uncomfortable or even overwhelming, don't label it as "bad." Instead, see it as a messenger trying to show you something important. Embrace it, understand it, and allow God to guide you through it. Our feelings are valid, and they don't make us "weird" or "wrong"—they make us human. It's not about avoiding uncomfortable emotions; it's about learning to sit with them, process them, and respond to them in healthy ways.

Rather than viewing emotions as inherently good or bad, think of them as tools for insight. They help us navigate life and draw us closer to the One who created us. Take them to God, explore His truth, and let Him provide comfort, direction, and healing when you need it.

Myth #2: "If I Feel It, It Must Be True"

This is another myth that has deeply influenced how we understand our emotions, and it affects how we communicate and relate with others. Many of us believe, "If I feel this way, it must be true." We assume that our emotions define reality and that our personal truth overrides objective facts. This myth often takes root in the modern concept of expressive individualism, which emphasizes the importance of personal expression and self-fulfillment. Expressive individualism encourages people to embrace and express their unique identities, values, and emotions as central to who they are. Within this framework, emotions are seen as inherently valid and defining of one's reality, leading to the belief that personal experiences and feelings are their "truth." However, the truth is that while our emotions are undeniably valuable in guiding us through life, they don't override reality.

Just because you feel like the sky is red doesn't mean it is; you can't say, "Well, the sky is red because that's how I feel." No—feelings aren't facts, and emotions don't always align with reality. Emotions are subjective experiences that reflect our unique perspectives, shaped by our physiology, life experiences, and personal beliefs. While emotions are valid, and they reflect our perceptions and experiences, they are not the same as facts. Knowing the difference between emotional truth and factual truth is essential, especially when making decisions or communicating with others. Ignoring facts in favor of emotions can lead to misunderstandings, conflict, and even harm.

Consider this example: Imagine that Kate has been feeling emotionally distanced from her fiancé, Austin, and one day tells him, "You don't love me anymore!" Caught off guard, Austin becomes defensive, listing all the ways he's shown his love for her. Kate, however, insists, "This is how I feel, so it must be true." But is it really? Just because Kate feels unloved doesn't necessarily mean that Austin doesn't love her. Her feelings are valid, but they aren't objective truth.

In this case, if Kate had instead expressed, "I've been feeling distant from you lately, and I miss the way you used to express your love," she would have communicated her emotions more clearly and invited Austin to understand and meet her needs.

Austin's response might be, "I'm sorry I haven't been as present or affectionate lately; I've been overwhelmed at work. I love you deeply and want to work on this with you." In this healthy communication, Kate's emotions are honored, and the truth of Austin's love is acknowledged. This approach helps foster understanding and trust rather than escalating into a conflict.

To truly improve our relationships and communication, we must recognize that while our emotions are valid, they aren't factual. Making all our decisions based on feelings alone would be not only dangerous but also a clear sign of poor emotional intelligence. In communication, expressing emotions as facts often leads to defensiveness, miscommunication, and unnecessary conflict.

As believers, it's important to remember that letting emotions override truth can lead to emotional idolatry. When we prioritize emotions as the ultimate authority, we risk letting them guide our decisions instead of God's Word. I often say this: there's a difference between what we feel and what we know. When your feelings clash with what you know, let what you know take precedence. If, for instance, you feel that God has abandoned you, ask yourself, "What does Scripture say?" In Matthew 28:20, Jesus promises, "And behold, I am with you always, to the end of the age." This truth reassures us of God's constant presence. So, when our emotions don't align with God's truth, we should place His Word first, letting it guide us as we bring our feelings under submission. The more we align with God's truth, the more He can refine and transform our emotions.

Your emotions are valid and important, but they are not "the way, the truth, and the life"—Jesus is. Don't let the enemy manipulate your emotions to lead you away from God's truth. When you idolize your emotions, you create room for the enemy to influence them, drawing you into alignment with his agenda rather than with God's Word. Instead, bring your emotions to God and let His truth ground you.

Moreover, treating emotions as absolute truth can create barriers in relationships. When we see our emotions as fact, it becomes harder to empathize with others' experiences, often leading us to dismiss, invalidate, or judge their feelings. This limits our ability to connect and communicate effectively. Your emotions matter just as much as the emotions of others do. Recognizing this balance and making room for objective truth is key to navigating the emotional landscape of your life and relationships with wisdom.

Myth #3: "Women Are More Emotional Than Men"

One of the most persistent myths about emotions is the notion that women are inherently more emotional than men. This stereotype suggests that women are governed by their feelings, while men are supposedly stoic, rational, and logical. But this view oversimplifies the complexity of emotions, ignoring individual nuances in how each of us feels and expresses what's inside.

This myth is especially damaging because it's dehumanizing for men, robbing them of the freedom to feel and express a full spectrum of emotions. It pushes men toward emotional suppression by perpetuating toxic masculinity and implying that being "strong" means hiding feelings. Phrases like "boys don't cry" and "stop crying like a girl" reflect a culture where men are conditioned to see emotional expression as weak or unmanly, so much so that "be a man" often implies being emotionless.

The impact of this myth is damaging to both men and women. For men, emotional suppression often leads to poor mental health, aggressive tendencies, and difficulty forming open, connected relationships. Under the weight of the expectation to be perpetually "strong," many men miss out on the benefits of emotional awareness and growth. With few acceptable outlets, repressed emotions can often find expression through anger—a response that society views as a more "masculine" display of strength. Over time, unprocessed emotions may surface as bullying, violence, or other toxic behaviors, as anger becomes a stand-in for sadness, vulnerability, or fear. Suppressing emotions doesn't make them disappear; it only redirects them, often in harmful ways.

For women, this myth fuels sexism by implying they are less rational and more emotional, as if emotional depth comes at the expense of logical reasoning. This bias has contributed to a long-standing mistrust of women in leadership and decision-making roles under the false assumption that they lack the steadiness to lead without being "overly emotional." Ironically, most wars and conflicts—often fueled by pride, revenge, or fear—were initiated by men, proving that emotional intensity is not gendered but human.

In truth, both men and women experience emotions equally. Research shows that we all feel a full spectrum of emotions, though we often express them differently due to influences like social conditioning, cultural norms, and personal experiences. Studies also indicate that women tend to score higher on emotional intelligence tests, likely because they're encouraged from a young age to explore, articulate, and communicate their emotions openly. As a result, women may be more outwardly expressive and are often provided with more outlets, such as close friendships, support groups, and events designed to nurture emotional connection. Men, however, often lack these spaces and may rarely feel encouraged to open up emotionally, even within their own homes, where they may feel pressured to be the "pillar of strength" for others.

If we want to encourage emotional health in men, we have to hold space for them. Creating a safe environment for men to express their emotions without judgment or expectation is essential because it leads to healthier relationships and a stronger community. The starting point is teaching young boys that it's okay to cry, feel, and be vulnerable. I once heard a story about a family who lost their father. As the family mourned, an uncle told the young son, "Don't cry. Now you're the man of the house; you need to be strong for your mother and sisters." This little boy had just lost his father, yet he was already being pressured to suppress his grief. If he doesn't process those feelings, they'll only grow heavier over time.

We need more conferences, small groups, and support systems for men where saying "I love you" and "I'm here for you" doesn't feel awkward or forced. God created men and women alike in His image as emotional beings. Scripture is filled with examples of men expressing their emotions. David openly expressed grief, danced with joy, and penned songs of praise. Job mourned his losses openly. Paul poured love and compassion into letters for his fellow believers. Nehemiah wept and prayed over Jerusalem's broken walls. Emotions are not "feminine"; they're human. They're a reflection of God's heart, meant to draw us closer to Him and to one another.

Reinforcing the idea that women are more emotional than men isn't just clinging to a falsehood—it actively limits growth and understanding for everyone. We were all created as emotional beings. While cultural conditioning may make women more expressive, this doesn't mean men are any less emotional. Emotional depth is not defined by gender. Recognizing this truth nurtures healthier relationships and creates a more compassionate and understanding society.

If you're on a journey to grow in emotional intelligence, throw this myth out for good. Let's pave the way for a richer understanding of emotions for both men and women, creating spaces where everyone feels safe to express and explore their feelings.

Myth #4: "Showing Emotion is a Sign of Weakness"

Much like the previous myth, this misconception is closely tied to outdated ideas of masculinity and femininity, where emotional expression is often equated with vulnerability and fragility. But as we've discussed, emotions are an essential part of being human. They add depth to our lives and contribute to our overall well-being.

The reality is that many of us care deeply about what others think of us—more than we may want to admit. We want to be seen as strong, capable, and composed. So, if showing emotion risks making us look weak, we hide it. We bottle it up. This is why, after sharing something deeply personal, we sometimes find ourselves anxiously replaying the moment, wondering if we "said too much" or fearing that others will judge us differently now. I know I've had those sleepless nights, cringing over moments of vulnerability, second-guessing every word I shared, and worrying about how I was perceived.

But here's the truth: showing your emotions doesn't make you weak. In fact, it's the opposite—it's a mark of real strength. It takes courage to be open and vulnerable, especially in a world that often discourages emotional honesty. Genuine strength lies not only in expressing your emotions but also in owning them, standing by your vulnerability, and being at peace with the fact that you are real and open, regardless of what others might think.

Hiding your emotions may seem like the "strong" thing to do, but it's actually a way of avoiding discomfort. Suppressing your emotions reflects an unwillingness to embrace vulnerability or confront others' perceptions. True strength lies in embracing and expressing our emotions—even the messy, unrefined ones—and trusting that those moments of openness will lead to greater self-knowledge and stronger connections with others. Embracing vulnerability not only shows strength but also conveys authenticity, making us relatable and trustworthy. When we allow ourselves to be fully seen, people connect with us on a deeper level, drawn to the honesty we share.

Conversely, hiding our emotions doesn't make us mysterious; it creates distance. When we constantly put up walls, it becomes difficult for others to know us fully, to trust us, or to feel close to us. Relationships deepen through shared vulnerability, through the moments when we allow ourselves to be human in front of others. If we constantly suppress how we feel, we build walls that push others away.

Believing that showing emotion is a sign of weakness can also lead to unhealthy coping mechanisms. People who suppress their emotions often turn to outlets like substance use, aggression, or detachment as ways to manage the unexpressed emotions building inside. No one wants to be seen as unpredictable or explosive, yet unaddressed emotions tend to manifest in these ways, creating tension in our lives and relationships.

Acknowledging and expressing emotions actually builds resilience, allowing us to face life's challenges with healthier coping strategies. As society becomes more aware of the importance of mental health, we're also beginning to recognize that emotional expression isn't a flaw or failure—it's a necessary strength. Embracing and processing our emotions with honesty prepares us for life's ups and downs and keeps us from being derailed by unexpected setbacks.

So, the next time you find yourself replaying a vulnerable moment in your mind, stop and remember: the fact that you were able to be open and real with someone is a strength. The fact that you allowed yourself to feel, to cry when you were hurt, is a testament to your courage. Each time you let yourself be seen in all your authenticity, you not only grow stronger but also inspire others to do the same.

Your friends, family, and loved ones who have seen these real moments aren't there because you're perfect—they're there because they value and love you for exactly who you are, flaws and strengths alike. Remember that someone may feel less alone in their struggles because they saw the courage you had to express yours. Remember Psalm 34:18: "The Lord is close to the brokenhearted." When you allow yourself to be vulnerable, you're giving God and those around you a chance to come closer, offer comfort, and share the journey with you.

Showing emotion doesn't define you as weak. It means you're strong, courageous, and human. And maybe, just maybe, those who can't handle your vulnerability feel that way because they're still learning to face their own.

Now, of course, expressing emotions openly doesn't mean sharing everything with everyone. It's essential to apply wisdom and discernment when opening up to others, taking into account the nature of your relationship and the setting. For instance, the way you express emotions with a close friend might not be appropriate in a professional environment. It wouldn't be wise, for example, to pour out the details of a recent breakup to your boss or an Uber driver. Reading the room and knowing when to maintain professionalism is key.

Likewise, in personal relationships, vulnerability should match the level of intimacy shared. Deep emotional openness should grow naturally as relationships deepen; sharing too much too soon can feel out of place or even create discomfort. Think of vulnerability as something to be revealed gradually, allowing trust to build in layers. By being thoughtful about where and how we share, we honor both our own emotions and the boundaries of those around us.

Myth #5: "My Emotions Are Uncontrollable.
I Have to Act Based on How I Feel."

Many people believe that their emotions are a force beyond control—a powerful current they're powerless to resist, leaving them feeling as though they must act impulsively just to release that emotional weight. Statements like, "I couldn't help it; the anger just boiled over" or "I had no choice but to react" are rooted in this myth. Often, people feel overwhelmed by their emotions and act as if they are at the mercy of their feelings, responding without considering the consequences. But the belief that emotions are uncontrollable is not only inaccurate; it's also damaging.

While emotions can indeed feel intense and overwhelming, the truth is that we can control our responses. We've been given free will, a powerful gift that allows us to choose how we react. Yes, emotions arise naturally, but how we respond to them is up to us. There's a difference between feeling an emotion and reacting impulsively to it. While you may not choose what you feel—emotions are instinctive responses—you do have a choice in how you express or respond to them. For example, if someone disrespects you, the natural reaction might be anger. What you choose to do with that anger, though, is up to you. You could punch them in the face because, hey, they "made you do it." But really, did they? That's a choice! No one made you clench your fist and throw a punch. They may have provoked you, but you still had the power to pause, breathe, and decide how to respond.

Even when provoked, we are still responsible for how we respond. Just as God doesn't give us a free pass to sin because we're tempted, He also doesn't give us a pass to act recklessly because we feel provoked. Knowing we'll face situations that stir up strong emotions, God has given us the Holy Spirit to help us cultivate the fruits of love, joy, peace, patience, kindness, goodness, faithfulness, gentleness, and self-control—qualities that reflect His character in our responses. God's not expecting perfection or emotional 'decorum' 24/7, but He does desire our growth in these qualities. Let's release the myth that emotions are an untamable force.

To debunk this myth, remember that you don't have to be a slave to your emotions. Jesus died to set you free, including freedom from being bound by impulsive reactions. Developing self-control isn't about denying your emotions but about honoring the power and freedom you have to respond thoughtfully, in alignment with your values and with God's Word. Each time we act impulsively, we're not only betraying our better judgment, but we're also betraying ourselves. Think about it: when you act out in ways that don't align with your core values, it erodes your confidence and trust in yourself. Just as a friend who constantly breaks trust would be hard to rely on, betraying yourself through unchecked reactions can damage your relationship with yourself.

The good news is that if you struggle with controlling your emotions, there's hope! God has provided the Holy Spirit to help you grow in this area. Additionally, here are some practical strategies to help you regulate intense emotions:

1. **Pause Before Reacting**: When emotions surge, take a moment to pause. This gives you a chance to check in with yourself and assess whether your initial reaction aligns with your values. If you're in an intense conversation, step away briefly to regain composure. Observe what you're feeling, where you feel it in your body, and allow yourself to fully process it. Emotions often feel less overwhelming when we acknowledge them and give ourselves a moment to sit with them.

2. **Practice Deep Breathing Techniques**: During moments of stress or overwhelm, our breathing often becomes shallow, which can heighten anxiety. Practicing deep breathing signals to your brain that it's okay to calm down, slowing your heart rate and helping you regain a sense of peace.

3. **Identify Triggers**: Understanding your triggers allows you to anticipate strong emotional reactions and prepares you to handle them better. Knowing what sets you off can help you develop effective strategies in advance to cope with similar situations in the future. At the end of this chapter, I've provided a couple of exercises designed to help you identify and manage your triggers more effectively.

4. **Worship**: Worship ushers you into God's presence, a space of peace that can help you recalibrate emotionally. By focusing on

God's goodness and sovereignty, worship allows you to cast your burdens on Him and receive His peace in return.

5. **Journaling**: Writing down your emotions can be incredibly therapeutic. Journaling helps you process feelings by translating them into words, allowing you to release pent-up emotions and gain perspective.

6. **Seek Support**: Talking to a trusted friend, therapist, or mentor can help you gain an outside perspective and support as you process difficult emotions. However, I encourage you to seek God's perspective first through prayer and Scripture. His Word offers wisdom and insight that can clarify and bring healing in ways human advice alone cannot.

It's okay if emotions sometimes feel overwhelming; that doesn't make them uncontrollable. The myth that emotions are unstoppable forces can be a barrier to emotional growth, leading us to impulsive reactions and strained relationships. Developing emotional intelligence means learning to pause, reflect, and choose responses that align with our values and God's Word. This approach empowers you to act thoughtfully and embrace emotional maturity.

While this chapter covered some of the most prevalent myths about emotions, countless others exist that we couldn't cover here. I encourage you to keep learning, studying, and seeking God's truth about your emotions. God's word is a light that can dispel any lingering myths. I pray that as you meditate on His truth, any darkness or confusion surrounding your emotions is replaced with clarity, peace, and freedom in Jesus' name. Amen.

Prayer

Heavenly Father,

Thank You for the gift of the Holy Spirit. Today, I invite You into my emotions. I ask You to refine them, helping me respond in ways that reflect Your image and align with the truth of Your word. Forgive me for the times I have acted based on my emotions rather than in accordance with Your word. Teach me to control and regulate my emotions with wisdom and grace.

Lord, if there are any myths or lies about emotions that I am holding onto—beliefs that hinder my spiritual and personal growth—I ask You to reveal them to me. Shine Your light of truth on any misconceptions I may have and help me replace them with Your wisdom. Transform my emotions so that I may honor You in how I feel, respond, and relate with others.

Thank You, Jesus, for Your sacrifice on the cross, which has set me free from the bondage of sin and from being a slave to my emotions. I surrender my emotions to You and ask that You cultivate in me the fruits of the Spirit so that I may reflect Your love, patience, and self-control in all that I do.

Thank You, Lord, for hearing me. In Jesus' name, Amen.

"GETTING TO THE ROOT" –
THE TRIGGER DISCOVERY EXERCISE

This exercise is a guided process to help you identify and explore your emotional triggers, digging deep to reveal those patterns, beliefs, and past experiences that may influence your emotional responses. Recognizing what prompts intense emotional responses is key to managing emotions effectively. By exploring the "why" behind our reactions, we can uncover hidden triggers or underlying beliefs that shape how we respond to situations. Use your emotions journal for this exercise so you can track your progress and insights over time.

Step-by-Step Guide:

1. **Pause and Identify the Emotion**
   Begin by pausing when you feel a strong emotional reaction (like frustration, anger, or sadness). Take a moment to name the emotion, separating yourself from it so you can look at it objectively. For instance, if you feel frustration, label it and record: "I feel frustrated."

2. **Ask the First "Why?"**
   With the emotion identified, begin digging to the root by asking yourself, "Why am I feeling this way?" Look for the immediate reason behind the emotion. For example, "I feel frustrated because my friend interrupted me twice during our group hangout while I was talking about my perspective."

3. **Ask the Second "Why?"**
   Now that you know why you're frustrated, go deeper: "Why does that situation make me feel frustrated?" Here, you're looking for a deeper reason beyond just being interrupted. For

instance, "That situation makes me feel frustrated because it made me feel disrespected, dismissed, and small."

4. **Ask the Third "Why?"**
Keep going deeper by asking, "Why does feeling dismissed, small, and disrespected bother me?" This level may reveal unmet needs or past experiences tied to unresolved emotional wounds. For example, "It bothers me because it makes me feel like I am not valued, and it reminds me of times in the past when I felt overlooked and small."

5. **Ask the Fourth "Why?" (and Beyond, if Necessary)**
Now, ask, "Why do I need to feel valued and listened to?" This question often uncovers a core desire, belief, or need influencing your reaction, such as a need for respect or affirmation. Sit with whatever insights arise and approach them with compassion. When you uncover your core desire or need, validate it. For example, it's valid to desire respect. If it reveals a core belief—like "I'm not smart enough, and that's why I'm being dismissed"—pause to check whether this belief is true. Seek guidance from God's word to ensure it aligns with His truth about you. If the belief is false, recognize that it may be rooted in an emotional wound and needs to be replaced with God's perspective.

If you still feel there's more to uncover, keep asking "why" until you feel you've reached the core reason behind your trigger. The goal is to uncover the deepest belief, desire, or need driving your emotional response. Once you've identified the root, true healing can begin.

6. **Reflection**
Once you've reached the core of your emotional response, take a few minutes to reflect. Are there patterns emerging? Is this a recurring trigger across different situations? Reflecting on these patterns helps you recognize similar triggers in the future, giving you the power to respond more calmly. Take this time to pray, asking the Lord to heal any emotional wounds

this exercise may have brought to light. If necessary, consider seeking therapy or counseling to support your healing journey.

By working through this exercise, you'll gain insight into your emotional triggers and strengthen your ability to manage them, bringing greater peace and emotional freedom into your life.

Additional Exercises to Explore Triggers

1. **Daily Trigger Journal:**
   For one week, use your emotions journal to track any strong emotional reactions you experience each day. Record the following details:

- **The Emotion:** Describe the specific feeling (e.g., frustration, sadness, excitement).

- **The Trigger:** Note what caused the reaction, whether it was a person, situation, or something specific that happened.

- **Your Reaction:** Reflect on how you responded emotionally and behaviorally.

- **Your Insight:** Consider what this reaction reveals about you and what it teaches you about yourself.

Review your entries at the end of the week and look for recurring patterns. Are there particular people, settings, or situations that consistently bring up strong emotions? This awareness will help you better understand and anticipate your triggers in the future.

2. **Values Reflection Exercise:**
   Identify three to five core values that hold the most importance to you (e.g., respect, integrity, honesty, independence). Over time, observe whether your triggers are connected to these values. When we feel that a core value is challenged or compromised, our emotional response may be heightened. Understanding this connection can guide you to approach triggering situations more calmly, focusing on solutions that honor your values.

REFLECTION QUESTIONS

1. What are some common myths about emotions that you believed before reading this chapter, and how have these myths shaped the way you express or suppress your emotions? As you reflect on the five myths discussed, which one(s) do you resonate with the most, and were there any you immediately recognized as false?

2. Reflect on the myth of "good" and "bad" emotions. Do you find yourself labeling your emotions as positive or negative? How has this impacted your ability to accept and process your feelings?

3. When you consider the myth that "emotions are uncontrollable," do you recognize times in your life when you've felt like you had to act on an intense emotion immediately? How might this new understanding change the way you respond in such situations?

4. In what ways has the belief that showing emotion is a sign of weakness affected your willingness to be vulnerable with others? What could change if you viewed emotional expression as a strength?

5. How has the myth that women are "more emotional" than men affected your perspective on emotional expression across genders? Has it influenced the way you engage with others' emotions, especially across gender lines?

6. Are there specific "trigger patterns" you've started to notice about yourself? How do you think these triggers are related to your values, past experiences, or personal beliefs?

7. When it comes to your relationship with God, do you feel you've believed any myths about emotions that limit how you bring your emotions to Him? How might this chapter encourage you to deepen your relationship with Him through honest emotional expression?

8. What does self-control look like to you in emotional situations? How can you balance self-control with being authentic about your emotions?

9. Reflect on a recent situation where you responded impulsively to a strong emotion. What do you wish you had done differently, and how might the strategies in this chapter help you respond more thoughtfully next time?

10. How does the idea of bringing your emotions in alignment with God's word resonate with you? What practical steps can you take to ensure your emotions are influenced by truth rather than myths?

04

PRIMARY AND SECONDARY EMOTIONS

I remember an experience from my teenage years, back when I lived in Lagos, Nigeria. My family lived on an estate—a term that has a slightly different meaning in Nigeria compared to how it's used in America. In Nigeria, an estate isn't one large property owned by a single person or family but rather a gated community with multiple homes or apartments owned or rented by different individuals.

One evening, I was out for a walk with my cousin. Strolling through our estate was something I enjoyed—breathing in the evening air and having meaningful conversations with her as we meandered through the neighborhood. During our walk, a man suddenly approached us.

This was a common experience for me as I was growing into a young woman. Men often stopped to chat or flirt when they found me attractive. This man was no different. He introduced himself, complimenting me by saying I was pretty and noting that he'd never seen me in the neighborhood before. After the initial pleasantries, he asked for my phone number so we could "get to know each other."

I had no interest in getting to know him—or any random stranger, for that matter—so I politely said, "No."

His face shifted ever so slightly, a subtle change that revealed his surprise. Laughing nervously, he tried again, this time with a bit more insistence. "Can I have your number?" he asked, his tone still light but tinged with disbelief.

Again, I refused, explaining, "I don't know you, and I don't give my number to strangers."

At this point, his expression changed even more noticeably. His initial flirty confidence gave way to frustration, and his tone hardened. I expected him to take the rejection gracefully and move on, but instead, his persistence escalated into demands. "Why won't you give me your number? It's just a phone number!" he exclaimed.

When I tried to end the conversation and walk away, his frustration turned into anger. He lashed out, saying things like, "Who do you think you are, some kind of celebrity? You're not even that pretty. I was doing you a favor!" What began with compliments about my beauty ended with insults and an angry tirade. Eventually, he stormed off, muttering under his breath.

If someone had asked this man at that moment why he was so upset, he likely would've said, "I'm angry because she was rude and refused to give me her number." But was that really it? Was anger truly the root of his feelings?

I watched as his emotions shifted throughout the encounter—first confidence, then confusion, frustration, and finally, anger. Beneath that anger, there was something deeper. At the core of his emotional response, he felt rejected. My refusal bruised his pride and triggered feelings of hurt and rejection.

For someone like him, admitting to feeling rejected or hurt likely felt too vulnerable. Perhaps he had been taught that vulnerability was a sign of weakness or that admitting to such feelings would damage his ego. Instead of processing those deeper emotions, he defaulted to anger—a secondary emotion that helped him mask the pain and preserve his sense of dignity.

If he had chosen to confront and process his primary emotions—rejection and hurt—the outcome could've been very different. He might have said something like, "Ouch, that rejection stings, but I respect your decision. Have a great evening." Later, he could have reflected on the situation: *Why did her refusal affect me so much? What can I learn from this experience?*

By bypassing his primary emotions, he leaned into anger, using it as a shield to protect himself from vulnerability. This interaction is a classic example of how primary and secondary emotions play out in our daily lives.

In this man's case, his primary emotions were rejection and hurt, while his secondary emotion was anger. His anger wasn't the core emotion; it was a response to the hurt and rejection he felt but didn't want to confront.

Primary and secondary emotions aren't unique to this man. We all experience them daily—whether we realize it or not. Yet, most of us rarely stop to reflect on what's happening beneath the surface. You may already be familiar with the concept of primary and secondary emotions, or it might be a completely new territory.

In this chapter, we're going to dive deep into the world of emotions—exploring what primary and secondary emotions are, the roles they play in our lives and relationships, and how we can identify and process them effectively.

By understanding and addressing primary emotions, we can avoid letting secondary emotions dominate our responses. The goal is to help you thrive emotionally, both personally and relationally, by equipping you to process emotions in a healthy, God-honoring way.

Primary Emotions

Let's start by understanding primary emotions. Primary emotions are our initial, instinctive emotional responses to a situation. They are universal, biologically driven feelings that humans experience across all cultures, genders, and ages. These emotions occur automatically, often without conscious thought or reasoning, and are deeply tied to our survival instincts.

Think of primary emotions as the raw, unfiltered reactions that arise in the moment. They are vulnerable, exposing how we truly feel about a particular situation or event. These emotions reveal what matters most to us and highlight the core of our humanity. Some examples of primary emotions include happiness, sadness, fear, anger, surprise, and disgust.

Examples of Primary Emotions in Action:

1. **Fear**: Imagine you're walking home at night with a friend, and suddenly, you hear loud footsteps rushing up behind you. Without thinking, your heart races, and you feel a jolt of fear. This is your brain's instinctive response to what it perceives as potential danger—a primary emotion designed to protect you.

2. **Happiness**: Now picture this: You receive an unexpected call from a sibling you dearly miss, who shares that they're coming to visit and bringing your favorite dessert. Your immediate response is joy. This happiness is a primary emotion, an instant and spontaneous reaction to the good news of reconnecting with a loved one.

3. **Sadness or Anger**: Consider this: Your partner forgets an important date, such as an anniversary. You immediately feel sadness or anger. These emotions, while vulnerable, reveal the value you place on being acknowledged and celebrated in your relationship.

Characteristics of Primary Emotions:

1. **Automatic and quick**: They arise instinctively, without much thought.

2. **Raw and vulnerable**: They expose your core feelings about a situation.

3. **Universal**: They are experienced by all humans, regardless of culture, age, or gender.

4. **Short-lived but intense**: They don't last long but are often powerful in the moment.

5. **Tied to survival**: They are hard-wired into us and often relate to basic needs or threats.

Secondary Emotions

While primary emotions are immediate and instinctive, secondary emotions are more complex. They emerge as reactions to our primary emotions and often involve layers of thought, reflection, and personal interpretation. Secondary emotions develop over time and are shaped by our upbringing, cultural norms, past experiences, and personal beliefs.

Where primary emotions are raw and universal, secondary emotions are nuanced and often unique to the individual. They are shaped by how we process and respond to our primary emotions and can linger longer, influencing our behavior in more subtle ways.

Examples of Secondary Emotions in Action:

1. **Guilt After Anger**: Imagine you feel anger as a primary emotion—perhaps someone cut in front of you in traffic, and you honked aggressively. Later, you reflect on your reaction and feel guilty, believing you overreacted. That guilt is a secondary emotion born out of your interpretation of your initial anger.

2. **Shame After Fear**: Let's say you feel fear as a primary emotion before speaking in front of a large crowd. You're nervous about making mistakes. Then, you begin to feel shame—embarrassed that you're afraid, perhaps worried about how others might perceive your fear. This shame, a secondary emotion, is layered on top of your initial fear.

3. **Jealousy After Insecurity**: Picture this: You're feeling insecure about where you are in life. You haven't been pursuing your goals, and you see someone else succeeding in ways you wish you were. That jealousy you feel toward them is not the core emotion. It's a secondary emotion, a response to the primary feeling of insecurity.

Secondary emotions often act as a form of protection, shielding us from the vulnerability of our primary emotions. For example, someone feeling hurt (a primary emotion) might express anger (a secondary emotion) instead because anger feels safer and less exposing than admitting pain or rejection.

While secondary emotions can provide temporary relief, failing to address the underlying primary emotion often leaves the root issue unresolved. For example, addressing jealousy (a secondary emotion) by avoiding someone's social media posts might provide temporary relief. Still, unless the primary insecurity is addressed, those feelings of jealousy will resurface in new situations.

Characteristics of Secondary Emotions:

1. **More complex**: They often involve multiple layers of feeling and thought.

2. **Cognitively processed**: They arise after reflection or judgment of the primary emotion.

3. **Influenced by social and cultural factors**: They are shaped by upbringing, expectations, and personal beliefs.

4. **Longer-lasting**: They tend to linger and influence behavior over time.

5. **Used as protection**: They often mask more vulnerable primary emotions.

Think of primary and secondary emotions like primary and secondary colors. Primary colors—red, blue, and yellow—are the foundation of all other colors. They are pure, unaltered, and cannot be created by mixing other colors. Similarly, primary emotions, such as happiness, sadness, and fear, are foundational. These emotions are universal across cultures and deeply rooted in our biology.

Just as primary colors combine to create secondary colors like orange, green, and purple, primary emotions blend to form more complex emotional experiences. Secondary emotions, such as guilt, resentment, and jealousy, arise when primary emotions mix with thoughts, beliefs, and experiences. These emotions are more nuanced and shaped by personal context, culture, and upbringing.

Like a specific shade of green that looks different depending on its surroundings, secondary emotions often require context to be fully understood. Primary emotions, much like primary colors, are raw and instinctively understood. Secondary emotions, like secondary colors, are layered and situational, shaped by our environment and individual experiences.

As we've explored earlier in this book, emotions require varying levels of vulnerability depending on the situation, the relationship, and the emotion itself. Primary emotions are often the most vulnerable because they are raw, unfiltered, and immediate.

Vulnerability is the state of being open to emotional exposure, where someone could potentially hurt or harm you. Primary emotions are especially vulnerable because they expose our emotional core—our deepest fears, desires, and needs. These emotions reflect the essence of who we are and what we value most.

For instance, feeling sad might reveal a fear of losing connection with someone you care about. Imagine feeling sad because a close friend hasn't reached out in a while. Expressing that sadness exposes your deep emotional need for connection and acceptance. But that same expression could feel risky if you fear your friend might misunderstand, dismiss, or even weaponize your vulnerability.

Likewise, if you feel fear because your partner isn't responding to your texts, expressing that fear is vulnerable because it reveals a deeper insecurity about the relationship. It shows your need for reassurance, making you feel emotionally exposed.

To illustrate this further, let's consider Emily's story.

Emily lost her mother—the person she was closest to—in a sudden and unexpected tragedy. The loss was devastating and left Emily with an unaddressed, subconscious fear of abandonment. Without realizing it, this fear began to shape her relationships and emotional responses.

A year later, Emily started dating Ian. Their relationship grew deeper, and Emily found herself falling in love. But as the relationship deepened, Emily's fear of abandonment began to surface in small, seemingly random ways.

For example, Emily often asked Ian to text her when he arrived at work. On one occasion, Ian forgot. Emily, feeling a wave of intense emotion, called him and unleashed her anger. Her tone was sharp, her words cutting. Ian was confused. He knew he had made a mistake, but her anger seemed disproportionate to the situation.

Another time, during an argument, Ian needed space to cool off. He walked out of Emily's apartment to clear his head. This triggered another intense response from Emily. She was overwhelmed by anger, yelling and venting her frustration. Ian, again, couldn't understand why such a simple request for space had caused such a strong reaction.

Eventually, the couple sought therapy. In one session, the therapist gently asked Emily what she felt at the root of these arguments. Emily broke down in tears.

She realized her anger wasn't about Ian forgetting to text or walking away during arguments. At the heart of her emotions was a profound fear of losing Ian, rooted in the trauma of losing her mother. When Ian didn't text her, her mind spiraled into worst-case scenarios: What if something happened to him? What if she lost him, too? When Ian walked out the door during an argument, it felt like he might never come back—just as her mother never did.

Emily's primary emotion was fear—a raw, vulnerable response to her deep-seated grief and fear of abandonment. But instead of expressing that fear, she masked it with anger—a secondary emotion that felt safer and less exposing.

Emily struggled to express her fear because doing so felt too vulnerable. It would require her to admit just how much Ian meant to her and how deeply afraid she was of losing him. In her mind, opening up in this way felt like giving Ian a weapon he could use against her. What if he used her vulnerability to manipulate, threaten, or hurt her?

In a toxic relationship, such fears could be valid. But in a healthy relationship, vulnerability opens the door to deeper intimacy and understanding.

By sharing her deeper feelings, Emily gave Ian the opportunity to understand her better. Through therapy, Ian realized that his actions—forgetting to text or walking away—weren't just small missteps. They triggered something much deeper in Emily. Armed with this understanding, Ian could respond with compassion, ensuring he communicated more clearly and addressed Emily's fears with love.

For Emily, vulnerability was a risk. But in a healthy relationship, it was a risk worth taking. Sharing her fears allowed her and Ian to grow closer, building a foundation of trust and emotional safety.

Primary emotions often feel risky because they expose our emotional core. But when expressed in the right context—especially in safe, loving relationships—they can lead to deeper connection and healing. Secondary emotions, while protective, can sometimes obscure the real issue, leaving it unaddressed.

Emily's story reminds us that vulnerability, while scary, is essential for emotional growth and relational health. When we dare to express our primary emotions, we create opportunities for greater intimacy and understanding, reflecting the heart of Jesus in our relationships.

Primary emotions often surface instinctively and without warning, leaving us with little time to filter or control them. When expressed in relationships—whether through tears of sadness or an outburst of anger—they can feel like handing over your emotional power to someone else. Showing these raw emotions makes you vulnerable to judgment, rejection, or misunderstanding.

Take an argument with a family member, for example. You might feel immediate anger when they criticize you. Expressing this anger in the heat of the moment can leave you feeling exposed because it reveals just how deeply their words hurt you.

Secondary emotions, on the other hand, aren't as raw and unfiltered as primary emotions. These are often used as emotional defenses, shielding us from the vulnerability of our primary feelings. They act as a protective layer, creating emotional distance and detachment.

For instance, if you feel neglected by your partner, your primary emotions might be sadness or hurt. But over time, if these emotions remain unaddressed, you might begin to feel and express resentment—a secondary emotion. Resentment feels less vulnerable than admitting sadness or longing because it shifts the focus away from your emotional needs and onto your partner's perceived shortcomings.

Expressing sadness or fear requires vulnerability because it exposes your emotional core:

- *What if your partner dismisses your feelings?*

- *What if they reject your needs or see you as too needy or clingy?*

Instead of risking those outcomes, you may retreat into resentment, withdrawing emotionally, keeping score, and even taking offense at small things. Resentment feels safer because it deflects from the deeper emotional wound, but it ultimately prevents healing and connection.

With secondary emotions, there is often more time to reflect and decide how to present your feelings. However, this detachment can sometimes lead to avoidance.

Imagine feeling fear because a close friend is spending more time with new people. Instead of admitting, *"I'm afraid I'm losing the closeness we once had,"* you might express jealousy. Jealousy shifts the blame outward, making it seem like your friend is the one at fault for neglecting the relationship. This avoids the vulnerability of admitting your deeper fear of losing their friendship and the importance of the relationship to you.

While secondary emotions offer a sense of protection, they can also create misunderstandings in relationships. Expressing jealousy instead of fear might make your friend feel judged, unfairly criticized, or even distanced from you, deepening the very gap you were trying to bridge.

Primary emotions are challenging to express because they open us up emotionally. But this very vulnerability is essential for building deeper, more authentic connections.

For example:

- Instead of allowing jealousy to cloud your interactions with your friend, you might say, *"I'm afraid I'm losing the connection we once had, and it's making me feel anxious."*

- Instead of expressing resentment toward your partner by saying, *"You don't care about me anymore,"* you might say, *"I feel hurt when we don't spend as much time together as we used to."*

While these vulnerable statements may feel risky, they open the door for empathy, understanding, and meaningful dialogue. Vulnerability is the bridge to intimacy. Without it, relationships can falter under the weight of unresolved feelings and miscommunications.

Using secondary emotions like resentment or jealousy as a mask can lead to missed opportunities for connection. It's easier to say, *"You don't care about me anymore,"* but this often leads to defensiveness or confusion. Your partner might feel inadequate or unsure of how to address the underlying issue.

On the other hand, expressing your primary emotion—*"I feel hurt when we don't spend time together"*—invites your partner into your emotional world. This vulnerability allows them to understand your feelings and respond with compassion.

Some of the friendships and relationships you've lost in the past may not have ended because of a single fight or disagreement. Instead, they may have unraveled due to a lack of vulnerability. When secondary emotions dominate, the true heart of the issue often goes unspoken.

Imagine a friendship where frustration and jealousy bubble up, but the core feeling of sadness over growing apart is never expressed. Without a heartfelt conversation to address the root cause, misunderstandings and assumptions take over, creating a distance that could have been avoided.

Vulnerability is the key to stopping the cycle of self-sabotage in relationships. While secondary emotions serve as a form of protection, they often hinder real connection. Expressing primary emotions—no matter how vulnerable—creates opportunities for healing, understanding, and deeper intimacy.

By daring to be vulnerable, you not only strengthen your relationships but also reflect the heart of emotional intelligence. Vulnerability requires courage, but it's a risk worth taking for the sake of genuine connection and love.

Many people are so terrified of vulnerability that they project secondary emotions, burying their primary emotions far below the surface. For some, these primary emotions have been hidden so deep, for so long, that they've become almost unrecognizable. Weeks turn into months, and months into years, with these core feelings—rejection, hurt, fear, sadness—left unaddressed, tucked away in the subconscious like forgotten secrets.

But here's the thing: emotions don't disappear just because we bury them.

Covering primary emotions with secondary ones like anger or resentment doesn't erase them. Your anger doesn't dissolve the sting of rejection, nor does your resentment erase the sadness that lies beneath. These primary emotions remain, quietly shaping your thoughts, behaviors, and relationships, even when you don't realize it.

Many people go through life only addressing and expressing their secondary emotions, leaving their relationships strained and the people around them confused. Why? Because the deeper, primary emotions remain buried and unresolved.

Imagine a sibling relationship strained for years. The resentment and frustration between them are evident, but no one dares to confront the root of it—a deep sadness or hurt buried since childhood, perhaps stemming from favoritism or a long-forgotten argument. The refusal to address these primary emotions keeps the relationship stuck in tension and misunderstanding.

Or consider married couples who end up divorcing over "irreconcilable differences." Often, those differences stem from years of unspoken feelings—fears, hurts, and vulnerabilities that were never addressed. Instead of tackling those core emotions together, the couple avoided them, burying them under layers of resentment, frustration, and detachment.

The longer you bury your primary emotions, the more damage they can do—not just to your relationships but to your emotional and mental health. Suppressed emotions don't just vanish; they fester, manifesting in self-sabotaging behaviors, toxic relationship patterns, and even physical or verbal abuse.

Take the man from the story at the beginning of this chapter—the one who became angry and verbally lashed out at me because I refused to give him my phone number. His primary emotion wasn't anger; it was rejection. His anger was simply a cover for the raw vulnerability of feeling rejected.

Now consider this: his reaction was relatively mild compared to countless other situations where buried primary emotions have led to devastating consequences.

There are tragic stories of individuals who lash out violently because they cannot cope with the vulnerability of their primary emotions. A man feels rejected by a woman who refuses his advances, and his feelings of hurt and rejection overwhelm him. Unable to process these emotions, he reacts with violence, harming or even killing her.

There are even cases of serial killers whose deep-seated childhood traumas—feelings of neglect, rejection, or abandonment—were never addressed. These unresolved primary emotions festered and grew into something monstrous, fueling actions that shocked the world.

While these are extreme examples, they highlight a critical truth: when primary emotions remain buried, they can lead to harmful, toxic, and even abusive behaviors.

Burying your emotions may feel safer in the short term, but it's a ticking time bomb. Suppressed primary emotions often resurface in destructive ways—lashing out at loved ones, sabotaging relationships, or harming others.

The interplay between primary and secondary emotions can be found even in the Bible. Many stories in Scripture reveal the emotional depth of its characters—real people with real feelings. One striking example is the story of Cain and Abel in Genesis 4:1–16. This narrative illustrates the dangerous consequences of suppressing primary emotions and masking them with secondary emotions, even leading to toxic and abusive behavior.

This account of the very first murder in the Bible offers a powerful lens through which we can explore the impact of unresolved emotions.

Cain and Abel were brothers, sons of Adam and Eve. Abel was a shepherd, while Cain worked the land as a farmer. Genesis 4:3–5 recounts:

"When it was time for the harvest, Cain presented some of his crops as a gift to the Lord. Abel also brought a gift—the best portions of the firstborn lambs from his flock. The Lord accepted Abel and his gift, but He did not accept Cain and his gift. This made Cain very angry, and he looked dejected."

The word "dejected" paints a vivid picture of Cain's emotional state. Another translation describes Cain as "despondent," meaning discouraged, disheartened, or low-spirited. These terms highlight that Cain's emotional response was more than just anger—it was layered with primary emotions like sadness, disappointment, and rejection.

At the core, Cain longed for acceptance and approval from God. When his offering was rejected while Abel's was accepted, he felt inadequate and exposed. These vulnerable emotions—sadness, rejection, and disappointment—were raw and immediate yet deeply tied to his desire to please God.

Genesis 4:8 reveals the tragic outcome of Cain's suppressed emotions:

"One day Cain suggested to his brother, 'Let's go out into the fields.' And while they were in the field, Cain attacked his brother, Abel, and killed him."

Notice how the verse begins: *"One day."* This wasn't an impulsive act carried out in the heat of the moment. The Bible doesn't specify whether this occurred days, weeks, or even months later. What we do know is that Cain allowed his primary emotions to fester, unchecked and unaddressed, over a period of time.

Instead of processing his feelings of anger, sadness, rejection, and disappointment, Cain buried these vulnerable emotions. In their place, secondary emotions—jealousy, resentment, and hatred—took root. These secondary emotions acted as a mask, shielding Cain from confronting his deeper feelings of inadequacy and worthlessness.

What's remarkable is that God saw Cain's emotional turmoil and directly addressed it. In Genesis 4:6–7, God said to Cain:

"Why are you so angry? Why do you look so dejected? You will be accepted if you do what is right. But if you refuse to do what is right, then watch out! Sin is crouching at your door, eager to control you. But you must subdue it and be its master."

Here, we see that God acknowledges Cain's emotions and calls them out by name—anger and dejection. God's words reveal His care and concern for Cain's emotional state. He warns Cain of the danger of letting these emotions go unchecked, likening sin to a predator crouching at the door, ready to take control.

God invites Cain to confront his feelings, reflect on his actions, and choose a better path. This moment shows that God cares deeply about our emotions and wants us to process them in His presence. Vulnerability before God allows Him to help us master our emotions, preventing them from evolving into harmful behaviors.

Cain, however, refused to take the vulnerable path. He did not address his primary emotions of anger and dejection. He did not seek reconciliation with God or ask for guidance on how to make his offering acceptable. Instead, Cain allowed his anger to fester, nurturing jealousy and hatred towards his brother.

These unchecked emotions created a feedback loop:

1. Primary emotions like anger, sadness, and rejection were buried.

2. Secondary emotions like hatred and jealousy grew unchecked, creating a distorted perspective.

3. These emotions culminated in toxic behavior—murdering his brother, Abel.

Cain's tragic story illustrates the destructive power of suppressing primary emotions. His inability to process his feelings led to a sinful act with devastating consequences—not just for Abel, but for Cain himself, as he was cursed and exiled.

Cain's story serves as a cautionary tale about the dangers of suppressing vulnerable emotions. When we bury our primary emotions, we give room for secondary emotions like jealousy, resentment, and hatred to grow unchecked. Over time, these emotions can distort our perspective, damage our relationships, and even lead to harmful actions.

Yet, this story also highlights God's care and compassion for our emotional health. God didn't ignore Cain's feelings. He named them, addressed them, and provided a way for Cain to master them. This is a powerful reminder that we can bring our emotions—no matter how raw or vulnerable—into God's presence, trusting Him to guide us toward healing and wholeness.

By choosing vulnerability and processing our primary emotions, we can avoid the dangerous consequences of emotional suppression and experience the freedom, peace, and relational health God desires for us.

When Primary Emotions Feel "Wrong"

The fear of vulnerability isn't the only reason we mask our primary emotions with secondary ones. Sometimes, the root runs deeper. We may hide our primary emotions because they feel inherently *wrong*. Society often imposes expectations on how we should feel in specific situations, dictating a framework of "acceptable" emotions. When our primary emotions deviate from these norms, we judge them—and ourselves—harshly. As a result, secondary emotions like guilt, shame, or resentment develop, masking the primary emotions we're too afraid to confront.

Let's explore two stories that illustrate this struggle.

Mary's Conflicting Emotions as a New Mom

Mary is a new mom, and her life should be filled with nothing but joy and gratitude—or at least, that's what everyone around her expects. She's just given birth to a beautiful baby, and her family is overjoyed, gushing about how exciting this new chapter must be for her.

But as Mary sits at home, holding her newborn, she feels an unexpected twinge of anger and resentment. Deep down, she feels overwhelmed by how much her life has changed in such a short time. Her body doesn't look the way it used to, and she's grappling with sleepless nights, hormonal shifts, and the mental toll of caring for a newborn. Social media only adds to her frustration as she watches friends and colleagues living their lives, traveling, and pursuing careers while she feels stuck at home.

Mary loves her baby deeply, but she also misses her old self—the version of her that had more freedom, energy, and time to do things like her hair and makeup. The emotional conflict within her is overwhelming. She feels both love and anger toward her baby, leaving her confused and ashamed.

Everyone around Mary assumes she's 100% overjoyed. This inten-sifies her guilt, as she begins to think, *"What kind of mother am I? I should be happy. Why am I feeling this way? I must be a terrible mom."*

Mary's fear of judgment stops her from being honest about her emotions. She's afraid people will think she doesn't love her baby or that she's ungrateful. Instead of processing her primary emotions—anger, frustration, and exhaustion—Mary suppresses them and devel-ops secondary emotions like guilt and shame.

Aisha's Conflicted Grief

Aisha has spent years as her father's primary caregiver. His terminal illness has taken a massive toll on her physical, mental, and emotional well-being. She has sacrificed her dreams, relationships, and personal time to prioritize his care, and the daily weight of seeing her father in pain has been heartbreaking.

When her father passes away, Aisha is devastated—but she also feels something unexpected: relief.

This relief stems from two places. First, she feels a sense of peace knowing her father is no longer suffering. Second, she feels a weight lifted as she can now begin to reclaim her life.

But society expects her to feel only sorrow and grief. Friends and family offer condolences, assuming she is entirely consumed by sad-ness. Meanwhile, Aisha feels torn inside. The relief she feels clashes with the sorrow, creating an emotional tug-of-war.

"I must be a terrible daughter," she thinks. "What kind of person feels relief after their father dies? People will think I'm heartless if they know."

Aisha judges her feelings and herself, burying her sense of relief under overwhelming guilt. This secondary emotion shields her from the vulnerability of admitting her true feelings, which she fears might invite judgment or rejection.

Both Mary and Aisha's stories reveal the complexity of human emotions. Primary emotions like anger, frustration, or relief arise in-stinctively, reflecting our inner realities. But when those emotions clash with societal expectations, we often suppress them, layering secondary emotions like guilt, shame, or resentment on top.

Mary isn't a bad mother for feeling anger or frustration. These emotions are natural responses to the overwhelming changes and challenges she's facing. Likewise, Aisha's relief isn't a sign that she didn't love her father. It's a natural release of tension after years of caregiving and witnessing his suffering.

These stories show us that it's possible for two contrasting emotions to coexist. You can love your child deeply while feeling frustrated by the demands of parenting. You can grieve a loved one's death while feeling relief that their suffering has ended.

Societal norms often dictate how we *should* feel, creating a blueprint for what's acceptable. When our emotions don't align with these expectations, we judge them—and ourselves. This judgment creates an internal conflict, driving us to bury our primary emotions and replace them with secondary ones that feel safer or more socially acceptable.

But burying these emotions only deepens the problem. Left unaddressed, they fester beneath the surface, creating confusion and strain in our relationships.

Mary's and Aisha's experiences remind us that emotions—no matter how complex or contradictory—are part of being human. The key to emotional health lies in confronting these feelings, not suppressing them.

When we allow ourselves to acknowledge and process our primary emotions, we open the door to compassion, understanding, and healing. Instead of judging ourselves for feeling a certain way, we can ask deeper questions:

- *What is this emotion trying to tell me?*

- *What need or value does this emotion reflect?*

By digging through the layers of secondary emotions like guilt and shame, we can uncover the primary emotions that reveal our truest selves. And when we allow ourselves to express those primary emotions—whether it's frustration, sadness, or even relief—we create space for connection and growth.

So, perhaps it's time to pick up the shovel and begin uncovering the layers of buried emotions that have been hidden for so long. In doing so, we can bring light to the vulnerable places in our hearts and experience the freedom that comes with true emotional honesty.

Societal Expectations and Gendered Emotional Expression

Did you know that gender significantly influences how we experience and navigate our primary and secondary emotions? Societal norms have long dictated which emotions are "acceptable" for men and women to express, shaping how individuals process, suppress, or display their feelings. These cultural expectations often create internal conflicts, influencing how men and women handle primary and secondary emotions.

Let's explore how these gendered norms affect emotional expression, starting with one of the most misunderstood emotions: anger.

Women are often socialized to prioritize relational harmony and avoid emotions perceived as disruptive—like anger. Society frequently portrays femininity as soft, gentle, nurturing, and agreeable, making anger seem incompatible with traditional ideas of what it means to be "feminine."

This dynamic creates an inner conflict for many women. When they feel anger, it often clashes with societal expectations, leading to guilt or shame for experiencing such a "masculine" emotion. Take, for instance, the harmful stereotype of the *"angry Black woman."* This trope not only diminishes a Black woman's valid emotional expression but also unfairly suggests that anger makes her less feminine, less attractive, or somehow less worthy.

As a result, many women suppress their anger to avoid being labeled as aggressive, bitter, or unladylike. Instead, they redirect their feelings inward, often masking their anger with secondary emotions like shame, guilt, or inadequacy.

For example, a woman may suppress her anger when her boundaries are crossed at work, internalizing her frustration. Over time, this pattern of suppression can prevent her from addressing the injustice or advocating for herself, leading to chronic self-doubt or even depression. Suppressed anger can also manifest in passive-aggressive behaviors, such as sulking, gossiping, or subtle criticisms—ways of expressing discontent without direct confrontation, which is often seen as "unfeminine."

While anger is deemed unfeminine, society views it as quintessentially masculine. Men are often encouraged to suppress vulnerable emotions like sadness, fear, or shame—emotions society associates with weakness and femininity. Instead, anger is framed as a "masculine" emotion that conveys strength, power, and dominance.

This cultural conditioning makes it easier for men to default to anger as a secondary emotion, masking deeper, more vulnerable primary emotions. For example, a man who feels rejected or disappointed may react with anger rather than expressing sadness or seeking support. Anger becomes a protective layer, shielding him from the perceived vulnerability of revealing his true feelings.

While this might temporarily preserve a sense of control or strength, the avoidance of primary emotions like sadness or shame prevents true emotional processing. This pattern can lead to unresolved emotional pain, strained relationships, and even destructive behaviors. Men who suppress these vulnerable emotions may find themselves trapped in cycles of conflict, unable to communicate their deeper emotional needs.

Societal norms create a stark divide in emotional expression between men and women. While women may feel more comfortable expressing sadness or shame—emotions seen as "soft" or "feminine"—they often suppress anger. Conversely, men may openly express anger but suppress emotions like sadness, fear, or shame, which are seen as "weak" or "unmanly."

These gendered norms result in emotional suppression for both men and women:

- A woman might internalize her anger, leading to chronic self-doubt or passive-aggressive behavior.

- A man might externalize his sadness through aggression, creating conflict and damaging relationships.

In both cases, individuals are left with unmet emotional needs, and their inability to process emotions authentically can have far-reaching consequences for their mental health and relationships.

Breaking free from these gendered norms requires a shift toward emotional literacy—learning to identify, understand, and express emotions without judgment or fear.

For women, this might mean learning to view anger not as a flaw but as a signal for change. Anger can be a powerful indicator that something is wrong, whether it's a boundary being crossed, an injustice occurring, or a need going unmet. Instead of suppressing anger, women can learn to express it constructively, using it to advocate for themselves and address underlying issues.

For men, breaking free involves creating safe spaces to express vulnerability without fear of judgment. By acknowledging primary emotions like sadness or fear, men can foster deeper connections and begin to heal unresolved emotional wounds.

Gendered expectations around emotions are deeply ingrained, but they are not immutable. By challenging these norms, we can create a culture where both men and women feel free to express their emotions authentically and constructively.

Imagine a world where women could express anger without fear of being labeled as "too much" or "too aggressive" and where men could openly share their sadness or fear without worrying about appearing "weak" or "less masculine." Such a world would allow individuals to process their emotions in healthier ways, leading to stronger relationships, greater self-awareness, and deeper emotional freedom.

The journey toward emotional authenticity begins with recognizing the societal pressures that shape how we express and suppress our feelings. By unlearning these patterns, we can reclaim the full spectrum of our emotions, honoring the humanity God designed in each of us.

Practical Steps to Work Through Your Primary and Secondary Emotions

1. Pay Attention to Your Reactions

In any given situation, pause and notice your immediate response. What are you feeling? Is it happiness, sadness, anger, relief, or disappointment? Naming the primary emotion is the first step in understanding your experience.

2. Examine the Secondary Emotion

Ask yourself, *"What am I feeling now that I've had time to reflect?"* or *"How do I feel about my initial reaction?"* Secondary emotions provide insight into how you're processing the event and may reveal deeper fears, desires, or unmet needs.

3. Express Emotions in Healthy Ways

Once you've identified both your primary and secondary emotions, practice expressing them constructively. This could mean having an honest conversation, journaling, or seeking counsel. Expressing your emotions authentically fosters better self-awareness and deeper understanding in your relationships.

4. Resolve Conflicts by Addressing Primary Emotions

Challenge yourself to move beyond secondary emotions when resolving conflicts. Instead of focusing on the protective layer of resentment, anger, or defensiveness, ask yourself, *"What's really going on here? What is the root of this feeling?"*

For instance, if sadness is at the core, explore why you feel sad and what can be done to address it before it evolves into more complex emotions like bitterness. When you center on the primary emotion, you can address the real issue and prevent further misunderstanding.

Suppressing primary emotions may feel easier in the moment, but it's not sustainable. Left unacknowledged, these emotions fester and grow, distorting your perception of yourself and your relationships.

Vulnerability is hard, yes—but it's also the key to emotional health, stronger relationships, and a more fulfilling life. When you address the core of your feelings, you don't just heal yourself; you create space for healthier, more authentic connections with those around you.

The first step to healing is acknowledging the emotions you've buried for too long. It requires courage, but it's necessary. By embracing vulnerability, you reflect the emotional intelligence and raw authenticity modeled by Jesus Himself.

When you allow yourself to process and express primary emotions, you break free from cycles of suppression, projection, and harm. You begin to understand yourself better, communicate more clearly, and cultivate relationships that are deeply rooted in trust and intimacy.

Your emotional well-being—and the health of your relationships—depends on this work. The journey isn't easy, but the reward is profound: healing, freedom, and the ability to live as your truest self, as God intended.

Take this step. Embrace the process. You are worth it.

The Importance of Understanding Primary and Secondary Emotions

As we conclude this chapter, it's essential to reflect on why understanding primary and secondary emotions is so transformative for our emotional well-being and relationships:

1. Identifying Core Feelings

Recognizing the difference between primary and secondary emotions helps you uncover the root of what you're truly feeling. When you address the core issue, you prevent it from escalating into something overwhelming, confusing, or even monstrous and unrecognizable.

2. Better Emotional Regulation

Understanding that secondary emotions stem from primary ones allows you to manage your reactions more effectively. For instance, instead of lashing out in jealousy, you can pause and explore its root—perhaps sadness or insecurity—and address those feelings directly.

3. Improved Communication in Relationships

In your relationships with family, friends, or partners, understanding your primary and secondary emotions equips you to communicate more authentically. It prevents sabotage, illuminates underlying issues, and fosters deeper connection and intimacy.

EXERCISES FOR NAVIGATING PRIMARY AND SECONDARY EMOTIONS

These exercises are designed to help you identify and separate primary and secondary emotions in specific situations, process your primary emotions more constructively, and embrace vulnerability. Use your emotions journal to record and reflect as you go through these activities. Repeat these exercises as often as needed throughout your personal development journey.

Exercise 1: Emotional Layering Chart

Objective: To uncover the layers of your emotions and better understand the connection between primary and secondary feelings.

Instructions:

1. Reflect on a recent emotionally charged situation where you had a strong reaction.

2. In your emotions journal, create a chart with two columns:

   - **Primary Emotion**: Identify the raw, instinctive emotion you felt initially (e.g., sadness, fear, disappointment).

   - **Secondary Emotion**: Pinpoint the emotion that developed afterward, influenced by thoughts, societal expectations, or past experiences (e.g., guilt, resentment, shame).

3. Answer the following questions for each column:

   - *What triggered the primary emotion?*

   - *Why did the secondary emotion develop?*

   - *How did I express or suppress these emotions?*

4. Reflect on what these emotions reveal about your needs, values, or emotional patterns.

Exercise 2: Vulnerability Practice

Objective: To help you process a primary emotion constructively and build the courage to express vulnerability.

Instructions:

1. Choose one primary emotion you've experienced recently but have not yet expressed.

2. Write your responses to the following prompts in your emotions journal:

   • *What is this emotion revealing about what I value or need?*

   • *What fears or hesitations do I have about expressing this emotion honestly?*

   • *How can I express this emotion constructively to someone I trust?*

3. Practice verbalizing this emotion with a trusted friend, partner, or family member in a safe environment. Focus on being honest, clear, and vulnerable in your communication.

REFLECTION QUESTIONS

1. Before reading this chapter, had you ever heard of primary and secondary emotions? What was your prior understanding of these concepts, if any? How has this chapter expanded your perspective?

2. Think of a recent situation where you felt a strong secondary emotion (e.g., jealousy, resentment, guilt). What primary emotion might have been buried beneath it? How can you work on addressing that primary emotion directly moving forward?

3. Do you find yourself masking your primary emotions with secondary emotions? Why do you think that happens? Does it vary depending on the relationship or situation?

4. How do you typically respond to vulnerability? Do you view it as a strength or a weakness? Why? How might embracing vulnerability improve your relationships and emotional health?

5. Have you ever judged yourself for feeling a certain emotion, especially one that didn't align with societal or cultural expectations? How did this self-judgment influence the way you expressed or suppressed that emotion?

6. In what ways have societal norms or cultural expectations shaped the way you express your emotions? Are there certain emotions you find yourself suppressing because of these norms? How does this affect your emotional well-being?

7. Reflect on a time when fear of vulnerability created distance or conflict in a relationship. How might expressing a primary emotion in that moment have changed the outcome?

8. Think about a strained or broken relationship in your life. What primary emotions might have been buried or left unaddressed in that relationship? How could addressing those emotions now bring healing or clarity?

9. How can understanding the difference between primary and secondary emotions help you improve your emotional health and communication in relationships? What practical steps can you take to integrate this understanding into your daily life?

10. After reading this chapter, what actionable steps will you take to uncover, process, and express your primary emotions more authentically? How do you think this will impact your emotional growth and your relationships moving forward?

PART II

05

EMOTIONS: GOD'S GIFT TO US

M any of you are probably familiar with the concept of the five love languages, introduced by Gary Chapman, a pastor, author, and speaker. According to Chapman, the five love languages describe how people give and receive love in relationships. They include words of affirmation, quality time, physical touch, acts of service, and receiving gifts.

For me, my top love language has been consistent for as long as I can remember—probably since childhood. Of all the five, my #1 love language is receiving gifts. Anyone who knows me well knows I love gifts. But here's the thing—it's not just about the gift itself. For me, a gift is like a tangible memory, a piece of a cherished moment that I can hold onto. It's about the story behind the gift.

I love it when someone asks me, "Where did you get this?" because it allows me to relive the moment and share the story of the relationship that inspired it. Gifts, to me, are a reflection of intentionality, thoughtfulness, and love. They represent the connection between the giver and me.

However, not everyone understands the love language of receiving gifts. There's a misconception that people who value this love language are shallow, materialistic, or high-maintenance. But let me set the record straight: for true lovers of receiving gifts, it's not about the price tag or the quantity. It's about the meaning behind the gift.

It's the thought behind the act. It's about someone walking into a store, seeing something, and thinking, "Ekemini would really love this." It's about the care and intention that goes into choosing something that reflects the relationship. It's the love poured into finding the perfect item that makes receiving gifts so meaningful.

The Three Categories of Gifts

Now, as much as I love gifts, not all gifts hit the mark. Over the years, I've noticed that the gifts I receive tend to fall into three categories:

1. **The Perfect Gift**: These are the gifts that make my heart sing—the ones that reflect me perfectly. These gifts feel personal and thoughtful, showing that the giver truly knows and values who I am. It's like receiving a piece of my own personality in a box.

2. **The Missed-the-Mark Gift**: These are the gifts that don't reflect who I am or what I love. If the giver is an acquaintance, it's understandable—they don't know me well and are simply being kind. But if the giver is someone close to me, it's a bit disappointing. You can often tell when someone grabbed something at the last minute without much thought.

3. **The "You Needed This" Gift**: Ah, the practical gifts. These are the ones I didn't ask for and wouldn't have picked out for myself, but I know deep down I probably need them. They can be both annoying and endearing.

Have you ever gotten a gift that you didn't want but secretly needed? These gifts always come with an interesting mix of emotions. It's like when someone knows you love novels but gets you a candle instead, saying, "You already have so many books, and I noticed you didn't have candles at your place." Or imagine someone knowing I'm a perfume lover—because I truly am—and deciding to get me a wellness planner instead. I mean, yes, I know my life is all over the place, and a planner might help me stay organized. But honestly, just get me another perfume! For someone like me who cherishes scents and collects perfumes with passion, a planner just doesn't hit the same. It's not that I don't appreciate the thought—it's just that when someone gives me what I need instead of what I want, it can feel like they're highlighting my flaws rather than celebrating my joy.

As much as I've rolled my eyes at those "you needed this" gifts—the ones that cater to my needs rather than my wants—my perspective on them completely transformed one unforgettable December in 2023. That Christmas, my now-husband, then fiancé, surprised me with a gift that blew my mind and completely shifted how I viewed this third category of gifts.

He knows me well—my love for perfumes, bags, and other beautiful things. Naturally, I was expecting something along those lines. That evening, he showed up at my apartment with a gleam in his eye and said, "I have a surprise for you."

Excited but nervous, I wondered, *what could it be?* My mind raced through my long perfume wish list, thinking, *"Surely, it has to be something from there!"* But oh, was I wrong.

With a smile, he revealed, "I got you some top-quality podcast equipment so we can take your podcast to the next level. Now you can record in higher quality and finally launch on YouTube."

Whoa. I was stunned. For those who don't know, I host **The Yellow Podcast**, a dream I launched on July 7, 2021. When I started, I didn't have much—just a single microphone and my trusty laptop to edit audio. My podcast episodes were audio-only, and while my mic wasn't the fanciest, it got the job done. Back then, my focus wasn't on perfection but on starting. I just wanted to create and share my voice with the world.

But this gift? This was on another level. My fiancé had gone above and beyond, investing in expensive, high-quality podcast equipment—two top-notch microphones (one for me and one for guests), a professional-grade audio interface, and everything I would need to upgrade my production. It was overwhelming—in the best possible way.

And yet, instead of jumping for joy and showering him with thanks, my first reaction was pure worry. "This is a lot," I said nervously. "I'm not tech-savvy. I don't even know how to use all this. How will I set it up? How will I edit YouTube videos? I don't know how to do any of that!"

In his gentle way, my fiancé reassured me, "You don't have to worry about any of that. I'll handle the equipment setup, production, and editing. All you need to do is what God has called you to do: speak into that mic and create content."

Wow. His words hit me like a wave. This wasn't just a practical gift—it was intentional, deeply meaningful, and perfectly aligned with my purpose. It wasn't about perfumes or handbags; it was about investing in my calling. This gift wasn't something I even dared to dream about, yet it was exactly what I needed to step into where God was taking me in the ministry of speaking, podcasting, and content creation.

More than that, this gift confirmed something profound. You see, back in 2019, God had spoken to me prophetically about my future husband. I'd written everything He revealed in a special journal reserved for His words. One detail stood out: God told me my husband would invest his resources in my calling and ministry. He would recognize the work God had called me to do and actively support it.

Before meeting my husband, I had dated a few men, but none of them believed in my podcast or the vision God had given me. They dismissed it as a fleeting hobby, something I'd eventually drop when "real life" set in. One even condescendingly told me I was dreaming too big and that he preferred a wife more focused on homemaking and catering to him.

Those experiences made me deeply grateful for the clarity God had given me. By holding on to what He had spoken about my future husband, I was able to discern the counterfeits that came my way. That Christmas, when my fiancé handed me the podcast equipment, it was more than just a thoughtful gift—it was a divine confirmation. This was the man God had spoken about. His belief in my purpose, his investment in my dreams, and his willingness to support my calling aligned perfectly with what God had told me years earlier. I couldn't help but feel tears of joy as my spirit recognized the confirmation.

Here's something just as beautiful as the story of the incredible gift my husband gave me: God is also in the business of giving gifts. In fact, He is the ultimate gift-giver. He doesn't just give us good gifts—He gives us the most perfect, purposeful, and intentional gifts, far beyond what any human could ever offer.

As much as my husband knows me and gives amazing, thoughtful gifts, the truth is, God knows me even more intimately. His gifts are so perfect that they often surpass my human understanding or expectations. Nobody knows you better than God, and that's exactly why He is the best gift-giver.

Now, here's the thing about God's gifts: they're not always based on what we want or desire. Sure, sometimes He gives us the things we ask for, those specific little blessings that make our hearts smile. For example, when you pray for something random—a parking spot on a busy day or for your favorite snack to still be in stock—He provides, simply because He's your loving Father. After all, Jesus did say to the disciples, *"Ask, and it will be given to you."*

But more often than not, God's gifts fall into the "you needed this" category. These are the gifts from God that go beyond our wants and cater to our growth, purpose, and ultimate well-being. God cares about our desires, yes, but His love for us is so deep that He gives us what we truly need, even when we don't realize it yet.

Even though we know that God is the ultimate gift giver, let's be honest—His gifts don't always *feel* like the perfect gifts to us. Why? Because they don't always align with the wish list we've carefully crafted in our minds—the things we've been fantasizing about, dreaming of, and hoping for.

Think about it: when the number one thing on your wishlist is a husband or wife, and you're still single, it doesn't exactly feel like God is handing you the perfect gift. Or maybe you've been dreaming of financial freedom, but you're still stuck in a job that just barely pays the bills. Perhaps you've been asking for a new car, and yet you're still navigating life without one. In these moments, it's hard to see God as the best gift giver because His gifts don't always satisfy our fleshly desires. Instead, He gives us those "you needed this" gifts—gifts that are essential and purposeful for fulfilling our calling and becoming more like Him.

So, what are some of these "you needed this" gifts from God? Let's start with the Holy Spirit. The Holy Spirit is one of the most ultimate gifts God has ever given us! Peter explicitly calls the Holy Spirit a gift in

Acts 2:38: *"...and you will receive the gift of the Holy Spirit."* The Holy Spirit is a divine gift from God that guides us, empowers us, and regenerates us. And the Holy Spirit didn't come empty-handed! He brought with Him a collection of other incredible gifts, as described in 1 Corinthians 12: the word of wisdom, the word of knowledge, the gift of faith, the gifts of healing, the gift of discerning of spirits, the gift of miracles, the gift of tongues, the gift of prophecy, and the interpretation of tongues. Each of these gifts is given to equip us to be more like Christ, fulfill our purpose, and spread the good news of the Gospel so that God's glory may be revealed on the earth.

But there's another powerful, thoughtful, and meaningful gift from God that we rarely think about. Are you ready for it? It's the gift of *emotions*. Yes, your emotions are a gift from God! Yet, when we think about the blessings He's given us, we often overlook this one.

Just like the other gifts I've mentioned, the gift of emotions is designed to help us reflect God's image on earth, build meaningful relationships and community, and walk in our God-given purpose. Your emotions are not random or purposeless; they are a tool God has given you to carry out your calling in whatever area He's placed you. Your emotions play a vital role in your purpose, serving as a way to not only reflect His image but also to reflect His heart to humanity.

God has also blessed us with the gift of emotions so that we can deeply connect with Him on a personal level. Our emotions are not just tools for navigating relationships with others—they are bridges that draw us closer to the heart of God. These emotions are divine gifts, and like every gift that comes from Him, they are inherently good because God Himself is good. Everything He creates, everything He gives, reflects His goodness. Emotions are no exception; they are a profound expression of His love, designed to help us experience Him more fully and intimately.

Emotions are a gift and a blessing. But let's be real—most of the time, they *feel* more like a burden than a blessing, don't they? They can be overwhelming, confusing, and difficult to navigate. And yet, when we start to see them as a divine gift, we begin to unlock their true purpose and beauty.

One of the most profound lessons I've learned is this: one of the enemy's greatest strategies to attack your faith and hinder your purpose is to convince you that your gifts are burdens rather than blessings. He cunningly twists our perception, making us believe that the very gifts God has given us to live a fulfilling and purposeful life are actually weighing us down.

Think about it—he convinces single people that the "gift" of singleness is a burden while simultaneously deceiving married people into believing that the "gift" of marriage is a burden. He does the same thing with emotions. The enemy works overtime to convince you that your gift of emotions is a liability, not an asset. He'll whisper lies, using the voices of others to tell you that you're "too much" because you feel deeply or express yourself passionately. He'll try to invalidate your emotions, making you believe it's wrong to feel the way you do. His goal? To make you resent the very emotions that God gave you as a gift.

How often have you found yourself saying things like, "I hate that this bothers me," or "I hate that I'm getting emotional about this"? Perhaps it's when a friend has deeply hurt you, and the sadness feels so heavy you wish you didn't care. Or when rejection stings, and you wish you could simply brush it off like it didn't matter. In these moments, emotions can feel like a burden we'd rather not carry.

But here's the truth: your emotions may feel like a burden because you haven't yet seen them for what they truly are—a profound gift and blessing. Maybe you're unsure how to handle and navigate this gift, which can make it feel overwhelming. I think back to the time my husband gave me the gift of podcast equipment. At first, I wasn't thrilled—I was worried because I had no idea how I was going to handle, use, or even begin to navigate that gift. But just as my husband reassured me that he would help me every step of the way, God also promises to help us with our gift of emotions.

God didn't just give you emotions and leave you to figure it out on your own. He walks with you, guiding and instructing you through His Word. The Bible is full of wisdom and instruction on how to manage and steward your emotions well. And God isn't a distant observer—

He deeply cares about your emotions and is actively involved, offering His help and support so you can fully appreciate this gift.

Just like any meaningful gift, emotions are designed to enrich your life and serve a greater purpose. God wants to help you navigate this gift so you can experience its blessings, use it to fulfill your calling, and glorify Him in the process. Emotions are not a burden—they are a reflection of His heart, a tool for connection, and a means to live out your purpose with authenticity and impact. With God's guidance, your emotions will no longer feel like a heavy load but a powerful instrument for good.

There was a time in my life when I truly felt like my emotions were more of a burden than a blessing. I'm someone who feels things deeply and passionately—a trait that's not inherently bad. However, when I was younger, I often struggled to navigate the depths of my emotional world, and this lack of understanding sometimes caused more harm to my relationships than good.

I vividly remember attending a two-week pneumatology school in North Carolina. During a prophetic presbytery session, one of the prophetic ministers shared something profound. She told me that God had revealed to her that I have a tendency to go deep—deep into situations, emotions, and understanding—and that He had designed me to dig to the root of things. Another prophetic minister spoke over me, saying that the Lord would use me to minister to people struggling with unforgiveness, anger, and hardened hearts. She said God would work through me to bring emotional healing, softening their hearts and breaking down the emotional walls they had built.

Those prophetic words planted themselves deep in my spirit, resonating in a way I hadn't expected. At that moment, something clicked. What I had once viewed as a burden, God was revealing to be a gift that He was refining and redeeming for His purpose. My emotions, which I had often wrestled with, were actually part of my calling. God was showing me that He could use my journey through emotions to help others struggling with their own, bringing healing and restoration to their hearts.

That revelation changed everything for me. It prompted me to pray intentionally about my emotions, asking God to give me wisdom and guidance. I wanted to use my emotions not as a source of chaos but as a tool to build His kingdom and strengthen my relationships. That prayer marked the beginning of a deeper understanding of the role my emotions play in my life and my calling.

Our emotions are far more than fleeting feelings—they are intentional gifts from God, designed to serve a purpose in our relationships, our calling, and our ministry as believers. Let's explore some of the incredible ways our emotions can be used as gifts to fulfill God's plan.

Emotions and Sexual Intimacy

Sexual intimacy within marriage is a God-given gift, designed not only to bring joy and unity to a husband and wife but also to glorify God. And yes, emotions are an integral part of this beautiful connection!

God created sex to unite a husband and wife, allowing them to become one flesh. It's not just a physical act but a sacred covenant reestablished and strengthened with each union. Sexual intimacy is meant to be enjoyed, deepening the bond and intimacy between spouses. This connection reflects God's desire for marriage to be a place where two people are truly known, accepted, and cherished.

In marriage, emotional intimacy often lays the foundation for physical intimacy. When spouses feel emotionally connected, it fosters trust, safety, and vulnerability—essential ingredients for a fulfilling and God-honoring sexual relationship. In fact, a couple's experience of sexual intimacy often mirrors their emotional connection and communication outside the bedroom. Emotions and sex are intricately intertwined, and when they work in harmony, they create a powerful bond.

From a Christian perspective, the emotional aspects of sexual intimacy reflect the profound closeness God desires with His people. Just as God invites us into a relationship marked by love, trust, and commitment, sexual intimacy invites couples to reflect that depth of connection with each other. Through physical closeness, spouses express love, admiration, and appreciation in ways that words alone cannot, nurturing one another on a deeper emotional level.

Sexual intimacy also facilitates bonding through the release of hormones like oxytocin, often called the "bonding hormone." This emotional and physical connection mirrors the "one flesh" principle in scripture, where two people become united as one. Beyond pleasure, sexual intimacy can be a space for healing and comfort. Emotions like empathy, compassion, and gentleness can be conveyed through physical touch, offering reassurance and strength. This nurturing aspect reflects God's love, where intimacy becomes a source of emotional support, not just physical fulfillment.

Trust and security—key emotional components—allow spouses to feel safe, valued, and cherished in each other's presence. This emotional foundation enables them to be vulnerable and authentic, strengthening their relationship and fostering a God-centered intimacy.

Your emotions are vital for a healthy sex life with your spouse! Isn't that incredible? Without emotions, marriage would lose its depth, intimacy, and connection. It would fail to reflect the relationship between Christ and the church, a union of love, sacrifice, and unwavering commitment. God has given you emotions to deepen your physical, spiritual, and emotional bond, enriching not only your relationship with your spouse but also glorifying the One who designed it all.

Emotions as A Weapon

Emotions are not just a gift and a blessing but also a weapon. Think about it: God, in His infinite wisdom, has given you the gift of emotions, not just to enrich your life but to empower you. This gift, in the form of a weapon, allows you to fight back against the kingdom of darkness and walk in the victory that Jesus has already won for you.

Love, for example, is a weapon. Scripture tells us in 1 John 4:18, "Perfect love casts out fear." This means love is not just a feeling; it's an active force that drives fear away. When you immerse yourself in the truth of God's perfect love, fear cannot stay—it has to flee.

Another weapon is **joy**. Joy, as Isaiah 61:3 reminds us, is the "oil of joy for mourning, the garment of praise for the spirit of heaviness." When you praise God through heavy and challenging emotions, He exchanges that heaviness for joy. This joy becomes a weapon, breaking through despair and defeating the enemy's attempts to weigh you down.

God didn't leave you defenseless in this world. Instead, He equipped you with emotions as a multifaceted gift: they're a blessing for connection and purpose, but they're also a weapon for spiritual warfare. Love, joy, and praise are just a few of the emotional weapons God has given you to stand strong, overcome fear, and push back against the enemy's schemes. Use them boldly, knowing that they come directly from the One who has already won the battle.

Emotions and Spiritual Gifts

Did you know that God redeems your emotions and uses them as instruments alongside the spiritual gifts He gives through the Holy Spirit? Your emotions play an integral role in how these gifts are activated and expressed, becoming a divine bridge between the natural and the supernatural. Let's explore this profound connection.

Take the gift of prophecy, for example. One fascinating mode of prophecy is visceral prophecy—a deeply felt, emotionally, and even physically charged prophetic experience. According to its definition, visceral prophecy involves revelation that is profoundly emotional, often accompanied by bodily sensations. It's not purely intellectual; it's instinctive and deeply personal. In this context, emotions are not just passive responses; they become active conduits through which the Holy Spirit communicates, allowing the prophet to connect with God's heart and convey His message.

When emotions are engaged in prophecy, they reflect the emotional dimensions of God's nature. For instance, a prophet may feel overwhelming sorrow, uncontainable joy, or fierce compassion—mirroring God's heart for a particular person or situation. These emotions amplify the urgency and depth of the prophetic word, transforming it into a more intimate and fuller expression of God's will. It's through this emotional engagement that the prophet can deliver a message that resonates deeply with its recipient.

Another beautiful example of emotions being intertwined with spiritual gifts is the gift of mercy. Mercy, as mentioned in Romans

12:6-8, is one of the gifts of grace and is marked by a heart of compassion and care for those in need. People with this gift are naturally drawn to those who are suffering, offering kindness, prayer, and practical support. The emotions tied to this gift—empathy, tenderness, and a deep sense of care—are not just byproducts but essential components. They allow the person with the gift of mercy to genuinely connect with the pain and struggles of others.

I vividly recall one evening in September 2024 when I was preparing to lead a Bible study. Out of nowhere, I felt an overwhelming sense of grief, so heavy that it brought me to tears. It was as if a dark cloud had settled over me, and I couldn't shake the weight of sadness. Feeling prompted, I began to pray and intercede for comfort and healing, though I didn't know why. Later that evening, I learned that at the exact time I had been praying, an inmate on death row was being executed—a man who had consistently claimed his innocence. I had no prior knowledge of this event, yet God allowed me to feel the grief likely carried by his family and loved ones, moving me to intercede on their behalf.

This is the heart of the gift of mercy—God uses your emotions to reflect His compassion, leading you to act as His hands and feet in moments of deep need. This emotional sensitivity aligns with God's heart, enabling His love, comfort, and healing to flow through you to others.

Similarly, consider the gift of discerning spirits. At times, God may place a strong emotional impression on your heart that aligns with the spiritual condition of a person or environment. For instance, I've had moments where I've met someone and suddenly felt a wave of anxiety or fear, only to have the Holy Spirit reveal that this person or someone close to them was battling a spirit of fear. That discernment allowed me to partner with them in prayer, addressing the root cause of their struggle and standing against it in the Spirit.

Another example is the word of knowledge, where God may stir your emotions to reveal specific insight into a person's life. These impressions can be deeply emotional, connecting you to God's heart for that individual and leading to a breakthrough or healing moment.

God engages our emotions not just as a part of our humanity but as a divine tool to activate and enhance our spiritual gifts. Emotions enable us to align with His heart, reflect His compassion, and step into divine encounters where healing, transformation, and breakthrough occur.

Your emotions are a powerful and sacred gift intricately woven into the spiritual gifts God has given you. They are instruments of connection, tools for ministry, and a reflection of God's own heart at work in and through you.

Emotions as God's Protection and Direction

Did you know that your emotions help to keep you alive? They are not just a part of your inner world but essential tools for your survival and spiritual journey. Emotions like fear, anger, sadness, and love are deeply tied to biological mechanisms designed to protect us. These emotions are part of God's intricate design, ensuring both our physical preservation and spiritual growth.

Take fear, for example. Biologically, fear is one of the most essential emotions in life-threatening situations. It activates the fight-or-flight response, preparing your body to act quickly in the face of danger. When your brain perceives a threat—like a fire or even a lion—your hypothalamus sets off a cascade of signals to the sympathetic nervous system. Your heart rate increases, your pupils dilate, and your body releases glucose for an energy boost, readying you to either fight or flee. This beautifully orchestrated system is a gift from God, keeping you alive and responsive to danger. Fear, often misunderstood as purely negative, is, in fact, a divine alarm system designed to preserve and protect you.

But God didn't stop at using emotions to protect us physically; He also uses them to guide and protect us spiritually. Your emotions are not just biological—they are spiritual tools. They can serve as channels through which God offers protection, direction, and insight into His will for your life. Through your emotions, God speaks, leading you away from harm and toward His purpose.

One way God communicates is through feelings—a form of divine direction often referred to as "feeling God's voice." This involves sensing His presence, guidance, or message through strong emotions, gut instincts, or an unshakable sense of peace or unease. When understood and stewarded well, these emotions can deepen your connection with God and align you with His heart.

Here are some ways God might speak to you through your emotions:

1. Peace in Uncertainty

Have you ever faced a difficult decision and felt an unexplainable peace about a choice, even when it didn't seem logical? This peace, described in Philippians 4:7 as "the peace of God, which surpasses all understanding," is often a confirmation of God's direction. It's a peace that doesn't depend on external circumstances but flows from the Holy Spirit. Even in the middle of chaos, God's peace can guide you to the right path, reassuring you that you're aligned with His will.

2. A Burden to Pray or Act

Sometimes, God places a specific person, group, or situation heavily on your heart. You might feel a deep emotional burden that compels you to pray, reach out, or act. For instance, have you ever felt inexplicably burdened to pray for someone, only to discover they were facing a significant challenge? That's not a coincidence; it's God engaging your emotions to intercede for others and protect them through your obedience.

3. Discomfort in Certain Environments

Have you ever felt unsettled or uneasy in a specific place or situation? Perhaps you walked into a room and sensed something spiritually off—an oppressive or dark presence. This is often God alerting you to pray and declare His authority over that space. Through the Holy Spirit, He uses your emotions to heighten your spiritual awareness, equipping you to discern and address what's happening in the spiritual realm.

While God uses emotions to speak and guide, discernment is critical. Not every emotion you feel is a message from God. Some emotions may arise from your flesh or external influences, including spiritual opposition. To discern whether an emotion is from God, align it with His Word and seek confirmation through prayer and wise counsel.

Take every emotion to God, asking Him to illuminate its source. Is He speaking through this emotion? Is it a call to action, prayer, or trust? Or is it a moment to reject a false influence? By inviting God into your emotional experience, you allow Him to clarify and refine what you're feeling, aligning it with His truth.

If you are someone who often feels deeply—what some call a "feeler"—recognize this as a gift. Through your emotions, God allows you to connect with Him on an intimate level, reflecting His heart and aligning your spirit with His. Emotions are a language God uses to draw you closer, to mold your heart to mirror His, and to guide you toward His purpose.

Remember, God created emotions not as a burden but as a blessing—a language for divine communication and a tool for protection and direction. By surrendering your emotions to Him, you open the door to deeper intimacy, clearer guidance, and a life that reflects His image and glory.

Emotions and the Soul

Your emotions are deeply intertwined with your soul, shaping how you experience life and connect with God. The human soul is a complex and multifaceted part of our being, often described in biblical and theological terms as comprising three key elements: the mind, the will, and the emotions. These elements work together to form the essence of who we are.

- **The Mind**: The intellectual aspect of the soul, encompassing thoughts, understanding, and reasoning. It's where we process information, form beliefs, and make sense of the world around us.

- **The Will**: The decision-making center of the soul, where desires, choices, and intentions are formed. It's where we exercise agency and free will, determining actions based on our values and priorities.

- **The Emotions**: The feeling dimension of the soul, reflecting our internal responses to external and internal stimuli. Emotions are tied to our experiences, relationships, and spiritual life.

Other faculties, like the **conscience** and **imagination**, are often considered extensions of these core components. The conscience, for example, functions as an internal guide to moral decisions, connecting the mind and will. Imagination, rooted in the mind, fuels creativity by enabling abstract thought and the ability to envision possibilities. Together, these elements reflect the complexity and beauty of the human soul.

Your emotions are a direct expression of your soul's condition. Throughout the Bible, emotions and the soul are closely connected.

Consider David's heartfelt cry in *Psalm 42:11*: *"Why, my soul, are you downcast? Why so disturbed within me?"* Here, David's emotions reflect the inner turmoil of his soul.

Jesus reinforces this connection in *Luke 6:45*, saying: *"For the mouth speaks what the heart is full of."*

Our emotions—whether joy, anger, sorrow, or peace—are windows into our values, beliefs, and spiritual state. They reveal what matters to us and where we stand in our relationship with God and others.

Even more, emotions are integral to the process of sanctification—the transformative journey where God refines the soul to reflect Christ's image. As believers, our emotions are gradually reshaped to align with God's character, reflecting His love, grace, and holiness. And here's the beautiful part: just as emotions are sanctified in this life, they will also play a role in our glorification in eternity.

Imagine a life where your emotions are fully redeemed, purified, and glorified. In the new heavens and the new earth, your emotions will be free from sin, pain, torment, or blemish. You'll experience the fullness of love, joy, peace, and awe—unhindered and pure.

Revelation 21:4 gives us a glimpse of this: *"He will wipe every tear from their eyes. There will be no more death or mourning or crying or pain, for the old order of things has passed away."*

Your emotions will become instruments of worship, reflecting God's glory in their truest form. They will deepen your intimacy with Him, allowing you to express eternal gratitude, joy, and awe in ways beyond what we can imagine on earth.

Another remarkable way emotions are connected to the soul is through conviction. When we stray from God's will, our emotions—stirred by the Holy Spirit—often act as spiritual signals, alerting us to areas that need alignment with God's truth. Jesus speaks of this work of the Holy Spirit in *John 16:8*: *"When He comes, He will convict the world concerning sin and righteousness and judgment."*

Feelings of sorrow or unease after sinning are not random—they are the Holy Spirit's loving way of drawing us back to God. Paul highlights this in *2 Corinthians 7:10*: *"Godly sorrow brings repentance that leads to salvation and leaves no regret, but worldly sorrow brings death."*

Godly sorrow is a gift. It stirs the soul toward repentance and restoration, drawing us closer to God's grace.

It's important to distinguish between conviction and condemnation:

- **Conviction** draws you closer to God, pointing you to His grace and truth.

- **Condemnation**, on the other hand, drives you away from Him, leaving you stuck in shame and fear.

Through the Holy Spirit, God uses your emotions to guide you back to Him, offering love and forgiveness rather than judgment. This is why it's so important to take every emotion to God. When you invite Him into your emotional experience, He will help you discern whether it's conviction or condemnation, aligning your heart with His truth.

The relationship between emotions and the soul emphasizes their divine purpose. Your emotions are not random or superficial—they are deeply intentional, designed by God to be an integral part of your spiritual life. They are tools for sanctification, worship, and connection with Him.

God doesn't just care about your physical body or spiritual state; He cares deeply about your emotions. They are a gift, a reflection of His heart, and a vital part of His plan for your life—both on earth and in eternity. Embrace them as a sacred part of your soul's journey with Him.

Engaging Your Emotions to Align with God's Will

I could go on and on about how purposeful and intentional the gift of emotions truly is. Your emotions are not just an accessory to your life—they are a divine gift from God, intricately designed to help you fulfill your God-given purpose and calling. As a disciple, your emotions are meant to equip and empower you to walk boldly in your calling, whether that's in ministry, relationships, or the marketplace.

Believe it or not, your emotions have a role to play, even in your career or corporate settings. Whether you work in the boardroom, the classroom, in a hospital, or at home, your emotions are a God-given tool to help you navigate your purpose with intentionality and impact.

But here's the real question: *How can you fully engage this gift to align with God's plan for your life?* What role do your emotions play in your personal, professional, and spiritual journey?

We need to shift our perspective and recognize our emotions for what they truly are—a blessing, not a burden. Perhaps it's time to reflect with the Lord:

- *What is your purpose?*

- *Where has God called you?*

- *How can you partner with Him to engage your emotions in fulfilling that purpose and calling?*

Consider the specifics:

- If you're a **therapist**, how is God calling you to use your emotions—like empathy or compassion—to create safe spaces for your clients to heal and grow?

- If you're a **nurse**, how is He asking you to show patience and gentleness with your patients, even in the most trying moments?

- If you're a **parent**, a **husband**, or a **wife**, how is God equipping you to engage your emotions in the ministry of parenting and marriage, reflecting His love to your family?

- If you're a **small group leader**, how can your emotional intelligence help you connect more deeply with your group members, fostering community and spiritual growth?

- If you're a **special education teacher**, how might God be asking you to use your emotions to bring comfort, patience, and understanding to your students?

Take some time to sit with the Lord and reflect on these questions. Allow Him to speak to your heart about how to redeem and embrace your emotions as a vital part of your identity and calling. Let Him redefine how you see your emotions—not as a liability but as a necessary and powerful tool for your purpose, ministry, and relationships.

Your emotions are a gift—a tool, a weapon, a blessing. When you invite God to transform your perspective and align your emotions with His will, you'll begin to see just how vital they are to living a life of impact, joy, and purpose.

Prayer

Heavenly Father,

Thank You for the precious gift of emotions. I humbly admit that I haven't always seen them as a gift, nor have I always used them intentionally to glorify You and walk in alignment with my purpose. Lord, I need Your guidance in this area. Teach me how to navigate my emotions and surrender them fully to You.

Holy Spirit, I invite You to refine and purify my emotions. Shape them to reflect the image of Jesus Christ and not the impulses of my flesh. Help me grow in emotional intelligence and give me a heart of surrender so that my emotions can be used for Your glory and not for selfish ambition or pride. Transform my perspective so that I see my emotions as a blessing and not a burden.

Expose any lies of the enemy that have caused me to view my emotions negatively or to misuse them. Thank You for the truth of Your Word, which reminds me that You've given me the Holy Spirit as my helper and guide, even in the sanctification of my emotions.

Lord, I love You, and I thank You for the work You're doing in my heart. Continue to lead me, refine me, and teach me to use every part of who I am—including my emotions—to reflect Your love and fulfill the calling You've placed on my life.

I pray all of this in the name of Jesus Christ, Your Son.

Amen.

REFLECTION QUESTIONS

1. What would you say is your top love language? How has under-standing your love language shaped the way you give and receive love?

2. Have you ever received a perfect gift, a missed-the-mark gift, or a "you needed this" gift? What did each of those experiences feel like, and how did they shape your understanding of intentionality in giving?

3. Do you struggle with trusting God when His gifts don't align with your personal desires? How can you surrender those expectations to align with His purpose for your life?

4. How do you currently view your emotions? Do you see them as a gift, a burden, or something in between? How has this chapter shifted your perspective on emotions?

5. Have you ever felt burdened by your emotions, like they were too much to handle? How does knowing that God designed your emo-tions with a purpose help you navigate those feelings?

6. How can you start using your emotions as a gift in your calling and daily life? Whether in your workplace, ministry, or relationships, think of practical ways to engage your emotions intentionally.

7. Which spiritual gifts mentioned in this chapter resonate most with how God engages your emotions? How can you surrender your emotions to Him to fully operate in those gifts?

8. Have you experienced God using your emotions to speak to you, such as through peace, conviction, or a burden for prayer? How did you respond, and what did that moment teach you about God's guidance?

9. How has the enemy tried to convince you that your emotions are a burden rather than a blessing? Reflect on how you can reject those lies and embrace the truth of your emotions as a gift from God.

10. In what ways can you invite the Holy Spirit to sanctify and refine your emotions? Think of specific areas where you want to grow in emotional intelligence, self-control, or empathy, and ask God for help.

06

THE MOST EMOTIONALLY INTELLIGENT MAN

When you think of someone who embodies emotional intelligence, who comes to mind? Is it a leader you admire, a close friend with an incredible sense of empathy, or perhaps someone you look up to for their self-control and wisdom? There are countless individuals we could name, but there's one person we often overlook in this conversation—someone whose emotional intelligence surpasses anyone else's.

For some reason, this person rarely comes up when we discuss emotional intelligence, yet I am absolutely convinced that He is the most emotionally intelligent man to ever walk the earth. That person is Jesus Christ—the Messiah, the Son of the living God.

The more I immerse myself in Scripture, the more I marvel at this truth: Jesus Christ embodied emotional intelligence in its purest and most perfect form. His life reveals an unparalleled understanding of emotions and a divine ability to navigate and steward them. Jesus didn't just demonstrate emotional intelligence—He defined it, setting the standard for us to follow.

From his mastery of self-awareness and self-management to his profound social awareness and relationship management, Jesus' life perfectly reflects the core components and pillars of emotional intelligence. As believers, we are often encouraged to "be like Jesus" and are called to reflect His image in every aspect of our lives. If that's true, shouldn't that also mean being emotionally intelligent like Jesus?

Jesus Christ is the epitome of emotional intelligence. In this chapter, we will explore His life in detail, analyzing how He embodied and exemplified the key attributes of emotional intelligence. Through His words, actions, and interactions, Jesus offers us the ultimate guide on how to live emotionally intelligent lives that glorify God and deepen our relationships with others. Let's dive into the life of Jesus Christ and discover what it truly means to reflect His emotional wisdom and grace.

His Self-Awareness

One of the most extraordinary qualities of Jesus Christ was His profound self-awareness. Jesus knew exactly who He was—His identity, His calling, and His purpose were absolutely clear to Him. This is one of my favorite things about Jesus. He was never confused about who He was, and He declared His identity without hesitation throughout His life and ministry.

Time and again in the New Testament, Jesus directly or indirectly revealed His divinity and expressed His authority with unwavering confidence. This confidence was not rooted in arrogance but in a deep, intimate awareness of His role and mission. Even when faced with harsh criticism, accusations, rejection, and betrayal, Jesus never allowed those things to define Him or shake His sense of identity. He stood firm as the Messiah, the Son of the living God.

One of the most compelling examples of Jesus' self-awareness is found in John 8:58, where He declared, "Truly, truly, I say to you, before Abraham was, I am." With this statement, Jesus used the divine name "I AM" (referencing Exodus 3:14) to claim eternal existence and identify Himself as God. The repetition of "truly, truly" was not just a cultural rhetorical device—it underscored the authority and weight of His words. Jesus was absolutely certain of His identity and authority, and He boldly proclaimed it.

In John 10:30, Jesus said, "I and the Father are one." This claim of unity with God led to accusations of blasphemy, as His listeners understood it as a declaration of divinity. But Jesus remained steadfast. He didn't alter His message to gain approval or avoid criticism. He stayed true to who He was.

In John 6:35, He declared, "I am the bread of life; whoever comes to me shall not hunger, and whoever believes in me shall never thirst." Here, Jesus identified Himself as the ultimate source of spiritual sustenance. How fascinating, then, that in Matthew 4, when Jesus fasted for 40 days and nights, Satan tempted Him, saying, "If you are the Son of God, command these stones to become loaves of bread." The "Bread of Life" was tempted to produce bread. Yet, Jesus didn't feel the need to prove His identity to Satan—or anyone else. His security in who He was enabled Him to resist the temptation with grace and authority.

Throughout His ministry, Jesus maintained clarity about who He was and what He was called to do. He didn't need external validation. He knew that truth exists independently of belief—it simply *is*. Jesus' identity didn't require acceptance to be valid, and His confidence wasn't contingent on others' opinions.

Despite being fully confident, Jesus remained humble. His certainty never crossed into arrogance. Instead, His self-awareness fueled His mission, empowering Him to fulfill His purpose with love, grace, and intentionality.

How different would our lives be if we were as secure in our identity as Jesus was in His? How often do we allow the opinions of others to dictate who we are and how we show up? The fear of rejection, criticism, or abandonment often influences our behavior and clouds our sense of self. Many people struggle with self-awareness because they've let the world define them instead of allowing God to shape their identity.

So often, we are more aware of our flaws and brokenness than the truth of who God says we are. But Jesus sets the perfect example for us to follow. He shows us how to remain anchored in truth, regardless of external pressures.

Do you have clarity about your identity and purpose? Do you know who you are in Christ? Do you understand your authority, strengths, and weaknesses? Do you trust God's promises for you? If not, perhaps it's time to ask God, "Who do you say I am?"

In Jeremiah 1:5, God says, "Before I formed you in the womb I knew you, and before you were born I consecrated you; I appointed you a prophet to the nations." Just as God knew Jeremiah, He knows you intimately. Before you were formed, God knew your spirit, and He gave you a specific calling and purpose. He knit you together in your mother's womb so you could fulfill the mission He has for you.

If God is the One who created you and called you, shouldn't He also be the One to define you? Only in Him will you find the clarity and confidence to walk in your true identity. Go to Him. Ask, "Who do you say I am?" Let Him reveal the truth of who you are so you can live with the same unwavering self-awareness that Jesus exemplified.

His Self-Management

Jesus Christ exemplified unmatched mastery over His emotions. The Bible shows us that He experienced the full spectrum of human emotions—compassion, anger, joy, sorrow, grief, and even fear. Yet, He managed them with extraordinary self-control, ensuring that His actions were always intentional and aligned with God's will.

Jesus' emotions never dictated His decisions. Instead, He anchored His actions in the Word of God, prioritizing His divine mission above fleeting feelings. As both fully human and fully divine, Jesus navigated the complexities of human emotions without allowing them to lead Him astray. His life shows us the power of self-management and what it truly means to steward our emotions with wisdom.

One of the most profound examples of Jesus' self-management is in Matthew 26:39, during His time in the Garden of Gethsemane. Knowing the torture and crucifixion that awaited Him, Jesus was overwhelmed with sorrow. Falling on His face, He prayed, "My Father, if it is possible, let this cup pass from me; nevertheless, not as I will, but as You will."

In this moment of deep anguish, Jesus did not suppress His emotions or deny their weight. He processed them in the presence of God, laying His fears and sorrow at the Father's feet. But Jesus didn't stop there. He surrendered those feelings, submitting them to God's will. That single, powerful statement—"not as I will, but as You will"—

demonstrates the epitome of self-management: feeling deeply yet aligning those emotions with divine purpose.

Jesus shows us the transformative power of praying through our emotions. Have you ever felt so weighed down by overwhelming feelings that it seemed impossible to move forward? In those moments, taking your emotions to God in prayer can shift the weight of those feelings. Something incredible happens: The intensity of your emotions begins to shrink while God's peace and presence grow larger.

As we pour out our hearts to God, He reorders the priorities in our lives. What seemed unbearable becomes manageable, and we can see clearly again. By processing emotions in prayer, we open ourselves to God's guidance, strength, and direction. Jesus modeled this perfectly in Gethsemane, where He prayed not just to express His sorrow but to align His heart with the Father's will.

Think about times in your life when emotions ran high—perhaps you were unjustly criticized, betrayed by someone you trusted, or mistreated in ways that cut deeply. Those moments can stir feelings of anger, sadness, or even the desire to retaliate. How often do we let those emotions drive us to act impulsively, seeking our own form of justice or relief?

But Jesus calls us to a higher standard. He invites us to follow His example: to bring our emotions to God and process them in His presence, ultimately surrendering them to His will. When we're tempted to lash out, defend ourselves, or seek revenge, can we pause and say, "Not as I will, but as You will"?

For example, if you're hurt by someone and the Holy Spirit prompts you to walk away instead of responding harshly, will you trust God's guidance over your own instincts? This is the essence of emotional self-management—surrendering your feelings to God and allowing His will to precede your fleshly desires.

Jesus didn't just show us what it looks like to manage emotions; He also gave us the tools to do so. God knows that our human nature often struggles with self-control. That's why He gave us the Holy Spirit, who cultivates the fruit of self-control within us. The Holy Spirit empowers us to manage our emotions in ways that honor God, helping us to reflect Christ's image in every situation.

Emotional management isn't about suppressing or ignoring your feelings—it's about surrendering them to God and allowing Him to guide your response. Jesus demonstrated this beautifully throughout His life. By following His example, we, too, can grow in self-control and emotional intelligence, becoming more like Him with each step of faith.

Let Jesus' life inspire you to handle your emotions with grace, aligning them with God's will and trusting that He will guide you through even the most overwhelming moments.

His Social Awareness

Social awareness, one of the four pillars of emotional intelligence, involves recognizing and understanding the emotions, needs, and perspectives of others and responding with empathy and care. Jesus Christ exemplified extraordinary social awareness throughout His life and ministry. He had a profound ability to connect with people, discern their emotional and spiritual needs, and meet them with compassion and love. Unlike a self-absorbed mindset consumed by personal experiences and emotions, Jesus was deeply attuned to the emotional realities of those around Him.

Jesus embodied "El Roi," meaning "the God who sees me." This name, first revealed in Genesis, perfectly captures the way Jesus made everyone He encountered feel seen. In Genesis 16:13, Hagar, a slave fleeing her abusive mistress, encountered God in the wilderness. Overwhelmed by her circumstances, she was met with divine comfort and reassurance. God gave her a promise for her future, and she declared, "You are the God who sees me." Hagar left that moment transformed, deeply comforted by the knowledge that she was not invisible to God.

The same was true for everyone who met Jesus. Whether in joy, sorrow, shame, or despair, they left His presence knowing they were seen, valued, and understood. Jesus' social awareness allowed Him to perceive and respond to people at the very core of their being, bringing healing, restoration, and affirmation.

One of the most striking examples of Jesus' empathy is found in John 11:35, the shortest yet one of the most profound verses in the Bible: "Jesus wept." At the tomb of His friend Lazarus, surrounded by Mary and Martha in their grief, Jesus didn't rush to invalidate their emotions or tell them to stop crying because He would raise Lazarus. Instead, He entered into their sorrow, weeping with them. This act wasn't just about their loss but a demonstration of His willingness to feel with them and validate their pain. Jesus teaches us that true social awareness is about stepping into the emotional worlds of others, not expecting them to shrink their pain or experience to fit our own perspective.

In Mark 5:25-34, when a woman with a twelve-year-long illness touched His garment in a crowded street, Jesus immediately stopped and asked, "Who touched my garments?" While the disciples dismissed the question, overwhelmed by the crowd, Jesus recognized the woman's unspoken need. Addressing her as "daughter," He restored her dignity and affirmed her faith. In this moment, Jesus wasn't just a healer; He was a restorer of worth, reminding her that she was seen and valued.

Another profound example of Jesus' social awareness is found in John 4:1-26 when He spoke with the Samaritan woman at the well. Cultural norms dictated that a Jewish man like Jesus should avoid Samaritans, let alone a woman of questionable reputation. Yet, Jesus engaged her in conversation and offered her hope and spiritual transformation. He acknowledged her struggles without condemnation and saw beyond her circumstances to her need for redemption. By the end of their encounter, she had not only received the truth but also felt profoundly seen and loved.

Jesus' awareness extended to the marginalized and overlooked, often challenging societal norms and injustice. In Luke 13:10-17, He healed a woman who had been bent over for 18 years. Despite knowing it would provoke criticism from the religious leaders, He called out their hypocrisy and declared that her healing mattered more than their rigid legalism. In Matthew 9:10-13, Jesus dined with tax collectors and sinners, facing backlash from the Pharisees. He responded by saying, "It is not the healthy who need a doctor, but the sick." Jesus understood societal judgments but never let them deter Him from meeting people where they were.

Jesus also discerned the unspoken emotions of those around Him. In Mark 2:1-12, when a paralyzed man was brought to Him, Jesus addressed the man's deeper need first: "Son, your sins are forgiven." While others focused on the man's physical condition, Jesus saw his need for spiritual restoration and ministered to his whole being—body, soul, and spirit.

Now, let's be real: we're not Jesus. We're not all-knowing or perfect, but as His followers, we are called to reflect His heart and His life. Social awareness is about being emotionally in tune with the people around us, and while we may not always understand their unspoken feelings, we have the Holy Spirit to guide us. Are we willing to let the Holy Spirit nudge us, burden us, and highlight people who need compassion and love?

For example, if a friend hasn't reached out in weeks, emotional immaturity would lead us to internalize their silence, taking it personally and maybe even responding with pettiness: *"If they don't call me, I'm not calling them either."* But what would Jesus do? Would He sit back and stew in offense? No. Jesus would be moved by compassion, wondering what pain or burden might be causing their silence. He would reach out, offering love and support rather than waiting for them to make the first move.

It is emotionally immature to expect people to always articulate their needs when we could cultivate sensitivity and discernment to perceive unspoken emotions. This isn't about mind-reading but about choosing empathy over indifference.

God has given each of us gifts through the Holy Spirit—gifts like discernment, prophecy, healing, and words of knowledge. How are you using these gifts to make others feel seen and valued? Are you praying for the homeless person on the street, the addict who feels invisible, or the friend who seems distant? Are you willing to love people who look, think, and act differently from you?

When people encounter you, do they leave your presence feeling seen and loved, just as the Samaritan woman, the woman with the issue of blood, and Hagar felt after encountering God? To love like Jesus is to see others—to truly see them in their pain, struggles, and hopes—and to respond with compassion, care, and empathy.

After all, to be loved is to be indeed seen, known, and understood. Let's reflect His image by making others feel seen, just as Jesus did.

His Relationship Management

The fourth pillar of emotional intelligence, relationship management, is the ability to navigate relationships with wisdom, resolve conflicts with grace, inspire and influence others, and foster genuine connections. Jesus Christ embodied this principle with unparalleled mastery throughout His life and ministry. His relationships were rooted in love, truth, and the desire for reconciliation. Whether interacting with His closest disciples, hostile authorities, or society's marginalized, Jesus managed relationships with wisdom and grace, leaving us a perfect example to follow.

Jesus intentionally invested in deep, meaningful relationships with a diverse group of people. When He called His disciples, He didn't choose based on status or qualifications but rather on their potential. Fishermen, a tax collector, a zealot—Jesus brought together individuals from vastly different backgrounds and molded them into a unified team. He taught, corrected, and empowered them with patience and love, creating an environment of trust where they could grow and ultimately lead others.

Jesus also demonstrated the value of friendship through His relationship with Mary, Martha, and Lazarus. He visited their home frequently, engaging with them on a personal and caring level. Yes, even as the Messiah, Jesus prioritized friendships. He showed us that life is not meant to be lived in isolation; we are created for connection, to love and to serve others selflessly. Jesus' relationships remind us that healthy connections require an intentional investment of time, care, and emotional energy.

Unity mattered deeply to Jesus. He worked tirelessly to bring people together, emphasizing love, forgiveness, and mutual service as the foundation of relationships. In John 17:20-23, just before His crucifixion, Jesus prayed for His disciples and all future believers to be united, just as He and the Father are one. Even among the twelve disciples, Jesus united people from conflicting ideologies and backgrounds. For example, Simon the Zealot and Matthew the tax collector were on opposite sides of the political spectrum, yet Jesus brought them together for a common purpose. He demonstrated that building an authentic community often requires helping diverse individuals work toward shared goals.

Jesus wasn't just a leader; He was the ultimate servant leader. His leadership style was rooted in humility, authenticity, and a vision of God's love. In John 13:1-17, on the night of His betrayal, Jesus performed an extraordinary act of servant leadership by washing His disciples' feet.

To grasp the magnitude of this act, we need to understand its historical context. In biblical times, feet were considered the dirtiest part of the body, as people wore sandals and walked dusty roads. Foot washing was typically reserved for the lowest-ranking servants. It symbolized subjugation, and those who received it were considered social superiors. Yet Jesus—the Messiah, the Son of God, the one through whom all creation was made—took on this role, washing not just the feet of His disciples but also of Judas, the very one who would betray Him.

When Peter protested, saying, "You shall never wash my feet," he revealed his own misunderstanding of humility. Peter saw Jesus' action through the lens of societal hierarchy, believing it inappropriate for someone of Jesus' status. But Jesus showed that true humility is not about clinging to status but about breaking down barriers of pride, superiority, and inferiority. In doing so, He demonstrated that healthy relationships require vulnerability and the willingness to serve others, even in their most "unclean" and broken parts.

To manage relationships effectively, we must also learn the art of "foot washing" metaphorically. This means being vulnerable enough to allow others to serve and love us in our own brokenness so we can, in turn, serve and love them in theirs. Giving and receiving love require humility and a willingness to step outside our comfort zones.

Conflict is inevitable in relationships, but Jesus modeled how to handle it with truth and reconciliation in mind. In Luke 22:24-27, when the disciples argued about who among them was the greatest, Jesus reframed the conversation, teaching them about servant leadership: "The greatest among you should be like the youngest, and the one who rules like the one who serves." He used the conflict as a teaching moment, realigning their values with God's Kingdom.

Even in moments of personal betrayal, Jesus showed grace. After Peter denied Him three times during His most difficult hour, Jesus didn't respond with anger or rejection. Instead, after His resurrection, Jesus restored Peter by asking three times, "Do you love me?" (John 21:15-17). Each question mirrored Peter's denials, but rather than dwelling on the offense, Jesus reaffirmed Peter's purpose, commissioning him to care for His followers.

If we were in Jesus' shoes, many of us would have cut Peter off completely. But Jesus saw the bigger picture. He understood that their relationship served a greater purpose and refused to let one failure define it. Through His example, Jesus showed that reconciliation often requires confronting failure with love, extending grace, and offering others a renewed sense of purpose.

Forgiveness was at the heart of Jesus' teaching and practice. In Luke 23:34, as He hung on the cross, Jesus prayed for His executioners: "Father, forgive them, for they know not what they do." Even in unimaginable pain, Jesus extended forgiveness, showing that it is a cornerstone of effective relationship management.

If you want to build healthy, long-lasting relationships, you must embrace forgiveness. People are flawed. Even those closest to you will disappoint and hurt you at times. Conflict, though uncomfortable, is an opportunity for deeper intimacy and growth when handled well. Jesus taught Peter to forgive not just seven times but seventy-seven times (Matthew 18:21-22), illustrating that forgiveness must be limitless.

Forgiveness is not a feeling—it's a choice. It's not a suggestion from God; it's a command. Holding onto grudges and cutting people off may feel easier in the moment, but they stifle emotional growth and prevent the flourishing relationships God desires for us. True forgiveness requires humility, grace, and a focus on the bigger picture of God's purpose for our relationships.

Jesus modeled what it means to manage relationships with love, grace, and intentionality. He showed us that healthy relationships require vulnerability, humility, and a servant's heart. Whether it's forgiving offenses, resolving conflicts with grace, or building unity among diverse individuals, Jesus set the standard for relationship management.

So, ask yourself: Are you modeling Christ's example in your relationships? Are you willing to humble yourself, serve others, and extend forgiveness, even when it's uncomfortable? Are you creating an environment where the people in your life can grow, thrive, and feel loved? Relationships mattered deeply to Jesus, and they should matter to you, too. To reflect His image, we must approach our relationships with the same love, grace, and purpose that He did.

His Healthy Boundaries

Boundaries often get a bad reputation. Some see them as selfish, mean, or controlling, but nothing could be further from the truth. Boundaries are essential for protecting our emotional health, safeguarding relationships, and stewarding our time and energy wisely. Jesus, the perfect model of emotional intelligence, demonstrated healthy boundaries throughout His life and ministry. His boundaries were not rooted in selfishness but in fulfilling His purpose and staying aligned with the Father's will.

While Jesus was incredibly kind, loving, and compassionate, He was *not* a people pleaser. He navigated complex relational dynamics, endless demands for His attention, and the overwhelming pressures of His mission with clarity and wisdom. Through His life, Jesus teaches us that boundaries are not just helpful—they are essential for living a life of love, purpose, and emotional health.

One of the most profound examples of Jesus' boundaries was His unwavering commitment to solitude and rest. Despite the constant demands of ministry, Jesus regularly withdrew from the crowds—and even His disciples—to spend time alone in prayer with the Father. Mark 1:35 tells us, *"Very early in the morning, while it was still dark, Jesus got up, left the house and went off to a solitary place, where He prayed."*

Think about this: Jesus, the Son of God, had people searching for Him constantly, clamoring for His attention, miracles, and teachings. Yet, He didn't try to be everything to everyone at all times. He honored His need for rest and spiritual renewal, refusing to compromise His time with God for the sake of people-pleasing.

Luke 5:15-16 reinforces this: *"Yet the news about Him spread all the more, so that crowds of people came to hear Him and to be healed of their sicknesses. But Jesus often withdrew to lonely places and prayed."* Despite the growing demands, Jesus recognized that He couldn't pour into others if He was spiritually and emotionally empty. He didn't let the demands of others dictate His schedule. He understood that without rest and spiritual renewal, He couldn't fulfill His mission effectively. He teaches us that prioritizing rest and reconnecting with God is not selfish—it's necessary.

Sometimes, the overwhelming emotions we feel—frustration, anxiety, resentment—stem from a lack of boundaries. Consider this: Have you ever lashed out at a customer service representative over a delayed package? Or have you found yourself experiencing road rage when someone cut you off in traffic? These moments often reveal deeper emotional depletion. When we don't prioritize time with God and neglect our need for rest, we run on empty, leaving us more reactive and less centered on His peace.

Jesus shows us that to love others well, we must first allow God to pour into us. Without that spiritual renewal, we risk becoming burned out, frustrated, and resentful. Even Jesus, though fully God, experienced the limitations of human flesh. He grew tired, burdened, and emotionally worn out. If He needed rest and solitude to stay aligned with His mission, how much more do we?

Another key way Jesus maintained healthy boundaries was by saying *no* to unrealistic expectations. He didn't allow the demands of others to derail His mission or dictate His actions. In Mark 1:37-38, Simon and others came looking for Him, saying, "Everyone is looking for You!" But Jesus replied, "Let us go somewhere else—to the nearby villages—so I can preach there also. That is why I have come."

That last sentence is key: *"That is why I have come."* Jesus knew His purpose. He didn't stay in one place to please the crowds or satisfy their demands. Instead, He stayed focused on His God-given assignment.

In John 6:14-15, after Jesus fed the 5,000, the people wanted to make Him king by force. Imagine the temptation to accept this offer—to be celebrated, elevated, and given earthly power. Yet Jesus withdrew to a mountain by Himself. Why? Because He already knew who He was and why He had come. He didn't need human approval or accolades to validate His identity or mission.

Perhaps we need to examine our own lives and the ways we allow people-pleasing to interfere with our boundaries. Do you start your mornings by immediately answering texts or emails, leaving no time for God? Maybe God is calling you to spend the first moments of your day in His presence, allowing Him to equip you with His peace and perspective. That small act of prioritizing time with Him could be the difference between reacting to daily frustrations or handling them with grace.

Jesus also set clear boundaries in His personal relationships. He loved deeply but with discernment and intentionality. For example, before choosing His 12 disciples, Jesus spent the night in prayer (Luke 6:12-13). Even within the twelve, He had an inner circle—Peter, James, and John—who witnessed intimate moments like the Transfiguration (Mark 9:2-8) and His prayer in Gethsemane (Matthew 26:36-39).

This shows us that while Jesus loved everyone, He didn't share everything with everyone. He used wisdom to determine the level of vulnerability appropriate for each relationship.

He even maintained boundaries with His family. In Mark 3:31-35, when His mother and brothers interrupted His teaching, Jesus said,

"Who are My mother and My brothers? Whoever does God's will is My brother and sister and mother." While Jesus loved His family, He prioritized His spiritual mission over their demands, showing us that boundaries often require tough but necessary choices.

Jesus also demonstrated boundaries in His ministry. In John 5:1-15, He healed one man at the pool of Bethesda, even though there was a multitude of sick people present. This wasn't about neglecting others; it was about staying aligned with the Father's guidance. Jesus didn't attempt to meet every need. Instead, He focused on the specific individuals and tasks God led Him to.

Compassion fatigue is real. It's the emotional and physical exhaustion that comes from caring for others, often leaving us detached, resentful, and less empathetic. I experienced this firsthand during my time in public health. After spending my days listening to the struggles and pains of others, I would come home to loved ones calling to vent or emotionally unload on me. I found myself feeling disconnected, unable to offer the empathy they needed, and even resentful at times.

It wasn't until I realized the importance of setting boundaries that I began to regain my emotional health. I had to create space for myself to recharge after work before engaging with others' emotional needs. It wasn't selfish—it was necessary. Even Jesus didn't try to heal or help everyone. Jesus discerned His specific assignment and stayed focused on it, showing us that it's not our responsibility to meet every need.

When we overextend ourselves, trying to fix everyone's problems, we risk not only compassion fatigue but also straying from the mission God has for us. Jesus teaches us to steward our time and energy wisely, trusting God to direct us to the people and situations He wants us to impact.

Jesus didn't just set boundaries—He enforced them. In Matthew 16:23, when Peter tried to dissuade Him from going to the cross, Jesus rebuked him, saying, "Get behind Me, Satan! You are a hindrance to Me. For you are not setting your mind on the things of God, but on the things of man." Setting healthy boundaries often means confronting behaviors that hinder our purpose and staying true to our values.

In John 2:13-17, Jesus drove out the money changers from the temple, declaring, "Stop turning My Father's house into a market!" This act demonstrates that boundaries protect what is sacred and are essential for preserving what aligns with God's will.

Jesus also modeled boundaries in how He handled rejection. In Mark 6:1-13, when His hometown of Nazareth rejected Him, He didn't force His teachings on them. Instead, He moved on to other villages. Likewise, He instructed His disciples in Matthew 10:14 to "shake the dust off their feet" and move on if a town rejected them. These boundaries weren't about rejection but about stewarding their time and energy for those who were receptive.

Jesus' boundaries were never about keeping people out but about creating space for love, growth, and alignment with His mission. They protected His emotional health, strengthened His relationships, and kept Him focused on the Father's will. Boundaries allow us to care for others without losing ourselves or straying from our purpose in the process.

Perhaps it's time to reflect on your own boundaries. Are you overextending yourself to please others? Are you neglecting rest, solitude, or time with God? Are you saying yes to everything and everyone, allowing people-pleasing to interfere with your priorities? Maybe God is calling you to establish new boundaries that protect your emotional health and keep you aligned with His will.

Jesus didn't just model boundaries—He invites us to embrace them, too. Boundaries are not selfish or mean. They are a gift from God to help us live with clarity, purpose, and peace. When we set and honor boundaries, we reflect Jesus' emotional intelligence, stay aligned with our mission, and love others from a place of wholeness. We also create space for a deeper connection with Jesus, with others, and with the purpose He has for our lives. Boundaries are not just a strategy for self-care; they are a spiritual discipline. Let's follow Jesus' example and embrace them fully.

Jesus: The Epitome of Emotional Intelligence

There's a reason Jesus is often considered the most emotionally intelligent person to have ever walked the earth, and I hope that as you've read this chapter, you've come to see why. More than that, I hope you've come to admire His example and aspire to emulate it in your own life.

Jesus consistently embodied emotional intelligence and emotional maturity. After all, He created emotions. But His mastery of emotional intelligence wasn't solely because He was God. It was because He lived in full submission and surrender to the will of the Father. His intimacy with God and unwavering obedience kept Him aligned with the Father's purpose, enabling Him to walk in wisdom, compassion, and grace in every situation.

Some might argue that it was easy for Jesus to exhibit such emotional intelligence because He was God—and that's partially true. But that's not the full story. Jesus wasn't just fully God; He was also fully human. He subjected Himself to life in the flesh, experiencing the same human limitations, emotions, and temptations that we do. He got tired. He got angry. He grieved. He felt sorrow and anguish. He faced rejection, criticism, and betrayal. He couldn't be everywhere at once, and He felt the weight of human frailty. Most significantly, He could die—and He did.

Jesus didn't take shortcuts. He didn't use His divinity to bypass the challenges of being human. He could have turned stones into bread when He was starving in the wilderness, but He chose to trust in God's provision. He could have accepted the crowd's offer to make Him king, basking in earthly power and approval, but He stayed focused on His heavenly mission. He could have exposed Judas and cut him off from His circle, but instead, He washed Judas' feet. He could have disowned Peter for denying Him three times, but He forgave Peter and entrusted him with building His church.

Time and time again, Jesus chose surrender over self-preservation. He chose obedience over convenience. He chose love over retribution.

At the Garden of Gethsemane, when His soul was overwhelmed with sorrow to the point of death, Jesus cried out to the Father for strength. He didn't suppress His emotions or pretend everything was fine. He faced them head-on, acknowledging the depth of His pain while surrendering to the Father's will.

Jesus wasn't afraid to express His emotions openly. He wept without shame. He displayed righteous anger when the temple was defiled. He showed compassion for the marginalized, the suffering, and the broken. He shattered cultural and gender stereotypes, refusing to conform to toxic masculinity or societal expectations.

Despite the pressures and provocations He faced, Jesus maintained remarkable self-control. He never lashed out impulsively or blamed others for His feelings. Even in the face of betrayal, mockery, and unimaginable pain, He remained composed, forgiving His executioners as He hung on the cross.

Jesus' ability to connect with people from all walks of life—whether rich or poor, respected or rejected—is a testament to His emotional intelligence. He saw people for who they were and met them where they were. He gave dignity to the overlooked, hope to the hopeless, and grace to the broken.

We all have role models—people we look up to and aspire to be like. But let me encourage you to place Jesus at the top of that list. Jesus perfectly demonstrated every pillar of emotional intelligence: self-awareness, self-management, social awareness, and relationship management. He set healthy boundaries for Himself and others, teaching us that love and service are not incompatible with rest and renewal.

In my own journey with emotional intelligence and personal development, I've read countless books, attended conferences, watched inspiring podcasts, and even invested in coaching sessions. All of these tools were helpful in their own way, but the real, transformative change in my emotions came when I fully surrendered them to Jesus.

When I stopped striving to "fix" my emotions on my own and instead submitted them to His perfect plan, I experienced a deeper level of healing and growth than I ever thought possible. My desire to be like Jesus—to reflect His emotional maturity and love—changed the way I viewed and responded to my emotions.

Here's the truth: You don't have to do this alone. You don't have to navigate the complexities of emotions or relationships in your own strength. Jesus offers a better way. By walking in intimacy with Him, surrendering your emotions to Him, and aligning yourself with the Father's will, you can experience true transformation.

Jesus is not just the most emotionally intelligent person who ever lived—He's also the ultimate guide for your emotional and spiritual growth. So, let Him be your role model. Let Him shape your emotions, refine your relationships, and guide you into a life of emotional intelligence that reflects His love, grace, and wisdom.

True transformation begins when we surrender our emotions to Jesus. Let Him lead you into the fullness of emotional health, and you'll find yourself not just managing your emotions but thriving in them, just as He intended.

Prayer

Heavenly Father,

Thank You for the gift of Your Son, Jesus Christ, who came to this earth to die for me and redeem me through His sacrifice on the cross. Thank You for giving us Jesus, who showed us what it truly means to live a life fully surrendered and submitted to You. Through Him, we see the perfect example of how You've called us to live, how to navigate relationships, and how to process, express, and submit our emotions in alignment with Your will.

Lord, I desire to be more like Jesus. Shape me, mold me, and transform me into His image. Help me to be as self-aware as He was, fully understanding my identity and purpose in You. Grant me the same level of self-control and emotional composure that Jesus demonstrated, even in the most challenging and overwhelming situations.

Lord, give me a heart that is empathetic and compassionate, a heart that mirrors Jesus' love for others. Teach me to serve with humility and sincerity, just as He did. Help me to steward my relationships well, cultivating connections that honor You and reflect Your purpose for my life.

Father, guide me in setting and maintaining healthy boundaries. Reveal any idols in my heart that may be fueling people-pleasing or a lack of boundaries. Remove the fear of man, the desire for human approval, or anything that hinders me from walking in Your truth and purpose. Show me where I need to establish boundaries and give me the courage and wisdom to honor them.

I surrender my life, my relationships, and my emotions to You, Lord. I trust You to lead me, heal me, and grow me in every area. Let Your will, not mine, be done in every aspect of my life.

In the precious name of Jesus Christ, I pray.

Amen.

BOUNDARIES REFLECTION EXERCISE

The purpose of this exercise is to guide you in identifying, setting, and maintaining healthy boundaries that protect your emotional and mental well-being. Boundaries are essential for reducing stress, avoiding emotional overload, and fostering healthier relationships. This exercise will help you assess where boundaries are weak or non-existent in various areas of your life, identify patterns in how and why boundaries are crossed, and build confidence in communicating your boundaries clearly and respectfully.

By engaging in this exercise, you'll strengthen all four pillars of emotional intelligence:

- Self-awareness: Understand your emotional triggers and recognize how a lack of boundaries affects your well-being.

- Self-management: Plan and practice how to handle situations when your boundaries are not honored.

- Social awareness: Become more comfortable with the concept of boundaries, allowing you to also respect and honor the boundaries of others.

- Relationship management: Improve your relationships by setting clear expectations and fostering healthier interactions.

This exercise is designed to be used with your *Emotions Journal* or a dedicated space for reflection. For best results, carry it out over the next week or two, tracking your thoughts, emotions, and progress. Revisit this exercise regularly as part of your emotional growth journey.

Instructions

Step 1: Create Categories

In your *Emotions Journal,* write down the following categories. You can draw a table for each category or designate a separate page for each, depending on how much space you think you'll need:

- Work (e.g., tasks, time, schedule, responsibilities, colleagues, work-life balance)

- Family (e.g., parents, siblings, extended family, in-laws, holidays, expectations)

- Friendships (e.g., close friends, acquaintances, social time, emotional labor, expectations, budget)

- Romantic Relationships (e.g., communication, expectations, time, physical/sexual boundaries, commitments)

- Personal Life (e.g., time for rest, self-care, personal time with God, alone time)

- Ministry (e.g., volunteering, serving, expectations, commitments, ministry work, availability)

Step 2: Reflect on Boundaries for Each Category

For each category, answer the following questions in your journal:

1. How do I feel about this category?

   - Reflect on where you feel overextended, uneasy, detached, drained, or even resentful.

2. Do I currently have boundaries in place for this category?

   - If so, have I communicated them clearly? If not, what might those boundaries look like?

3. Are there any situations within this category where I feel my boundaries are being crossed or not honored?

4. What emotions tend to surface when my boundaries in this category are not respected?

5. Are there specific people or behaviors within this category that consistently challenge my boundaries?

   - Write down their names and the specific actions, behaviors, or statements that cross your boundaries.

Step 3: Define and Write Your Boundaries

For each category, identify one to three boundaries you'd like to establish or strengthen. Write them down clearly.

Step 4: Script Your Boundary Statements

For each category or specific situation, craft a boundary statement using this formula:

"When you [specific action], it makes me feel [emotion]. I need you to [specific request] so that I can [desired outcome]."

Examples:

- **Work:**

  "When you call me after hours to discuss work, it makes me feel overwhelmed and unable to rest. I need you to save these discussions for business hours so I can recharge and be more productive."

- **Family:**

  "When you comment on my weight during family gatherings, it makes me feel uncomfortable and disrespected. I need you to stop making comments about my weight so that I can feel safe and enjoy our time together."

- **Friendships:**

  "When you cancel plans at the last minute, it makes me feel unvalued. I need you to prioritize our commitments or let me know in advance if something comes up so I can feel respected in our relationship."

Step 5: Practice Saying Your Boundaries

1. Practice saying your boundary statements aloud.

2. Reflect on the experience in your journal:

   • How did it feel to express your boundaries?

   • What fears or hesitations came up?

   • How can you overcome these challenges to communicate confidently in real-life situations?

Step 6: Plan for Enforcing Boundaries

1. Write down one action step you can take to protect and enforce each boundary if it's not honored.

   • Example: If someone consistently calls you after hours, consider setting your phone to "Do Not Disturb" mode or politely reminding them of your boundary.

Step 7: Reflect on Your Progress

As you implement these boundaries, track your experiences over the next week or two:

• What changes have you noticed in your emotions and relationships?

• Were there moments where you successfully enforced a boundary? How did it feel?

• Were there moments when your boundary was crossed? What did you learn from those situations?

Use This Exercise Regularly

Boundaries are an ongoing practice, not a one-time fix. Revisit this exercise regularly to refine your boundaries, assess their effectiveness, and deepen your emotional awareness. Healthy boundaries not only protect your peace but also create space for thriving relationships. By practicing this exercise, you are taking an important step toward living with greater emotional intelligence and purpose.

Living Like Jesus:
Relational Exercises for Emotional Growth

These activities are designed to help you reflect the image of Jesus in your relationships and cultivate His emotional intelligence. By modeling His love, forgiveness, and compassion, you'll not only grow in emotional maturity but also transform your relationships.

Activity 1: Modeling Jesus in My Relationships

Objective:

To identify ways you can reflect Jesus' relational principles in your most significant relationships.

Instructions:

1. Write down 2–3 significant relationships in your life (e.g., your spouse, a close friend, a family member, or a colleague).

2. For each relationship, reflect on the following questions and write your responses in your journal:

   • How can I prioritize love in this relationship?

   • What would it look like to serve this person as Jesus served?

   • Are there unresolved conflicts that require forgiveness or reconciliation?

   • How can I empower and encourage this person to grow in their purpose?

3. Based on your reflections, write one actionable step you will take this week to strengthen each relationship.

   • For example: "I will schedule quality time with my spouse this week," or "I will send a note of encouragement to my sibling."

Activity 2: Forgiveness Inventory

Objective:

To practice forgiveness and release resentment, following Jesus' example of unconditional grace.

Instructions:

1. Write down any relationships where you feel hurt, resentment, or tension.

2. Reflect on how Jesus forgave even in the most painful circumstances, such as when He prayed for His executioners while on the cross (*"Father, forgive them, for they do not know what they are doing"* — Luke 23:34).

3. Say a prayer or statement of forgiveness for each person on your list. Example:

"Lord, I choose to forgive [name] for [specific offense]. I release them into Your hands and surrender any bitterness or resentment I've held in my heart. Just as You have forgiven me, help me to extend the same grace and love to them."

4. Visualize yourself walking this person up to Jesus on the cross. Imagine holding their hand and releasing them to Jesus, recognizing that the cross represents forgiveness for *all* sins, including theirs.

5. Repent for any offense, unforgiveness, or bitterness you've held toward this person. Ask God for forgiveness and the strength to walk in love.

6. If appropriate, consider taking a step toward reconciliation, such as initiating a conversation or sending a kind message.

Activity 3: Encouragement Challenge

Objective:

To cultivate habits of encouragement and reflect Jesus' compassion by speaking life into others.

Instructions:

1. Choose three people in your life who may need encourage-ment. These could be individuals facing challenges, feeling unappreciated, or in need of affirmation.

2. Spend time in prayer, asking God to reveal His heart for each person. Invite the Holy Spirit to show you how to encourage them specifically. Reflect on these questions:

   - What is a strength or quality I admire about this person?

   - How might God want to speak hope, affirmation, or love to them through me?

3. Write a note, send a message, or have a heartfelt conver-sation with each person. Share words of affirmation, en-couragement, or appreciation based on what God revealed to you.

Examples:

- "I see how hard you've been working, and I want you to know how much I admire your dedication and perseverance. God sees your efforts and is proud of you."

- "I felt led to remind you that you're deeply loved and valu-able, not just to me but to God. You have such a unique gift that impacts everyone around you."

4. Reflect in your journal:

   - How did this act of encouragement impact the recipient?

   - How did it impact you?

As you engage in these activities, consider how they challenge and stretch you to reflect the emotional intelligence of Jesus. Through these intentional practices, you are modeling His love, forgiveness, and encouragement, creating space for healthier relationships and emotional growth.

REFLECTION QUESTIONS

1. Who is someone you consider a role model in your life, and why? What qualities or characteristics do you admire most about them? How do they inspire you in your personal growth journey?

2. What aspect of Jesus' emotional intelligence—self-awareness, self-management, social awareness, or relationship management—stood out to you the most in this chapter? Why?

3. How did Jesus' ability to process and express His emotions (e.g., weeping, showing compassion, or expressing righteous anger) challenge or inspire your view of emotional health and expression?

4. Jesus often demonstrated remarkable self-control, even in the most difficult circumstances. Are there areas in your life where you struggle with self-control? How can you follow His example to improve in those areas?

5. Jesus was deeply empathetic and always attuned to the emotional needs of others. In what ways can you grow in social awareness, becoming more mindful of others' needs? What specific steps can you take this week to practice empathy and compassion in your interactions?

6. Think about your relationships. Are there any that feel disconnected or strained? Is there someone you need to forgive or reconcile with? How might reflecting Jesus' example of love, humility, and grace help you nurture or repair those relationships?

7. Do you consider yourself a people-pleaser? If yes, could this tendency stem from idolatry in your heart, such as fear of man or seeking approval from others? Reflect on whether Jesus is truly enough for you and how surrendering this need to Him could bring freedom and peace.

8. Jesus set healthy boundaries while still living a life of service and love. Are there areas in your life where you feel called to set better

boundaries? How could doing so help you align more closely with God's purpose for you?

9. Think about a conflict you've experienced recently. How did you handle it? How might Jesus' example of handling conflict with truth, humility, and reconciliation guide you in resolving conflicts moving forward?

10. In what ways has this chapter helped you see Jesus not just as your Savior but also as a role model for emotional intelligence? How will you apply His example to your own emotional growth journey?

07

EMOTIONAL IDOLATRY: LIFE AFTER EDEN

The book of Genesis holds a special place in my heart—it's my all-time favorite book of the Bible. I love Genesis for so many reasons. First, it's the beginning of everything. Genesis reveals the foundation of creation, the intricate design of humanity, and the nature of God's relationship with us. It offers subtle but profound details about God's character, such as His unity within the Trinity and His intentionality in creation. Every time I revisit Genesis, I uncover something new—a truth I hadn't noticed before, a layer of meaning I'd previously overlooked.

Genesis is more than a historical account; it's the origin story of humanity, sin, and redemption. It takes us from the perfection of creation to the heartache of the fall, showing us how the first humans navigated life with God and the consequences of sin. In this chapter, as we delve into the topic of emotional idolatry, it's only fitting that we return to Genesis. To understand emotional idolatry, we must start where it all began.

Genesis opens with the story of creation. God creates the heavens and the earth and then methodically fills them with life and beauty. Finally, He forms humanity in His own image, as it says in Genesis 1:26:

"Then God said, 'Let us make man in our image, after our likeness.'"

And in Genesis 1:27:

"So God created man in His own image, in the image of God He created him; male and female He created them."

These verses remind us that we were designed to reflect God's image. Just as God has emotions—experiencing love, compassion, anger, and joy—He gave us emotions to mirror His nature. Our emotions are a gift designed to help us reflect His character and connect deeply with Him and others.

One key theme in the creation narrative is God's repeated declaration of what is *good*. After each act of creation, we read, *"And God saw that it was good."* God, as the Creator, is the ultimate authority on what is good. He decided what was good for food, for life, and for flourishing. Everything He created was good—except for one thing.

In Genesis 2:18, God says:

"It is not good that the man should be alone; I will make him a helper fit for him."

This is the first time God declares something that is *not good* in His creation. Why? Because man was created to reflect God's image, and God is a God of community. God exists in perfect communion within the Trinity—Father, Son, and Holy Spirit. We see this unity reflected in Genesis 1:26, where God says, *"Let us make man in our image."* That "us" signifies the divine fellowship of the Trinity, present at the very beginning of creation.

Since man was made in God's image, it wasn't a reflection of God's nature for man to be alone. So, God created Eve. When Adam first saw Eve, his response was one of deep emotion and excitement. In Genesis 2:23, Adam exclaims:

"This one is bone from my bone, and flesh from my flesh! She will be called 'woman,' because she was taken from 'man'."

Adam's exclamation reflects the first recorded emotion of humanity—joy. His words are filled with excitement and wonder. Adam's emotions were tied to Eve, and God gave these emotions to help Adam and Eve bond, reflect God's unity, and care for creation with compassion.

In this perfect state, everything was good. Genesis 2:25 says:

"Now the man and his wife were both naked, but they felt no shame."

This is such a powerful and beautiful picture of humanity before sin—pure in heart, free from shame, and in perfect harmony with God and each other. Shame didn't exist in their lives because their image was an unbroken reflection of God's image.

But everything changed when the serpent entered the picture.

In Genesis 2:16-17, God gave Adam a clear instruction:

"You may freely eat the fruit of every tree in the garden—except the tree of the knowledge of good and evil. If you eat its fruit, you are sure to die."

This was the first parameter, boundary, or warning God gave humanity, even as He entrusted them with dominion over all creation. This instruction wasn't arbitrary; it was a boundary of love designed to protect humanity and preserve their intimacy with God.

Then came Genesis 3. The serpent, described as crafty—clever, skillful, and deceptive—approached Eve. His opening line was a question designed to distort God's word:

"Did God really say you must not eat the fruit from any of the trees in the garden?"

The serpent twisted God's words to plant a seed of doubt in Eve's heart. When Eve corrected the serpent, stating what God had actually commanded, the serpent contradicted God's warning:

"You won't die! God knows that your eyes will be opened as soon as you eat it, and you will be like God, knowing both good and evil."

This interaction is so layered. With his first question, *"Did God really say?"* the serpent subtly undermined God's word and intentions, making Eve question the clarity of God's command and the goodness of His character. That seed of doubt weakened Eve's trust in God's authority and promises, opening the door for temptation. The serpent didn't stop there; he implied that God was withholding something good from Eve—wisdom and the opportunity to "be like God." Ironically, Eve was already made in God's image, already like Him! Yet, the serpent's cunning suggestion made her question her identity, God's goodness, and His intentions.

Then came a pivotal moment. Genesis 3:6 says:

"So when the woman saw that the tree was good for food, and that it was a delight to the eyes, and that the tree was to be desired to make one wise, she took of its fruit and ate, and she also gave some to her husband who was with her, and he ate."

This is the first recorded instance of humanity deciding for themselves what was good, apart from God's authority. Eve looked at the tree and, rather than relying on God's wisdom and command, determined for herself that it was good for food, pleasing to the eyes, and desirable for wisdom. She elevated her own judgment above God's word. Eve's decision-making was now driven by her desires rather than trust in God's wisdom. She ate the forbidden fruit and shared it with Adam. Together, they committed the ultimate act of rebellion, attempting to dethrone God and take authority into their own hands. This was the birth of idolatry.

The Root of Idolatry

At its core, idolatry is putting something—anything—in the place of God. It's elevating a person, object, or desire to a position of ultimate authority, trust, and devotion that belongs only to God. It is treason, an act of "de-godding" God and crowning something or someone else as sovereign. At the root of *all* sin is idolatry, and at the root of idolatry is doubt.

The serpent planted doubt in Eve's heart, making her question God's goodness, promises, and commands. He made her believe that God was withholding something good. That doubt led her to elevate her desires above God's authority, to rely on her own judgment of what was "good," and ultimately, to disobey.

This same pattern plays out in our lives today. Consider money as an example of idolatry. The serpent's whisper may sound like this: *"Will God really provide for you? Will He really meet all your needs?"*

The seed of doubt takes root, and suddenly, God's command to tithe or to live honestly feels negotiable. Perhaps you withhold your tithe or accept a bribe because you've decided that your financial security is more pressing than obeying God. Take marriage as another example. The doubt sounds like this: *"Is God really going to give me a spouse? Is He really enough for me in my singleness?"*

Doubt leads to desperation, and desperation leads to poor decisions—ignoring red flags in a relationship, pursuing ungodly connections, or even dabbling in new-age practices to "manifest" a spouse.

This, too, is idolatry. It's the elevation of our desires above God's word and God's timing.

The Birth of Emotional Idolatry

After Adam and Eve's disobedience, everything changed. Genesis 3:7 says:

"At that moment their eyes were opened, and they suddenly felt shame at their nakedness. So they sewed fig leaves together to cover themselves."

The first emotion humanity experienced outside of God's presence was *shame*. Before sin, Adam and Eve were naked but unashamed, reflecting their purity and innocence in God's presence. Now, their nakedness exposed their vulnerability, and with it came shame—a painful emotion tied to the consciousness of wrongdoing.

What did Adam and Eve do in response? They covered themselves with fig leaves. They didn't run to God for help or guidance; they acted independently, relying on their own efforts to address their shame. This pattern of taking matters into their own hands didn't stop there. When God came walking in the garden, calling for Adam, Adam hid. Genesis 3:10 recounts his response:

"I heard you in the garden, and I was afraid because I was naked, so I hid."

The second emotion recorded outside of God's presence was *fear*. The God they once walked with in intimacy now felt distant and threatening.

Doubt had led to disobedience. Disobedience had birthed shame. Shame had led to fear. And fear drove Adam and Eve further from God.

In their shame and fear, they made decisions based on their emotions rather than seeking God's guidance. They relied on their feelings as their authority, which is the essence of emotional idolatry.

What Is Emotional Idolatry?

Emotional idolatry occurs when we place our emotions in the position of God. It's when we allow our feelings to guide our decisions, define our truth, and take priority over God's word and will. Emotional idolatry is dethroning God and crowning our emotions as the ultimate authority in our lives.

For example:

- *"I'm angry, and I know God's word says to honor my parents, but right now, my anger is in control, so I'll yell at my mom anyway."*

- *"I'm stressed, and I know God says to flee from sexual immorality, but my frustration is pushing me to watch pornography to cope."*

Emotional idolatry, like all idolatry, starts with doubt. Doubting God's word or His intentions causes us to rely on our emotions to determine what is "good" for us in the moment. It's an attempt to dethrone God and replace Him with what *feels* right.

Adam and Eve's fall illustrates how idolatry begins with doubt, progresses to disobedience, and results in emotional chaos—shame, fear, and separation from God. Their story is a cautionary tale, but it's also a mirror. How often do we rely on our emotions rather than God's truth? How often do we let our feelings sit on the throne of our hearts?

Think about it. Our doubts are often projected through the manifestation of our brokenness. We doubt God, and as a result, we don't trust Him. When you're consumed by anger and offense toward someone, it becomes incredibly hard to obey God's word and forgive them. The temptation to cling to your anger, to let it dictate your actions and decisions, can feel overwhelming. Why? Because at the root of holding onto that offense is doubt: deep down, you doubt that God is just. You doubt His justice. You doubt that He sees the wrongs committed against you and that He will defend you and right those wrongs.

Letting go feels almost impossible because you don't fully trust that God will fight for you. So, instead of releasing the offense to God, you let anger decide for you what justice looks like. Anger takes the throne where God should sit. This is emotional idolatry—replacing God's authority with your feelings.

The same pattern happens with jealousy. When you allow jealousy to take root in your heart, dominating your relationships and actions, it often stems from a deeper mistrust. Perhaps you don't believe God has something good for you, too. Your feelings of insecurity and envy may be tied to a deeper struggle to trust God's definition of your worth, identity, and sufficiency. You may begin questioning whether God truly loves you or whether His promises for you are true.

At its core, emotional idolatry is deciding for yourself what is good and right based on what *feels* good in the moment rather than submitting to God's word and His way.

We often think of idols as tangible things: golden calves, material possessions, social status, or even people. But idols can also be intangible—they can be emotions. You make your emotions an idol when you elevate them above God and His word.

This is precisely what Adam and Eve did. They put their desires and judgment above God's command and wisdom. Their rebellion birthed sin, which distorted their hearts and led to a battle between the flesh and the spirit.

As discussed in a previous chapter, our emotions reside in the soul. While God has a divine purpose for our emotions, sin has given the flesh the power to manipulate them. The flesh seeks to use our emotions to rebel against God's will. Each day, we face a choice: Will we submit our emotions to God, or will we allow our feelings to dictate our actions, contrary to His word?

The emotional chain of events in the Garden is both sobering and illuminating:

- **Doubt** was the seed planted by the serpent.

- **Disobedience** grew from that seed.

- **Shame** sprouted after the disobedience.

- **Fear** followed shame.

- **Hiding** was the ultimate outcome, separating Adam and Eve from God.

This sequence is a blueprint for how emotional idolatry takes root. Doubt leads to disobedience, which opens the door for shame and fear to dominate, driving us further from God.

The Three Pillars of Emotional Idolatry: Doubt, Fear, and Shame

In my opinion, doubt, fear, and shame are the foundational pillars of emotional idolatry. I call them *"the weapons of mass emotional destruction"* because of their pervasive and destructive influence on emotional health and spiritual well-being.

Let's start with **doubt**. Many emotional wounds and traumas begin with doubt—doubt in our worth, identity, abilities, or even God's goodness. Doubt destabilizes our emotional foundation and creates fertile ground for fear and shame to take root.

For example, consider a child with an absent father. That child might doubt they are lovable, doubt they are worthy of love, and even doubt the love of their Heavenly Father. This doubt can lead to a fear of abandonment and a deep-seated insecurity. That fear might drive them to overcompensate in relationships, idolizing love, control, or approval as a way to avoid further abandonment.

Next, **fear**. Fear often leads to emotional attachments to idols like people, perfectionism, or material possessions. Fear of rejection, failure, or loneliness can cause us to prioritize human approval or earthly comfort over God's approval and eternal promises.

Finally, **shame**. Shame tells us we are unworthy of love, grace, or acceptance. It causes us to hide, suppress our true selves, and seek validation from idols like status, beauty, or achievements. Shame can distort our identity and lead us to seek worth through external means rather than God's unconditional love.

Doubt, fear, and shame are intertwined at the root of emotional wounds, trauma, and idolatry. They distort how we see God, ourselves, and others, leading to cycles of emotional bondage and unhealthy patterns.

At the core of idolatry is a trust issue. We doubt God's word, His character, His promises, His justice, and His sufficiency. Because we don't trust Him fully, we look for idols—things that can serve as our "plan B" in case God doesn't come through.

This is especially true in emotional idolatry. We don't trust God with our feelings, so we let our emotions take the lead.

- *"I don't trust God's justice, so I'll hold onto my anger and seek my own form of revenge."*

- *"I don't trust God to comfort me, so I'll turn to alcohol or another coping mechanism to numb my pain."*

- *"I don't trust God's timing, so I'll compromise my values to secure what I think I need right now."*

The enemy uses this lack of trust to manipulate our emotions and drive us further from God's will. Sin distorts and perverts our emotions, making them unreliable guides when detached from God's truth.

Biblical Examples of Emotional Idolatry

The Bible is full of examples where emotional idolatry led to destructive consequences:

- **Joseph's Brothers**: Bitterness and resentment drove them to sell Joseph into slavery (Genesis 37). Their unchecked emotions led to years of family strife.

- **David and Bathsheba**: David's lust led him to commit adultery and murder (2 Samuel 11). He allowed his desires to override God's word.

- **Peter in the Garden**: Overwhelmed by fear and anger, Peter cut off the ear of a soldier, acting impulsively rather than trusting Jesus' plan (John 18:10).

Each of these examples shows the devastating consequences of putting emotions on the throne instead of God.

To dethrone God and put our emotions in His place is an act of rebellion, the same rebellion that led to humanity's fall in the Garden of Eden. Emotional idolatry is no less sinful than any other form of idolatry, and it requires repentance.

If we want to break free from emotional idolatry, we must start by trusting God with our emotions. We must surrender our feelings to Him, allowing His word—not our emotions—to guide our actions. This is not easy, but it is the path to freedom, healing, and restored intimacy with God.

The War on Your Emotions

When sin came into the picture, everything changed.

God created a world full of beauty, harmony, and order—everything in its perfect place. He saw all that He had made, and He declared it "good." But sin entered, and its nature is perversion—it twists, distorts, and corrupts what God originally created for good.

Sin brought division where there was once unity. It turned harmony into chaos and peace into conflict. In the Garden of Eden, Adam and Eve existed in oneness with each other and with God. But after sin, everything was fractured. The same Adam who once exclaimed, *"This one is bone of my bone and flesh of my flesh!"* (Genesis 2:23) turned and blamed Eve for his disobedience and even pointed fingers at God for giving her to him.

Sin didn't stop at disrupting humanity's relationship with God; it disrupted humanity's relationship with themselves, with others, and even with creation. The animals, once peaceful, became hostile. The earth, once fruitful, began to resist. And our emotions—once a pure reflection of God's heart—became entangled with brokenness.

God designed our emotions to reflect His character: love, joy, peace, compassion, justice, and truth. Our emotions were intended to connect us to God, to others, and to the beauty of creation. They were meant to help us carry out His purposes with tender care and devotion. But sin corrupted the way we process and express our emotions.

Instead of our emotions drawing us closer to God, they now often lead us astray.

Instead of peace, we feel shame.
Instead of joy, we feel jealousy.
Instead of love, we harbor resentment.

Sin introduced a war—a war between the spirit and the flesh. The spirit, connected to God, desires to align our emotions with God's will. But the flesh, tainted by sin, manipulates our emotions, pulling us away from God and into self-destruction.

And here's the truth: **there is a war on your emotions.**

I don't write this lightly. Right now—yes, at this very moment—there is a battle over your soul, and your emotions are at the center of it. Why? Because your emotions reside in your soul, the seat of your mind, will, and conscience.

God is after your soul. But so is the enemy.

God wants to redeem your emotions, sanctifying them so they can reflect His image and advance His kingdom. But the enemy wants to hijack your emotions—manipulating and twisting them to bring destruction, division, and bondage into your life. He wants to use your emotions to drive you further from God, from your purpose, and from the freedom Jesus died to give you.

This is why God warned Cain in Genesis 4:7:

> *"Sin is crouching at the door, eager to control you.*
> *But you must subdue it and be its master."*

The same warning applies to us today. Sin is crouching at the door of our hearts, eager to exploit our emotions for destruction. It whispers lies, plants seeds of doubt, and waits for the perfect moment to take root. Like Cain, if we don't guard our emotions and submit them to God, sin can gain a foothold and wreak havoc.

Cain allowed unchecked emotions of anger and jealousy to fester, and it led him to commit murder against his own brother. That same pattern exists today. The enemy sows seeds into our hearts to manipulate our thoughts and emotions—pushing us into isolation, broken relationships, and sin.

Proverbs 4:23 gives us a powerful warning:

"Guard your heart above all else, for it determines the course of your life."

Think about that. If the enemy can plant a single seed of doubt, bitterness, or shame in your heart, it can literally reroute the course of your life. The words and actions you take—driven by unchecked emotions—can sabotage relationships, dreams, and your God-given purpose.

Now that we've identified the battle, let's examine how the enemy plants seeds in our hearts to manipulate our emotions.

1. Through Your Thoughts

Proverbs 23:7 warns us:

"For as he thinks in his heart, so is he."

Your thoughts have tremendous power—they shape your emotions, influence your behaviors, and, ultimately, direct the course of your life. This is why it's critical to guard your mind and protect the flow of thoughts entering and leaving it.

The enemy knows this truth well. He plants negative, deceptive thoughts in your mind, hoping they'll take root in your heart and grow into something destructive. Here's the sad reality: Many people lack the discernment to recognize when these thoughts aren't their own. They assume every thought that crosses their mind belongs to them, unaware that the enemy has infiltrated their thinking.

This is where discernment comes in. The gift of discernment isn't just for identifying external demonic influences in people or places; it's also for recognizing when your own thoughts have been infiltrated by the enemy.

When Eve first encountered the serpent in Genesis 3, her first mistake wasn't eating the fruit—it was entertaining the serpent. She engaged with a voice that twisted God's words and planted doubt. Instead of rejecting the serpent outright, she entertained his words, entertained the lies, and allowed the seeds of doubt to take root.

We do the exact same thing today. The enemy whispers lies into our minds like:

"Nobody loves me."
"I'm a failure."
"I'll never be good enough."

And instead of rejecting those thoughts immediately, we entertain them. We dwell on them. We have a back-and-forth dialogue with the enemy as if he's worthy of our attention. Every time you sit with those thoughts, ruminate on them or allow them to take root, you're doing exactly what Eve did—you're entertaining the serpent.

But here's the truth: your mind is not a playground for the enemy.

You must filter every thought through the Word of God. If a thought doesn't align with His truth, it doesn't belong in your mind. The longer you let it sit, the deeper it takes root and the harder it is to uproot.

Imagine this: someone isolated and tormented by thoughts of worthlessness didn't get there overnight. It likely started with a single thought: *"Nobody loves me."* That thought wasn't challenged, and over time, it grew. It became a tree with branches of depression, isolation, and hopelessness, bearing fruit that only brought destruction.

To stop this cycle, you must catch the thought immediately. Recognize it for what it is—a lie—and reject it before it can take root.

2 Corinthians 10:5 reminds us:

"We destroy arguments and every lofty opinion raised against the knowledge of God, and take every thought captive to obey Christ."

This isn't a passive process; it's an active, intentional one. Taking a thought captive means grabbing it by the collar, examining it in the light of God's Word, and deciding whether it aligns with truth or needs to be thrown out.

Let's make this practical. Suppose a thought comes into your mind:

"I'm such a failure. I can never do anything right."

If you let that thought linger and speak it aloud, you're coming into agreement with it. By saying, *"I'm such a failure,"* you align yourself with the enemy's agenda to sabotage your purpose.

Instead, here's how you fight back:

- **Recognize the lie.**

  - "This thought is not from God. I reject it."

- **Speak God's Word against it.**

  - Say: *"No, I rebuke that thought in the name of Jesus! I am not a failure. I can do all things through Christ who strengthens me."* (Philippians 4:13)

- **Declare the truth aloud.**

  - Pray: *"Satan, I rebuke you and resist you. My mind is not your playground. I plead the blood of Jesus over my thoughts, and I declare that my mind belongs to Christ. Flee in the name of Jesus!"*

Do you see how powerful this is? When you actively fight back with God's Word, you silence the lies and refuse to give the enemy access to your emotions or your heart.

Proverbs 18:21 reminds us:

> *"Death and life are in the power of the tongue,*
> *and those who love it will eat its fruit."*

Your words have the power to either agree with the enemy's lies or align with God's truth. Choose life. Choose truth. Speak the Word of God over yourself and watch as the lies lose their grip on your heart.

Your thoughts are the battlefield where the war on your emotions is fought. But you are not powerless—you have the authority of Christ, the truth of God's Word, and the power of the Holy Spirit to overcome. Don't let the enemy's lies take root. Refuse to entertain the serpent. Guard your thoughts, take them captive, and align your mind with the truth of God's Word.

You are victorious when you choose truth over lies, life over death, and faith over doubt.

2. Through The Words and Actions of Others

Whether we like it or not, the words and actions of people in our lives hold immense power—they can uplift us or tear us down. The enemy is well aware of this and often uses the words of those we care about most—parents, siblings, friends, mentors, or significant others—to plant seeds of doubt, insecurity, and emotional wounds deep in our hearts.

These seeds aren't random. They are often strategically planted attacks designed to derail your identity, purpose, and emotional health.

Think about this: there are grown adults today still carrying the weight of words spoken to them in childhood—words from parents, teachers, or caregivers that became the foundation of their self-image. Some have even given up on their goals, dreams, or God-given purpose because of a single discouraging sentence spoken years ago.

That's how powerful words can be.

I remember a time when someone I deeply cared about said three simple but heavy words to me: "You're too much." At first, I brushed it off, thinking it didn't affect me. I never brought it to God in prayer or processed it. I thought I was fine. But over time, the enemy used those words to plant seeds of doubt, fear, and insecurity in my heart.

I started to believe it. I began shrinking myself, dimming my light, and suppressing the very personality God gave me. I spoke less, expressed myself less, and worked tirelessly to take up less space because I didn't want to scare anyone off or be "too much" for them.

As I grew deeper in my walk with Christ, I wrestled internally because my real self—my joyful, passionate, expressive self—kept trying to resurface. Yet I pushed it back down, afraid that embracing my true personality would make me undesirable or unlovable.

At one point, I even convinced myself that being "soft and quiet" was the ideal image of femininity and holiness and that my vibrant personality wasn't Christian enough. But then the Holy Spirit began speaking to me:

"Who gave you this personality?"

God showed me that my personality was tailor-made for me, designed specifically for the purpose and calling He has for my life. By dimming my light, I wasn't just betraying my identity—I was hindering my own growth and purpose. I was trying to wear someone else's clothes, and they didn't fit because they weren't mine.

What seemed like a "harmless" three-word comment— *"You're too much"*—wasn't harmless at all. It was a strategically orchestrated attack from the enemy to keep me from fully embracing my identity in Christ and stepping into my calling.

What words are you still carrying? Who you are today may still be shaped by words that were spoken over you years ago:

- A parent's harsh comparison that made you feel less than.

- A teacher's dismissal that planted seeds of failure.

- A friend's rejection that made you question your worth.

Maybe you grew up being compared to your siblings, with a parent always favoring one child over the other. No matter how casually spoken, words of comparison can sow seeds of jealousy, inadequacy, and insecurity. Now, as an adult, you struggle to feel "good enough," constantly battling feelings of inadequacy or resentment.

Those seeds from childhood, if unchecked, can grow into emotional turmoil, sabotaging your relationships, goals, and ability to receive the good things God has for you.

But let me be clear: those words were not just "harmless comments." They were weapons, tools the enemy used to launch a spiritual attack against your future, your identity, and your purpose.

This is why forgiveness is so important. Forgiveness isn't about excusing what someone said or did. It's about refusing to let their words and actions take root in your heart and hold you captive.

Unforgiveness is like water for a seed—it allows the offense to grow, take root, and bear bad fruit. But forgiveness nullifies the power of those words. It uproots the lies and allows the Holy Spirit to come into your heart, heal your wounds, and restore your identity.

When you forgive, you:

- Release the offense so it can no longer hold you back.

- Surrender your pain to God, trusting Him to heal what was broken.

- Break the enemy's influence over your heart, emotions, and thoughts.

Matthew 6:14-15 reminds us:

"For if you forgive others their trespasses, your heavenly Father will also forgive you, but if you do not forgive others their trespasses, neither will your Father forgive your trespasses."

Forgiveness is not just obedience—it's freedom.

Not every word spoken over you is truth. People often project their own brokenness, insecurities, and wounds onto others. That's why it's critical to filter every word you hear through the truth of God's Word.

- When someone says, *"You're not good enough,"*

  God says: *"You are fearfully and wonderfully made."* (Psalm 139:14)

- When someone says, *"You'll never succeed,"*

  God says: *"For I know the plans I have for you, plans for welfare and not for evil, to give you a future and a hope."* (Jeremiah 29:11)

The only voice you need to believe is the voice of your Heavenly Father.

The enemy uses the words and actions of others to sow doubt, fear, and shame into your heart. But Proverbs 4:23 urges us:

"Guard your heart above all else, for it determines the course of your life."

Guarding your heart doesn't mean building walls or shutting people out. It means surrendering your heart to God so His truth can be the filter through which every word and action passes.

Don't allow the enemy to weaponize the words and actions of others against you. Recognize those seeds for what they are—an attack on your identity, purpose, and emotional health. Bring every offense to God. Forgive those who've spoken hurtful words, release the weight of their actions, and allow the Holy Spirit to heal you.

When you do, you'll begin to see yourself the way God sees you: loved, chosen, worthy, and beautifully created for a purpose.

You are not defined by anyone's words but God's. Hold on to His truth, and let Him renew your mind and restore your heart.

3. Through Your Dreams

This might surprise you, but it's absolutely true: The enemy can sow seeds into your heart through your dreams, manipulating your emotions and influencing your behavior. While God uses dreams for divine purposes, the enemy distorts them to plant fear, confusion, offense, and doubt, driving you further from God's will.

From a biblical perspective, dreams are visions or experiences during sleep that can serve different purposes:

- **Divine Dreams**: Directly from God for revelation, encouragement, instruction, deliverance, or warning.

- **Natural Dreams**: A product of the mind processing your thoughts, emotions, and experiences. Ecclesiastes 5:3 tells us, *"Too much activity gives you restless dreams."*

- **Demonic Dreams**: Manipulated or influenced by the enemy to deceive, disrupt, or plant seeds of destruction.

God often communicated through dreams in Scripture. He used dreams to reveal Joseph's future (Genesis 37:5-10) and to warn Pharaoh about an impending famine (Genesis 41). God also used King Nebuchadnezzar's dreams (Daniel 2, 4), interpreted by Daniel, to reveal His sovereignty and humble the king. In the New Testament, He guided Joseph, the husband of Mary, through dreams to protect Jesus (Matthew 1:20; 2:13).

While God uses dreams for good, the enemy seeks to pervert them. Jesus said in Matthew 13:25, *"But while men slept, his enemy came and sowed tares among the wheat and went his way."* While this parable isn't directly about dreams, it's significant that Jesus used *sleep* to illustrate how the enemy operates. Sleep makes us vulnerable. We are not conscious, alert, or on guard, and the enemy takes advantage of this to plant seeds of deception, fear, and destruction.

I've personally experienced this. Many years ago, I applied for a particular job that I was incredibly excited about. I prepped for days, picked out my outfit the night before, and went to bed confident about my in-person interview. That night, however, I had a vivid and frightening dream: I was trapped inside an elevator, crying out for help, but no one answered. I panicked and felt completely stuck.

Now, here's the twist—the interview was on the 15th floor of a building. I had always been fearful of elevators, and when I woke up, that dream left me overwhelmed with a crippling sense of fear. I almost didn't go to the interview because the fear felt so real.

Looking back, I can clearly see how the enemy sowed a seed of fear in my dream to sabotage me. If I hadn't discerned it as a demonic dream and prayed to cancel its influence, I might have missed an important opportunity. I prayed fervently, broke the spirit of fear in Jesus' name, and went to the interview with peace and confidence.

The enemy can use your dreams to manipulate your emotions and actions in subtle but destructive ways. He plants fear, anger, or confusion into your subconscious so that when you wake up, those feelings linger and influence how you respond throughout the day.

Early in my marriage, the enemy tried to plant seeds of division through my dreams. I would have vivid, intense dreams where my husband and I were arguing or offending one another. The emotions in the dream were so strong that I'd wake up feeling unsettled. I would remind myself, *"It's just a dream. He didn't actually do anything to offend me."* Still, throughout the day, I found myself snapping at him, easily annoyed, and picking up unnecessary arguments.

What was happening? The dream had planted a seed of offense in my heart. I didn't realize it at first because I was dismissing it as "just a dream," but my emotions told a different story. The real enemy wasn't my husband—it was the devil, the same one who used the serpent to plant seeds of doubt in Eve's heart. The enemy was using my dreams to manipulate my emotions and disrupt the unity in my marriage.

This happens more often than people realize. I've also heard countless stories of individuals waking up from vivid sexual dreams. The dream plants a seed of lust in their hearts, and without discernment, they carry that seed into their day. Suddenly, they're struggling with temptation, battling thoughts of pornography, masturbation, or fornication. What they think "just happened" in the middle of the day actually started the night before, in a dream.

Dreams are powerful. Just as God can use dreams to stir compassion, intercession, and direction, the enemy can manipulate them to carry out his destructive agenda. But you don't have to be a victim of demonic dreams. Here's what you can do:

- **Pray Before You Sleep**

Cover your sleep with prayer. Plead the blood of Jesus over your dreams and ask God to protect your mind and heart while you sleep. Pray Psalm 4:8: *"In peace I will lie down and sleep, for you alone, O Lord, will keep me safe."*

- **Pray When You Wake Up**

If you wake up from a disturbing or demonic dream, don't ignore it. Pray immediately. Cancel the dream and its effects in the name of Jesus. Ask the Holy Spirit to uproot any evil seed that may have been planted in your heart. Declare: *"I reject this dream in Jesus' name. No weapon formed against me shall prosper"* (Isaiah 54:17).

- **Pay Attention to Your Emotions**

How do you feel when you wake up? If you're overwhelmed by fear, anger, lust, or offense—emotions that push you away from God or His peace—those feelings may have been planted by the enemy. Invite the Holy Spirit to bring clarity and discernment.

- **Combat the Lies with Truth**

Speak God's Word over your life. Replace fear with faith, offense with forgiveness, and lust with purity. For example:

- *"God has not given me a spirit of fear, but of power and of love and of a sound mind"* (2 Timothy 1:7).

- *"I will walk in purity and honor because I am a temple of the Holy Spirit"* (1 Corinthians 6:19-20).

- **Recognize the Real Enemy**

Your spouse, family, or friends are **not** the enemy. The devil is. Ephesians 6:12 reminds us: *"For we wrestle not against flesh and blood, but against principalities, against powers, against the rulers of the darkness of this world, against spiritual wickedness in high places."*

The enemy is cunning, but God is greater. Don't allow emotions planted in your dreams to go unchecked. Bring every dream before the Lord in prayer, discern its source, and refuse to allow the enemy's seeds to take root. Your dreams—and your emotions—belong to God, and He alone deserves the authority over them.

There are countless ways the enemy plants seeds in our hearts to manipulate our emotions. It's critical to understand this: if your emotions are not fully submitted to the Lord, they can easily become idols, tools the enemy uses to gain control over you.

I once heard a powerful quote from Pastor Steven Furtick that has stayed with me for years: "Sin is meeting a legitimate need illegitimately." Let that sink in.

- Your need for acceptance is legitimate, but meeting that need through people-pleasing is not.

- Your need for connection is legitimate, but fulfilling it through gossip is not.

- Your need for companionship is legitimate, but engaging in fornication or pornography is not.

- Your need for justice is legitimate, but seeking revenge is not.

God gave us these needs, and He has provided legitimate solutions for meeting them—solutions that align with His Word. He is our source, and His answers to our needs are pure, life-giving, and satisfying. But when we elevate the need itself above God, the enemy finds an opening. He manipulates our emotions, tempting us to meet those needs illegitimately. When we allow emotions to guide us over God's Word, we step into emotional idolatry.

Outside of God's presence, our legitimate needs—acceptance, love, justice—can become overwhelming and all-consuming. We allow them to drive us to *illegitimate solutions*. However, in God's presence, our emotions are steadied. He satisfies those needs, providing peace and answers that align with His will.

This brings us back to a foundational truth: Emotions are not good or bad—they are neutral. God created emotions as tools to help us navigate life, relate to Him, and fulfill His purposes. Joy, love, anger, and even fear were originally designed to reflect His nature.

However, the fall of humanity introduced sin, distorting the way we experience and express emotions. For example:

- **Fear**: Before the fall, fear was likely tied to reverent awe and respect for God. After sin entered the world, fear became associated with hiding, avoidance, and distrust (Genesis 3:10).

- **Shame**: There was no shame in the Garden of Eden. Adam and Eve were "naked and unashamed" (Genesis 2:25). Shame only emerged after their disobedience. It became a destructive emotion that drove them to cover themselves and hide from God.

Sin twists emotions, corrupting their original purpose. Fear, which should inspire reverence for God, becomes paralyzing anxiety. Anger, meant to confront injustice, turns into hatred, unforgiveness, and bitterness. Emotions that were tools for connection now drive disconnection and isolation.

But here's the key: Emotions remain neutral. It's not the emotion itself that is sinful; it's our response to the emotion that determines whether it leads us to righteousness or sin.

- Fear can lead us to trust God for wisdom and protection, or it can spiral into anxiety and distrust.

- Anger can empower us to establish boundaries or intercede for justice, but left unchecked, it can fester into unforgiveness and hatred.

Our emotional responses reveal whether we are aligned with God's will or allowing sin to take root. They expose whether we've placed our feelings above God's truth, revealing emotional idolatry.

Emotions vs. Demonic Spirits

Now, you may have heard phrases like *"spirit of anger"* or *"spirit of fear,"* especially in deliverance settings. This can be confusing: *How can anger be a God-given emotion and also a demonic spirit?* Let's clarify.

1. Emotions

Emotions—like anger, sadness, or fear—are designed by God. They are neutral, temporary, and part of being human. For example:

- **Anger**: Scripture shows us that anger can reflect God's righteous nature. Psalm 7:11 says, *"God is a just judge, and God is angry with the wicked every day."* Anger, when managed under the guidance of the Holy Spirit, can lead to righteous action and sanctification.

   However, Paul warns in Ephesians 4:26-27: *"Be angry and do not sin; do not let the sun go down on your anger, and give no opportunity to the devil."* Unchecked anger can open the door for the enemy to gain a foothold.

2. Demonic Spirits

A demonic spirit, on the other hand, is an oppressive and persistent influence designed to enslave. The spirit of anger, for example, isn't just a moment of anger—it's a stronghold where anger becomes uncontrollable, destructive, and all-consuming. It drives a person's thoughts and actions beyond their will.

- **Example**: Saul's unchecked jealousy and anger toward David (1 Samuel 18:10) opened a door for a tormenting spirit. What began as an emotion became a demonic stronghold, driving Saul to irrational violence.

Similarly, the spirit of fear goes beyond natural fear. It's a crippling stronghold that torments and paralyzes. 2 Timothy 1:7 tells us, *"For God has not given us a spirit of fear and timidity, but of power, love, and self-discipline."* Fear, when left unchecked, can open the door for this spirit, leading to bondage and separation from God's love.

Distinguishing Emotions from Demonic Spirits

Here's the distinction:

Emotion	Demonic Spirit
God-given and neutral	Destructive, sent by the enemy
Temporary, natural response	Persistent, oppressive influence
Can be managed through self-control and the Holy Spirit	Requires discernment, deliverance, and spiritual authority
Leads us to discern situations with clarity	Leads to bondage, sin, and confusion, and blurs our discernment

Example:

- Emma feels anger when hurt but takes it to God in prayer, choosing forgiveness. Her anger is processed under the Holy Spirit's guidance.

- Taylor feels anger but doesn't address it. Over time, anger becomes her default response, turning into uncontrollable rage and bitterness. This unresolved emotion opened the door to a spirit of anger, influencing her actions and thoughts.

The good news is this: Jesus Christ has all authority over emotions and spirits. As believers, we can submit our emotions to Him, allowing the Holy Spirit to help us steward them. Through discernment, we can identify when emotions become strongholds or when a demonic influence is at play.

Your emotions were never meant to sit on the throne of your heart.

Anxiety is not your identity. Fear is not your identity. Shame is not your identity.

Your identity is in Christ. Jesus defines you, not your emotions. Emotions are a gift from God, but when they take His place, they become dangerous idols. Recognizing emotional idolatry is the first step to restoring God's rightful place in your heart and dethroning feelings that have been elevated beyond their purpose.

There is a war on your emotions, but Jesus has won the victory. Repent from emotional idolatry, submit your emotions to Christ, and let Him heal and sanctify them so they become a beautiful reflection of His image.

Prayer

Heavenly Father,

Thank You for the wisdom and truth You have revealed through this chapter by the power of Your Holy Spirit. Lord, I come before You today humbly acknowledging my sin. I confess that I have stored up idols in my heart and committed the sin of emotional idolatry.

I repent for every time I placed my emotions above You and Your Word. I repent for allowing my feelings to take the throne of my heart, where only You belong. Forgive me for the moments when I doubted that You were enough, seeking fulfillment in people, emotions, and things instead of in You. Lord, I lay these idols at Your feet and ask for Your mercy and cleansing.

Wash me, Lord, with the perfect and sacrificial blood of Jesus Christ. Purify my heart and soul. Create in me a clean heart, O God, and renew a steadfast spirit within me. Refine my thoughts and desires with the fire of Your Holy Spirit. If there are idols or deceptions hidden in my heart that I am unaware of, I ask that You reveal them and uproot them by Your power.

Transform my mind, O Lord. Renew my perspective and give me the gift of discernment so I may filter my thoughts and recognize when the enemy tries to sow seeds of doubt, fear, or shame. Reveal every demonic stronghold that has kept me bound and hindered my relationships—with others and with You. Let every stronghold be exposed and destroyed by the blood of Jesus.

Thank You, Father, for the work of Your Holy Spirit within me. I fully receive Your forgiveness and grace. Today, I surrender my heart, my mind, my soul, and every part of who I am back to You. I renounce every idol and false god, taking back my desires and will and placing them firmly in Your hands. Align my heart and desires with Your will and purpose for my life.

Thank You for Your love, Your mercy, and Your faithfulness. I trust You to guide me, heal me, and make my emotions a reflection of Your image.

In the mighty and holy name of Your Son, Jesus Christ, I pray.

Amen.

REFLECTION QUESTIONS

1. Have you ever studied the story of Adam and Eve in the Garden of Eden through the lens of emotional idolatry? How has this chapter expanded your understanding of how disobedience and emotional idolatry began with their actions?

2. What is emotional idolatry, and how have you seen it manifest in your own life? Can you recall specific instances where your emotions took precedence over God's authority?

3. Reflect on your personal experiences: Have doubt, fear, or shame acted as "weapons of mass emotional destruction" in your life? Can you identify an emotional chain reaction that began with doubt, led to shame, and culminated in fear? What was the seed of doubt the enemy planted in your heart, and how did it shape your decisions or beliefs?

4. Think about an identity struggle you are currently facing—whether it's perfectionism, fear of rejection, low self-esteem, people-pleasing, or seeking validation. Can you trace its root? Was it shaped by a past experience, a seed of doubt, or hurtful words spoken over you? How does this struggle reveal areas where you may be struggling to trust God?

5. Have negative words or actions from others influenced you, creating emotional wounds or insecurities? Reflect on those experiences. How can forgiveness and inviting the Holy Spirit into that pain bring healing and freedom?

6. Consider the quote, "Sin is meeting a legitimate need illegitimately." Are there needs in your life—such as acceptance, connection, or justice—that you've sought to fulfill in ways that contradict God's Word? Reflect on those legitimate needs and how you've sought to meet them. What steps can you take to trust God to meet those needs His way?

7. How has sin distorted your understanding and expression of emotions? Reflect on moments when your emotional responses were submitted to God versus moments when they were influenced by the flesh. What were the differences in the outcomes of each scenario?

8. What is the difference between God-given emotions and demonic influences, such as the spirit of fear or anger? Have you ever felt that an emotional struggle has become a stronghold? How can the Holy Spirit and your local church community support you in experiencing healing and deliverance?

9. In what ways have you allowed emotions like anger, fear, or disappointment to define your identity or dictate your actions? How can you shift from letting emotions define you to allowing God's Word and your identity in Christ to lead the way?

10. What practical steps can you take to dethrone emotional idols and ensure that God reigns on the throne of your heart? How can prayer, repentance, and reliance on the Holy Spirit guide you toward freedom and emotional health?

PART III

08

EMOTIONAL HEALING

We live in a broken world—a world fractured by sin. Sin entered and quite literally ruined everything. It didn't just break the world around us; it infiltrated our hearts and began its work within our flesh, distorting and perverting all that God declared "good." As a result, we are broken, too.

Paul captures this reality so powerfully in Romans 7:22-24:

"I love God's law with all my heart. But there is another power within me that is at war with my mind. This power makes me a slave to the sin that is still within me. Oh, what a miserable person I am! Who will free me from this life that is dominated by sin and death?"

Paul's lament is profound. He describes himself as miserable—"wretched" in other translations—because of sin's grip. The truth is, we are all emotionally broken because of the sin at work in the world and in us.

And here's a sobering thought: we often love others from this place of brokenness. Whether we like it or not, our love is filtered through the lens of our emotional wounds, and those around us are doing the same. This creates a cycle where we are both recipients and distributors of brokenness—a heartbreaking loop of pain that perpetuates itself.

The reality is we all need emotional healing. While our wounds may differ based on our unique experiences, we each carry the scars of a broken world. No one is capable of loving you perfectly 100% of the time, not because they don't care, but because they, too, are broken. Even the most compassionate, altruistic people—your parents, your friends, your mentors—are loving from places that have been shaped by their own doubts, fears, and wounds.

Emotional brokenness is inevitable. And here's the hard truth: there are things that haven't even happened yet in your life that you will one day need healing from. As you grow older, you will face more complex emotions, situations, and challenges. While we often prepare for the good things in life, we must also acknowledge the inevitability of difficult moments in this fallen world. These moments will require emotional healing when they come.

But here's the hope: Emotional healing is a choice and an invitation. God, in His mercy and goodness, foresaw the chaos sin would unleash, and He has provided both practical and spiritual resources for healing. The question is whether you will choose to embrace the healing He offers.

A Reflection of Experience or God's Design?

Who you are today is a culmination of your life experiences, external influences, and relationships. From birth until now, every moment has shaped how you think, feel, and relate to others. This is a profound reality because it means the version of yourself you see in the mirror may be more a reflection of your experiences than of God's original design for you.

God had a vision for you before you were born—a version of you that was perfect and complete, fully aligned with His purpose and image. This is the version He knew before you were formed in your mother's womb. But the version of yourself you see today might be distorted by wounds, sin, and life's hardships. Emotional healing is the process of realigning yourself with the version of you that God envisioned before you were born. It's about becoming aware of your brokenness, addressing the distortions, and committing to the journey of restoration. As you heal, you grow closer to reflecting God's image and the 'you' He envisioned when He created you.

The story of Jeremiah beautifully illustrates this. In Jeremiah 1:4-5, God says:

"I knew you before I formed you in your mother's womb. Before you were born I set you apart and appointed you as my prophet to the nations."

God knew Jeremiah before his physical body was formed. He knew the whole, healed, and complete version of Jeremiah—the version untouched by the brokenness of the world. God had already set Jeremiah apart with a clear purpose and calling. Yet when God called him, Jeremiah responded from a place of insecurity:

"O Sovereign Lord," I said, *"I can't speak for you! I'm too young!"* (Jeremiah 1:6)

Jeremiah's insecurity reflected the accumulation of his cultural, social, and relational experiences. In ancient Israel, age and experience were highly valued, and Jeremiah's youth likely made him feel inadequate to confront elders and authority figures. But God responded with reassurance:

"Don't say, 'I'm too young,' for you must go wherever I send you and say whatever I tell you. And don't be afraid of the people, for I will be with you and will protect you. I, the Lord, have spoken!" (Jeremiah 1:7-8)

This interaction reveals how Jeremiah's insecurities were rooted in his brokenness. God did not create Jeremiah to live in fear or insecurity. Yet, like us, Jeremiah was shaped by his environment and experiences. God did not see the insecure version of Jeremiah shaped by societal expectations; He saw the bold prophet He had created and called. Jeremiah's healing journey involved trusting God, confronting his insecurities, and embracing his calling despite his fears.

Jeremiah's story reminds us that emotional healing is a journey of moving from the distorted version of ourselves to the true version God intended. It's about shedding insecurities, fears, and wounds that hold us back from fulfilling His purpose.

Take a moment to ask yourself: "If God showed me the version of myself He knew before I was born, would it match the person I am today? Would the life I'm living reflect the life He intended for me?"

Perhaps God has destined you for thriving relationships, but fears of rejection or abandonment have caused you to self-sabotage. Perhaps He's called you to creative or ministry work, but imposter syndrome has held you back. Or maybe God wants you to bring peace and unity to your family, but unforgiveness and offense have created division instead.

Emotional wounds and traumas often hinder us from fully embracing God's love and stepping into our God-given identity and purpose. This is why emotional healing is so vital. Without it, no amount of knowledge about emotional intelligence will allow you to truly thrive. Emotional brokenness will continue to pull you back unless you confront it and embrace the healing that God offers.

Emotional healing is God's gift to help us shed the broken version of ourselves and step into His divine image and purpose. But it requires intentionality. Like a physical wound that requires surgery, emotional wounds won't heal on their own. Emotional healing is a process that demands effort and commitment. The process may be painful, but it is worth it. Healing allows you to live with freedom, love, and peace. It transforms your relationships, softens your heart, and aligns you with God's image and purpose.

God offers this healing as a gift, but you must choose to accept it. The journey won't always be easy, but it will always be worth it. On the other side of healing is a life that reflects God's glory—a life of flourishing relationships, inner peace, and a heart free of bitterness and unforgiveness.

Healing is God's invitation to you. All you have to do is take the first step and intentionally begin.

What Is Emotional Healing?

Emotional healing is the process of recovering from wounds, traumas, and emotional distress in a way that restores inner peace, emotional balance, and psychological well-being. It involves addressing and resolving negative emotions, unhealthy thought patterns, and unresolved pain caused by past experiences while cultivating healthier ways to process and manage emotions.

In other words, emotional healing is not just about alleviating pain—it's about growing through it, building resilience, and achieving a sense of wholeness. It's not only about removing the emotional wounds and traumas but also replacing them with healthier mindsets, thought patterns, and coping mechanisms. It's about strengthening your emotional "muscles" so that when life throws more challenges your way, you are equipped with better tools to handle them, leading to healthier and more productive outcomes.

Think of it like recovering from a physical injury. If you injure a muscle, recovery doesn't stop at healing the injury itself; it includes strength training to prevent further stiffness, pain, or reinjury. Emotional healing works the same way—it involves an intentional effort to build emotional strength and resilience so that future challenges don't leave you devastated but instead lead to growth and maturity.

While it's important not to dwell on the past, your past experiences matter because they hold lessons that can help build emotional resilience and healthier coping strategies. From a faith-based perspective, emotional healing involves surrendering pain to God and allowing His love, grace, and truth to bring restoration. Scripture reminds us of God's role as the ultimate healer:

"He heals the brokenhearted and binds up their wounds"
(Psalm 147:3).
"Come to me, all you who are weary and carry heavy burdens,
and I will give you rest"
(Matthew 11:28).

In essence, emotional healing is as spiritual as it is practical. Embracing one without the other results in incomplete healing. True and holistic healing requires both dimensions: the spiritual aspect connects you to God's restorative power, while the practical and psychological aspects provide the tools and strategies to navigate your healing journey. Together, they form a well-rounded and balanced approach to emotional healing—one that not only restores the mind and heart but also renews the soul.

However, it's important to address certain truths and debunk common myths about emotional healing. In our society, the term 'healing' is often used loosely, tied to self-love journeys that can sometimes perpetuate misconceptions. These misunderstandings may inadvertently hinder genuine emotional restoration. Let's delve into some of these key aspects and clarify the path to true emotional healing.

Time Does NOT Heal All Wounds

You've probably heard the saying, "Time heals all wounds." But this is a myth—misleading and untrue. Time alone does not heal wounds, and believing otherwise can lead to a passive and ineffective approach to emotional healing. If you truly want to embrace the journey of emotional healing, you must let go of this mindset.

The truth is time does not heal all wounds. In fact, time can often make a wound worse if left untreated. Imagine having a deep physical wound but neglecting to care for it, hoping it will heal on its own with time. What happens? The wound festers, potentially leading to severe infection, tissue damage, and, in extreme cases, the need for amputation. If left untreated long enough, it could even become life-threatening.

The same principle applies to emotional wounds. When left unaddressed, they don't just disappear; they deepen. These untreated wounds take root in the heart and mind, festering below the surface and affecting every area of life—relationships, work, and even spiritual health. Over time, the damage spreads, creating a ripple effect of pain and dysfunction.

Time doesn't heal wounds—intentional treatment does. Emotional healing requires deliberate effort and action. You must take ownership of your healing journey. Placing your emotional healing in the hands of time alone is not only unproductive but often a form of avoidance. It's a way to sidestep the hard work of confronting your pain, unpacking your trauma, and seeking restoration.

Time can reveal how deep a wound truly is, but it cannot heal it. Instead, time often amplifies the consequences of leaving a wound untreated. Think about it: the longer a father and daughter leave an emotional rift unaddressed, the more complicated the journey to reconciliation becomes. The hurt grows, resentment builds, and the process of healing becomes even longer and harder.

Time can do more than allow wounds to fester—it can also harden your heart. An untreated emotional wound, left for years, builds layers of bitterness and defensiveness, forming a hardened shell that makes it increasingly difficult to connect with God or others. A hardened heart desensitizes the conscience, blocking the flow of love, empathy, and grace that is essential for true healing.

So, let go of the saying, "Time heals all wounds." It doesn't. Only intentionality will move you toward emotional restoration. Your healing requires active participation: identifying the pain, seeking help, and working through it with determination and courage. Time alone can delay your healing, but your intentional choices are what bring transformation and freedom.

Emotional Healing Is a Journey, Not a Destination

Emotional healing is not a final destination but a continuous journey—a process of growth and transformation that unfolds throughout your entire life. As long as you live on this earth and walk in the flesh, you will remain on this healing journey. This mirrors the process of sanctification, which is also lifelong. Sanctification is the gradual transformation by which believers are conformed to the image of Christ through the work of the Holy Spirit.

Sanctification continues until the day we die or until Christ returns. Its culmination, glorification, is when we are united with Christ in eternity. At that moment, we will be perfected, free from sin and brokenness, and wholly transformed into His image. Glorification brings perfect holiness, resurrected bodies, and eternal union with God. At that point, the need for healing will cease. But as long as we remain in this broken world, sanctification—and, by extension, emotional healing—will continue.

The journey to emotional healing is about realigning yourself with God's image, making it inherently intertwined with sanctification. Just as sanctification is ongoing, so is emotional healing. There will always be new dimensions of healing that God desires to walk you through—whether through heartbreaks, losses, disappointments, or traumas yet to come. Healing is continuous because life itself is full of experiences that refine and shape us.

This understanding is crucial, especially in a world where many believe they must be fully healed before stepping into significant roles or relationships. You've likely heard statements like:

- "I'm not ready to date; I need to be completely healed first."

- "I can't be a parent until I've fully healed."

While these sentiments reflect a desire for self-awareness, they can also create an unrealistic expectation of perfection. The truth is, you will never be completely healed or fully ready to be a spouse, parent, or anything else. Waiting for total healing may mean waiting forever.

The key is not achieving perfection but pursuing awareness and intentionality. You must acknowledge your emotional wounds, identify areas needing healing, and take deliberate steps toward restoration. If you are completely unaware of your patterns, triggers, or toxic behaviors, it's wise to invest time in self-reflection and growth before pursuing significant relationships. But you don't need to be flawless to step into the roles God has called you to.

In fact, part of your healing is often found within the relationships and community you might be avoiding. Healing isn't something you accomplish in isolation. Relationships serve as mirrors, reflecting parts of ourselves we might not otherwise see. They reveal wounds, fears, and areas of growth, offering opportunities for healing that no self-help book or therapy session can fully replicate.

Imagine someone who has attended therapy and feels "ready" to date, only to find their old wounds resurface when faced with relational challenges. This is normal because healing isn't static—it evolves as you navigate life with others. Similarly, as a parent, no matter how much you prepare, you will occasionally fall short. Yet, your children will witness your growth and healing, learning alongside you. This is the beauty of life: healing and growing together.

So, don't isolate yourself in the name of "healing." Avoidance isn't healing—it's fear or discomfort disguised as self-protection. Cutting people off to shield yourself from emotional challenges only delays your growth. True healing is evident when you can engage with life, face difficult people and situations, and respond in ways that reflect Christ, not your past wounds.

Healing is a journey of becoming, not arriving. The ultimate sign of healing isn't perfection; it's progress. It's seeing your responses to difficult people and situations evolve. It's watching your behavior, thoughts, and emotions align more with Jesus and less with the pain of your past. As you walk this path, you will encounter God's grace and transformation in ways that draw you closer to Him and closer to the person He created you to be. Embrace the journey, knowing that healing is continuous and that God walks with you every step of the way.

Emotional Healing Requires Forgiveness

Yes, friends, healing requires forgiveness. This is a hard truth to accept, but it's an essential part of emotional healing. To truly recover from your emotional wounds and pain, you must **choose** to forgive those who hurt you and those connected to the wound. Notice the word "choose." Forgiveness is not a feeling; it's a decision. It's not something you do because you feel ready or because the pain has subsided. Forgiveness comes from your will. It's a choice you make, regardless of your feelings.

As believers, we don't forgive because the offender is remorseful or has apologized. Sometimes, you'll need to forgive people who will never acknowledge their wrongdoing or seek reconciliation. Why? Because forgiveness is not about their actions—it's about the grace God has extended to us through Jesus Christ. We forgive because Christ forgave us. He bore our sins on the cross and offered us forgiveness freely despite our unworthiness. As recipients of such grace, we are called to extend the same grace to others, regardless of whether they've "earned" it.

Holding on to offense and unforgiveness doesn't punish the person who hurt you—it punishes you. It binds you to emotional pain, turmoil, and bitterness, delaying your own healing. Let's take the example of Ariana, who was deeply hurt by her ex-boyfriend, Michael.

Ariana held onto the hurt for years, refusing to forgive Michael because she felt forgiving him would "let him off the hook." But over time, that unforgiveness grew into resentment and bitterness, affecting every aspect of her life. In her new relationships, she became easily triggered, lashing out at anything that resembled past mistreatment. Her wounds led her to self-sabotage relationships that God intended for her good.

Offense and unforgiveness are not contained emotions—they spill into every area of life. For Ariana to break free, she had to choose to forgive Michael. Forgiving him didn't mean he wasn't wrong or that her pain wasn't valid. It meant releasing the offense to God, removing the power it had over her emotions, and trusting the Lord with her healing. Forgiveness is about surrendering the debt someone owes you to God, trusting Him to handle it in His perfect justice and love.

Sometimes, the hardest person to forgive is yourself. Self-hatred, shame, and judgment can stem from an inability to forgive your own mistakes, flaws, or regrets. You might project that shame onto others, becoming critical or harsh because of the unresolved pain within. Emotional healing requires self-forgiveness. To embrace the version of yourself that God knew before He formed you, you must release the version of you that fell short in the past. Forgive yourself for your ignorance, your mistakes, and even your future shortcomings.

It's also important to remember that forgiveness is not always a one-time event. Even after forgiving someone, feelings of hurt may resurface when something reminds you of the pain. When that happens, you must choose forgiveness again and again. Jesus instructs us to forgive not just seven times but seventy-seven times (Matthew 18:22)—an ongoing act of grace. This doesn't mean you excuse or overlook wrongdoing but that you continue to release the offense whenever it resurfaces.

Some of you may still be holding onto offense from what your ex did, what your parents said, what a friend betrayed, or what an authority figure mishandled. While your pain is valid, clinging to unforgiveness only keeps you bound. God cares deeply about your pain, and He is big enough to handle it. You can trust Him with your burdens, knowing He is both just and loving.

Forgiveness doesn't always mean returning to the same relationship dynamic. Depending on the severity of the wrongdoing, it may not be wise or safe to return to the way things were. But forgiveness does mean choosing peace and reconciliation in your heart. It means not using the offense against the person anymore and leaving it at the cross, where Jesus died for all sins.

Forgiveness is hard, but it is necessary. It's a step toward the freedom and emotional healing God desires for you. By choosing to forgive, you open the door for God's love, grace, and restoration to flow into your life, replacing bitterness with peace and brokenness with wholeness.

Healing Is Not Linear

Understanding that healing isn't linear is a foundational truth for navigating emotional, physical, or spiritual recovery. Healing doesn't follow a straight line from pain to wholeness. It's more of a winding road filled with ups and downs, setbacks, and breakthroughs. This is a lesson I learned firsthand the year I began writing this book.

That year, I faced a medical emergency that required immediate surgery. It was my first surgery, and since it was an emergency, I had no time to prepare myself. Thankfully, the surgery went well, but the recovery process turned out to be far more challenging than I ever anticipated. Recovery tested me in ways I didn't expect.

I vividly remember waking up the morning after surgery in excruciating pain. The medication had worn off, and even simple tasks like walking or showering felt impossible. Like most people, I assumed my recovery would be linear—a straight path from pain to painless. But that wasn't the case. While I improved each day, my healing journey was marked by good days and bad days. On day three, I felt almost normal and thought I was healed, only for day four to arrive with the pain returning full force. Weeks later, I would experience sudden, sharp pains that left me concerned something had gone wrong. But when I called the hospital, I was reassured that these pains were part of the healing process. The sharp twinges were my body forming scar tissue, a natural and expected part of recovery. They even told me to anticipate these random pains for several months.

This taught me a profound truth: **healing is rarely linear.** Emotional healing is much the same. It's a journey marked by progress and setbacks, moments of triumph, and unexpected pain. There will be good days when you feel like you're moving forward and bad days when old emotions, triggers, or habits resurface, making you feel as though you've made no progress at all. But these setbacks aren't failures—they are simply part of the process.

Think of healing as peeling back layers of an onion. Each layer you uncover gives you deeper insight into yourself and the situation, even if it's uncomfortable. Progress often looks more like a spiral than a straight line. You may revisit old wounds from different angles, but each time you do, you're still moving closer to growth and restoration.

Imagine healing as a road trip with unexpected detours. When you plan a trip, you might expect to drive directly from point A to point B. But the reality is that you'll need to stop for gas, food, or even to stretch your legs. Without allowing time for these detours, you'll end up frustrated and disappointed when the trip takes longer than expected. Healing works the same way. You must create room for the unexpected—setbacks, bad days, and unforeseen challenges—and see them as part of the journey, not as barriers to progress.

Comparison can also derail your healing journey. Everyone's process is unique. While one person might experience rapid breakthroughs, another might go through slower, more gradual healing. Both are valid. Resist the urge to compare your journey to someone else's, as this can lead to frustration and unnecessary pressure. Your healing path is your own, shaped by your unique experiences and circumstances.

Healing can also surprise you by uncovering areas you didn't even know needed attention. For instance, I once saw a therapist after a difficult breakup. During one session, after venting about my ex, the therapist asked, "What was your relationship with your parents like growing up?" The question felt completely unrelated, but as we dug deeper, I realized there were unresolved childhood experiences influencing my attachment style and patterns in relationships. Healing one area often reveals deeper roots in others. For example, addressing people-pleasing tendencies might lead you to explore a lack of emotional validation during childhood. These revelations, though unexpected, are invaluable parts of the healing process.

Even when healing feels chaotic, God's word offers reassurance: *"And we know that God causes everything to work together for the good of those who love God and are called according to his purpose for them" (Romans 8:28).*

The non-linear path of healing often leads to outcomes more profound than we could imagine. God knows the areas in your life that need attention, so trust Him as He gently reveals them, layer by layer.

Embracing the truth that healing isn't linear allows you to extend patience and compassion to yourself and others. It encourages you to surrender the process to God, trusting His presence even in the valleys. Celebrate the small victories, and remember: forward movement, no matter how small, is still progress. Healing is a journey, not a destination; every step brings you closer to wholeness.

Healing Is Not Pretty

My mum has this saying: *"I thank God that I don't look like what I'm going through."* It always makes me smile because, in my family, we firmly believe in staying composed and put together, even when life is challenging. Despite our struggles, we refuse to let them define our appearance. We don't want people to look at us and immediately see our battles. Why? Because while we may strive to look pretty on the outside, our healing journeys are anything but pretty. Healing is messy, raw, and often downright ugly.

In a world that romanticizes healing as a serene and beautiful journey, the reality is much grittier. Healing is often depicted through aesthetically pleasing journals and wellness routines, complete with inspirational quotes and calming visuals. But your healing process is unlikely to look like that pristine journal you just bought. Some people own several healing journals yet remain unhealed because true healing isn't found in appearances but in the hard, messy, and uncomfortable work of confronting the pain within.

Healing is like cleaning out a wound: painful but necessary. It requires facing buried emotions, memories, and truths that disrupt your emotional "status quo." The messiness doesn't mean you're failing; it's a sign that the emotional clutter hidden deep within is finally being dealt with. It's akin to doing a deep cleaning of your home. You know—the kind that takes a whole weekend and leaves your room looking worse before it looks better. Clothes are pulled out of closets, forgotten items are unearthed, and surfaces long ignored are dusted and scrubbed. For a while, the chaos might make you feel like you're not making progress, but the truth is, the mess is evidence that you're cleaning from the inside out.

Surface-level cleaning might make your room appear tidy, but open the closet, and everything spills out. Similarly, some people look put together on the outside but have unresolved emotions and trauma stuffed away. Then there are those whose lives might look messy because they're in the midst of deep healing and refinement. The mess is proof of progress—it's the path to something beautiful, wholesome, and clean.

I once had a Bio Lift Facial at a luxurious spa, and the experience taught me a profound lesson about healing. The treatment was designed to rejuvenate my skin, reduce wrinkles, and make it firmer and more youthful. Afterward, my esthetician warned me to expect a few acne breakouts due to skin purging. The facial had brought hidden impurities to the surface—a necessary step for true purification and renewal. Isn't that just like emotional healing? The gunk is buried beneath surfaces. During the process, it is brought to the surface, and while it's not pretty at first, it's a sign of deeper transformation.

Healing can hurt before it heals. Much like disinfecting a wound stings before it soothes, emotional healing often involves sitting with painful feelings. Grieving loss means facing the ache of absence. Processing trauma might require reliving difficult experiences in therapy, prayer, or inner healing sessions. Breaking toxic patterns can feel disorienting and isolating before it becomes liberating. The discomfort and mess are signs that you're stretching and growing.

True healing pushes you beyond the familiar. It may involve setting boundaries with loved ones who've caused harm, a task that feels awkward and guilt-inducing. It may require deep self-reflection, repentance, and forgiveness, which can be humbling and exhausting. It forces you to remove the mask you wear to appear strong, demanding vulnerability and authenticity instead. Growth requires unlearning deeply ingrained lies, like *"I'm unworthy of love"* or *"I have to act tough to survive."* Rebuilding healthier beliefs and behaviors is messy but necessary work.

Healing often calls you to let go of what no longer serves you: toxic relationships, resentment, or unrealistic expectations. Letting go is hard and can feel like a loss, even when it leads to freedom. And healing rarely happens in isolation. It often takes place within the messiness of relationships—through counseling, friendships, or spiritual mentorship. Vulnerability with others can feel risky, but it's a vital part of learning to trust again.

Amid the mess, remember this: *Jesus Christ is the beauty in the mess.* God meets us in our brokenness, using the mess to refine, renew, and restore us. The process may feel long and overwhelming, but it's a lot like refining gold. When gold goes through the fire, the process is anything but pretty. It's intense and messy. But when the gold comes out of the fire, it's beautiful, radiant, and valuable—nothing like what it was before.

Just as God was with Shadrach, Meshach, and Abednego in the fiery furnace (Daniel 3), Jesus Christ is with you in your own refining fire. Trust Him through the process. Let Him take the mess and transform it into something extraordinary. Healing may not look pretty now, but in God's hands, it will be worth it.

Emotional Abuse and Emotional Neglect

Emotional healing is a deeply personal journey, with each person's wounds shaped by unique experiences. Heartbreak, loss, trauma, betrayal—there are countless sources of emotional pain, each deserving of careful attention. While this chapter cannot address every source of emotional distress, it will focus on two particularly impactful and often overlooked areas: emotional abuse and emotional neglect. These wounds are not only pervasive but also subtle in their effects, often leaving people unaware of the depth of their harm.

Emotional abuse and neglect shape how we see ourselves, God, and others, often distorting our sense of worth and trust. By shedding light on these areas, my prayer is to guide you toward paths of healing, restoration, and wholeness in Christ. Let's dive into what emotional abuse and neglect truly entail so we can better understand the steps toward recovery.

Emotional Abuse

When most people hear the word *abuse*, they think of physical violence. While physical abuse is serious and damaging, it is not the only form of harm. Emotional abuse, though often less visible, is just as real and equally serious. Because it is so subtle, emotional abuse can be difficult to detect, yet its long-term effects are profound. Over time, it can erode self-esteem, distort self-worth, and create patterns of dependency.

What is Emotional Abuse?

Emotional abuse is a form of psychological harm in which words, actions, or behaviors are used to manipulate, control, demean, or invalidate another person. According to the National Domestic Violence Hotline, *"emotional abuse includes non-physical behaviors that are meant to control, isolate, or frighten you."* This type of abuse often seeks to undermine the victim's sense of self, making them dependent on the abuser for validation or security.

Emotional abuse can occur in any relationship—between partners, family members, colleagues, or even within friendships. Its impact is often amplified by its subtlety and repetition, making it difficult to recognize and validate. Below, we'll explore the characteristics and signs of emotional abuse to help identify and address it.

Characteristics of Emotional Abuse

1. Power and Control

Emotional abuse involves an imbalance of power, where the abuser seeks to dominate the victim's emotions, thoughts, or actions.

2. Repetition

It is typically not a one-time occurrence but a repeated pattern of behavior.

3. Subtlety

Emotional abuse is often covert, making it harder to detect compared to physical abuse.

Common Signs of Emotional Abuse

1. Manipulation and Control

- Constantly monitoring your activities or whereabouts.

- Demanding access to your phone, passwords, or social media.

- Controlling decisions about your appearance, friendships, or finances.

- Using guilt trips or emotional blackmail to ensure compliance.

2. Gaslighting

- Denying events or making you question your memory or perception of reality.

- Dismissing your feelings as overly sensitive or invalid.

- Saying things like, *"That never happened. You're imagining things."*

- Breaking down your ability to trust your own perspective.

3. Criticism and Belittling

- Making harsh or unfair comments about your appearance, abilities, or decisions.

- Humiliating you in private or public settings.

- Using sarcasm or "jokes" as a cover for hurtful comments.

4. Verbal Abuse

- Insulting you, name-calling, or using demeaning language.

- Yelling excessively or mocking your words and actions.

5. Emotional Withholding

- Refusing to provide affection, attention, or emotional intimacy.

- Using the "silent treatment" as a form of punishment.

6. Isolation

- Discouraging or preventing you from spending time with loved ones.

- Making you feel guilty for seeking emotional support outside the relationship.

7. Jealousy and Possessiveness

- Constant accusations of infidelity without cause.

- Acting overly jealous or possessive of your relationships with others.

8. Blame-Shifting

- Refusing to take responsibility for their actions.

- Blaming you for their behavior, saying things like, *"Look what you made me do. This is all your fault."*

9. Sabotaging Independence

- Discouraging you from pursuing personal or professional goals.

- Undermining your aspirations or efforts toward growth.

10. Undermining Your Self-Worth

- Making you feel unworthy or incapable.

- Using subtle put-downs disguised as humor or concern.

11. Emotional Unpredictability

- Frequent mood swings or outbursts of anger.

- Making you feel like you're constantly "walking on eggshells."

12. Constant Need for Power and Control

- Creating an imbalance in the relationship that leaves you feeling powerless.

- Insisting on always having their way without compromise.

Signs That Someone Has Experienced Emotional Abuse

Recognizing the signs of emotional abuse is crucial, not just for understanding others but for identifying whether someone is operating from a place of unresolved emotional trauma. These signs can help distinguish between deliberate harm and unintentional reactions rooted in past wounds. Indicators of emotional abuse include the following:

1. Low Self-Esteem

- Feeling unworthy, inadequate, or perpetually flawed.

- Internalizing negative messages from the abuser, such as: *"I'm the only person capable of loving you. No one else will want you."*

2. Chronic Guilt or Shame

- Feeling guilty for asserting needs or expressing emotions.

- Carrying shame even when not at fault.

- Frequently apologizing, saying *"I'm sorry"* excessively.

3. Anxiety or Hypervigilance

- Constantly anticipating conflict or criticism.

- Being overly sensitive to others' moods or reactions.

4. Depression or Emotional Numbness

- Persistent feelings of sadness, hopelessness, or emotional detachment.

- Losing interest in activities that once brought joy.

5. Fear of Rejection or Abandonment

- Struggling with attachment or dependency issues in relationships.

- Overanalyzing interactions out of fear of losing connection.

6. People-Pleasing Tendencies

- Going to great lengths to avoid conflict or seek approval.

- Struggling to say "no" or set healthy boundaries.

7. Difficulty Trusting

- Being overly guarded or suspicious of others' intentions.

- Hesitating to form close relationships.

8. Conflict Avoidance

- Avoiding necessary conversations due to fear of confrontation.

- Suppressing opinions or emotions to keep the peace.

- Exhibiting passive-aggressive behaviors.

9. Self-Sabotaging Behaviors

- Undermining personal success or happiness due to feelings of unworthiness.

- Turning to destructive coping mechanisms, such as overeating or substance abuse.

10. Inability to Trust Themselves

- Doubting their memory or reality due to gaslighting effects.

- Recording conversations to verify what actually occurred.

- Constantly seeking validation from others for decisions, no matter how small.

Long-Term Effects of Emotional Abuse

Emotional abuse can leave lasting scars that affect every facet of life, including the following:

- Emotional Dysregulation: Difficulty managing anger, sadness, or fear.

- Negative Self-Talk: Replaying the abuser's harmful words mentally.

- Relationship Challenges: Struggling to form healthy, trusting relationships.

- Mental Health Issues: Increased risk of anxiety, depression, PTSD, or complex trauma (C-PTSD).

Emotional Neglect

Emotional neglect, though less visible than abuse, can be just as damaging. It occurs when a person's emotional needs are consistently ignored, dismissed, or unmet by those responsible for their care. Unlike emotional abuse, which involves harmful actions, emotional neglect is defined by an absence of emotional attention and support.

Signs of Emotional Neglect

In Childhood

- **Lack of Emotional Validation:** Caregivers dismiss or fail to acknowledge a child's feelings, using phrases like *"Stop crying"* or *"You're overreacting."*

- **Minimal Affection or Encouragement:** Rarely expressing warmth, giving physical affection, or offering praise.

- **Ignoring Emotional Distress:** Overlooking signs of fear, sadness, or anger without providing comfort or help.

- **Overemphasis on Practical Needs:** Prioritizing physical care (e.g., food, shelter) over emotional connection.

- **Discouraging Emotional Expression:** Punishing or shaming children for expressing emotions like sadness, anger, or fear.

In Adulthood

- **Emotional Disconnection:** Avoiding emotional intimacy or deep conversations.

- **Inconsistent Availability:** Being physically present but emotionally distant.

- **Invalidation:** Minimizing or disregarding emotional needs, expecting independence without support.

Signs That Someone Was Emotionally Neglected

- **Difficulty Identifying Emotions:** Struggling to recognize or name their own feelings.

- **Low Self-Worth:** Feeling undeserving of love, attention, or care.

- **Fear of Asking for Help:** Hesitating to express needs out of fear of rejection or being a burden.

- **Avoidance of Emotions:** Suppressing feelings or feeling overwhelmed by intense emotions.

- **Struggles with Boundaries:** Difficulty setting limits and advocating for personal needs.

- **Emotional Over-Attunement to Others:** Prioritizing others' emotions at the expense of their own.

- **Loneliness or Isolation:** Feeling unseen or disconnected, even in relationships.

- **Perfectionism or Overachievement:** Seeking validation through accomplishments to compensate for unmet emotional needs.

Long-Term Effects of Emotional Neglect

- **Emotional Dysregulation:** Struggling to manage anger, sadness, or anxiety.

- **Chronic Emptiness:** Feeling persistently numb or hollow.

- **Attachment Challenges:** Developing insecure attachment styles (e.g., anxious, avoidant, or disorganized).

- **Mental Health Issues:** Increased risk of depression, anxiety, or PTSD.

- **Difficulty Trusting Others:** Fear of vulnerability and emotional reliance on others.

- **Unhealthy Coping Mechanisms:** Turning to distractions, substances, or overworking to avoid pain.

Distinguishing Between Emotional Abuse and Neglect

Although emotional abuse and neglect share similarities in their impacts, their roots differ significantly.

Aspect	Emotional Abuse	Emotional Neglect
Action vs Inaction	Active, harmful behaviors like insults.	Passive absence of emotional care.
Intent	Often deliberate, aimed to harm or control.	Often unintentional, due to ignorance or stress.
Focus	Causing emotional harm directly.	Failing to meet emotional needs.

Recognizing these distinctions is essential in understanding the unique challenges faced by those who've experienced either—or both—and provides insight into the paths to healing.

Healing From Emotional Wounds

The journey to healing from emotional wounds—whether caused by abuse, neglect, or other sources of pain—requires two essential dimensions: the practical path and the spiritual path. When these paths are intertwined, they form a holistic approach to emotional healing, addressing both surface-level behaviors and the deeper roots of the pain.

Practical steps alone, while beneficial, often lack the lasting impact needed to bring about complete healing. Without addressing the spiritual aspect, the deeper soul wounds and the renewal of the mind—which only Jesus can provide—remain unresolved. On the other hand, focusing solely on the spiritual path while neglecting the tools and resources God has given us through science and psychology can limit our progress.

It's important to remember that God, in His goodness, created all things and called them *"good,"* including science and psychology. These are gifts from Him, designed for our benefit. By embracing the tools and insights they offer, alongside the transformative power of God's truth and grace, we can fully experience the restoration and renewal He intends for us.

Let's explore both the practical and spiritual steps needed to heal from emotional wounds, pain, and trauma. Together, they form a comprehensive guide to achieving true, sustainable healing.

The Practical Path

1. Acknowledge and Validate

Begin by recognizing and validating your experiences. Emotional abuse and neglect are legitimate forms of pain, and understanding that they weren't your fault is a critical first step. Allow yourself to feel anger, sadness, or grief over unmet needs—it's okay to process these emotions as part of your healing.

2. Seek Professional Help

Professional support is invaluable in navigating emotional wounds. Therapists and counselors can provide tools and strategies tailored to your unique experiences. Depending on your situation, you might explore:

- Grief counseling, trauma counseling, or therapy specializing in attachment theory.

- Techniques like Cognitive Behavioral Therapy (CBT) or Eye Movement Desensitization and Reprocessing (EMDR).

- Inner Child Work or Emotionally Focused Therapy (EFT) to address emotional neglect.

A licensed therapist can guide you in unpacking childhood experiences, rebuilding emotional awareness, and developing effective coping mechanisms.

3. Build Emotional Awareness

Emotional awareness is essential for healing. Practice identifying, naming, and processing your emotions. Journaling can be a powerful tool to help you connect with and articulate your feelings.

4. Set Boundaries

Learning to set boundaries is a key step toward emotional recovery. Consider working with a boundaries coach to:

- Identify and advocate for your needs.

- Set clear and healthy boundaries in your relationships.

- Practice asking for help and expressing your emotions.

5. Build Healthy and Supportive Relationships

Surround yourself with people who are loving, supportive, and safe. Be intentional about cultivating relationships that align with the emotional dynamics you aspire to have. Through positive relationships, you can relearn trust, vulnerability, and healthy connection.

The Spiritual Path

The spiritual journey to emotional healing involves seeking God's love and relying on His Word to guide and restore you. Through the redemptive work of Jesus Christ, you can break free from emotional bondage and embrace God's identity for your life.

It's vital to clarify what "spiritual" truly means. In today's culture, the term often carries a range of interpretations, some of which are deeply misleading. Practices like astrology, tarot readings, crystals, sage burning, and chakra healing are widely promoted as paths to emotional wellness. However, these practices are rooted in new-age spirituality, false ideologies, and even occultism.

New-age spirituality is not the path to emotional healing; it is idolatry and witchcraft. While these practices promise peace, healing, and wholeness, they deliver the opposite. They invite spiritual darkness into one's life, causing torment and disruption instead of freedom. God's Word warns us about such practices in Deuteronomy 18:10-12:

"Let no one be found among you who sacrifices their son or daughter in the fire, who practices divination or sorcery, interprets omens, engages in witchcraft, or casts spells, or who is a medium or spiritist or who consults the dead. Anyone who does these things is detestable to the LORD..."

These practices over-promise and underdeliver. Your need for peace, love, and healing is legitimate, but fulfilling those needs through these means is not. Crystals, sage, and astrology cannot provide the answers or the healing you seek—only God can.

Jesus is the ultimate source of healing. Only He can fill the voids in your heart, deliver you from emotional bondage, and restore you to wholeness. As believers, we must reject false promises and turn to the truth of God's Word.

Healing is found in surrendering fully to Jesus and allowing the Holy Spirit to work in your life. As we explore the spiritual path to emotional healing, remember this foundational truth: the path to wholeness is through Christ alone.

Now, let's delve deeper into the steps of the spiritual path to healing.

Inner Healing and Deliverance

We cannot discuss the spiritual path to healing without delving into the profound ministries of inner healing and deliverance. These two approaches, rooted in Christianity, focus on emotional, psychological, and spiritual restoration. Both aim to bring freedom, healing, and wholeness through the transformative power of Jesus Christ. While inner healing and deliverance often overlap in purpose and are sometimes used interchangeably, they differ in focus and methodology.

Inner Healing

Inner healing addresses the emotional wounds, traumas, and negative thought patterns that hinder spiritual and emotional well-being. It centers on healing the heart and mind through the power of the Holy Spirit and God's Word.

Characteristics/Steps of Inner Healing

1. **Focus on Emotional and Spiritual Wounds**

   - Targets past traumas, hurts, and unresolved emotional pain (e.g., rejection, abandonment, abuse, neglect).

   - Brings awareness to lies or false beliefs formed from negative experiences.

2. **Renewing the Mind**

   - Replaces distorted thinking with the truth of God's Word.

   - Helps individuals see themselves through the lens of their identity in Christ.

3. **Healing Through Prayer**

- Invites Jesus into painful memories or emotional wounds through prayer to bring healing.

- Encourages surrendering pain to God.

4. **Forgiveness**

- Central to inner healing is the act of forgiveness—whether forgiving others or oneself or even releasing resentment toward God.

- Forgiveness releases bitterness, unlocking emotional freedom.

- See "Activity 2: Forgiveness Inventory" in Chapter 5 for a forgiveness prayer template.

5. **Repentance**

- Acknowledges and turns away from sinful behaviors, attitudes, or coping mechanisms (e.g., bitterness, anger, self-hatred).

- Clears spiritual and emotional barriers, allowing God's healing power to flow.

- Deepens intimacy with God and aligns the individual with His will.

6. **Restoration of Wholeness**

- Focuses on emotional wholeness and peace, enabling individuals to trust, love, and engage in healthy relationships.

Deliverance

Deliverance is the process of freeing individuals from demonic influence, oppression, or bondage. It focuses on spiritual strongholds that hinder a believer's walk with God.

Characteristics/Steps of Deliverance

1. **Focus on Spiritual Bondage**

- Addresses demonic oppression, torment, or influence in a person's life.

- Identifies strongholds such as fear, addiction, shame, or generational curses.

2. **Authority in Christ**

   - Operates through the authority of Jesus Christ, as believers have power over demonic forces (Luke 10:19).

   - Involves rebuking and casting out demonic spirits (Luke 9:1).

3. **Breaking Demonic Agreements**

   - Renounces agreements, sins, or generational patterns that give the enemy a foothold.

   - Includes severing ungodly soul ties (e.g., unhealthy attachments from toxic relationships).

   - Breaks demonic vows, such as self-destructive declarations ("I'll never trust anyone again").

   - Addresses generational curses, such as patterns of anger, fear, or addiction within family lines.

4. **Restoring Freedom**

   - Frees individuals from spiritual oppression, allowing them to experience Christ's fullness.

5. **Spiritual Warfare**

   - Involves prayers of protection, binding demonic forces, putting on the full armor of God (**Ephesians 6:10-18**), and pleading the blood of Jesus.

Key Differences Between Inner Healing and Deliverance

Aspect	Inner Healing	Deliverance
Focus	Emotional wounds and traumas	Demonic oppression, influence, or torment
Primary Goal	Emotional and psychological healing	Spiritual freedom and breaking demonic strongholds

Method	Prayer, forgiveness, renewing the mind	Rebuking demons, renouncing agreements
Cause	Emotional hurts, lies, negative thought patterns, false beliefs	Demonic oppression, generational curses, demonic vows, soul ties
Key Scriptures	Isaiah 61:1-3, Romans 12:2	Luke 10:19, Ephesians 6:12

Other Steps on the Spiritual Path to Healing

- **Faith-Based Counseling**

  Engage in counseling rooted in Scripture for emotional restoration and guidance.

- **Meditation on God's Word**

  Consistently renew your mind with Scripture to replace lies with truth.

- **Prayer and Intimacy with God**

  Deepen your relationship with God through consistent prayer and communion, allowing Him to heal the broken places in your heart.

- **Worship and Praise**

  Shift your focus from pain to God's greatness and love, creating an atmosphere for healing.

- **Fasting**

  Practice fasting to intentionally seek God's presence and healing.

- **Confession and Accountability**

  Share your struggles with trusted believers, allowing them to pray for you and provide encouragement.

- **Seeking Community and Support**

  Healing often happens in the context of healthy, godly relationships. Isolation can hinder emotional healing, while community fosters growth and prayerful support.

God's Path to Emotional Healing

We all need emotional healing. Life brings moments of loss, betrayal, trauma, and disappointment that leave wounds on our hearts. Whether it's losing a loved one, enduring a devastating breakup, experiencing emotional abuse or neglect, or suffering through trauma, emotional pain is inevitable in this broken world. But there is hope. Jesus is our hope, and emotional healing is the path He has lovingly laid out for us.

You are not alone in your struggles, and your pain is not new to the human experience. The Bible offers countless examples of people who faced emotional abuse, neglect, and deep wounds and who navigated their healing through faith and resilience:

- Hannah endured years of emotional abuse from Peninnah, her husband's other wife, who mocked her for being barren. Overwhelmed by shame, grief, and inadequacy, Hannah turned to God in prayer, pouring out her heart in His presence. God met her at her point of need, healed her, and restored her joy.

- Joseph suffered emotional abuse and betrayal from his own brothers. Out of jealousy and envy, they mocked him, plotted to kill him, and sold him into slavery. Despite these deep wounds, Joseph clung to his faith in God. Over time, God turned Joseph's pain into purpose, leading him to forgiveness and restoration with his family.

- David was subjected to ongoing emotional abuse by King Saul, who, fueled by jealousy and fear, hurled false accusations, threats, and outbursts at him. David, constantly on the run, faced rejection and fear. Yet he chose to respond by turning to God in prayer and worship, as seen in the Psalms, trusting God to protect and vindicate him.

- Naomi and Ruth experienced profound grief and emotional neglect from their community after the deaths of their husbands. Naomi felt abandoned, even believing God had turned against her. Yet, through their faith and trust in God's provision, He restored their lives, leading them to blessings through Boaz.

- Jesus Christ endured the ultimate emotional abuse during His trial and crucifixion. Mocked, falsely accused, spat on, and abandoned by those closest to Him, He carried the weight of humanity's sin.

Despite the rejection and humiliation, Jesus exemplified ultimate forgiveness, saying, "Father, forgive them, for they do not know what they are doing" (Luke 23:34).

These stories remind us that emotional abuse and wounds, no matter how deep, are not beyond the reach of God's healing power. God sees your pain, He cares deeply, and He offers comfort, restoration, and freedom.

When you invite Jesus into your healing journey, the places of pain become landmarks of redemption. They are transformed into testimonies of where Jesus met you, healed you, and delivered you. God has the power to renew your mind and redeem your experiences. In biblical times, people didn't have access to therapy or counseling; all they had was God. Yet He was enough. Today, we not only have God but also the tools and resources He has graciously provided through science and psychology. Let us embrace both.

Forgiveness and healing are possible, though they often require time, grace, and divine intervention. Whether you've been wounded or you've caused wounds, God desires healing for you. I know this to be true because I've walked this road myself. I've carried emotional wounds so deep I thought I would never recover. But God had other plans. He not only healed and delivered me but also restored me, turning my pain into purpose. One of those purposes is this very book you are holding.

Just as He did for me, God can work all things together for your good. He can use the emotional wounds that once seemed unbearable to transform and strengthen you. The key is surrender. Surrender your pain to Him, invite Him to heal your heart, renew your mind, and walk the practical and spiritual paths He has laid out for your holistic healing.

Remember, there is purpose in your pain. God is not finished with you yet. Trust Him to bring beauty from the ashes of your wounds and to lead you into a future filled with hope, healing, and restoration.

Prayer

Heavenly Father,

Thank You for Your healing power and boundless love. Lord, I come before You, broken and wounded, carrying the weight of emotional pain, betrayal, grief, and disappointment. In this moment, I invite You, Jesus, into the deepest, most fragile places of my heart and soul. I ask You to heal every emotional wound and restore every part of me that has been broken.

Renew and transform my mind, Lord. Cleanse it of every unhealthy thought pattern and false belief that does not align with Your truth. Let the blood of Jesus wash over my mind, removing anything that is not of You. Father, if there are emotional traumas or wounds hidden deep within me—buried so long that I am unaware of their influence—please send Your Holy Spirit to reveal them. Illuminate those hidden places, and let Your healing power flow freely through my heart, mind, and soul. Touch every broken part of me with Your divine hand, reviving and restoring me.

Lord, I repent for the emotional wounds I have inflicted on others, knowingly or unknowingly. I also repent for the ways I have contributed to my own pain and bondage. Today, I choose forgiveness. I choose to forgive myself. I choose to forgive those who have inflicted emotional pain, trauma, and wounds upon me. I release them to You, Lord, and I ask that You also forgive me for the ways I have caused hurt to others.

Deliver me, Lord, from the strongholds and demonic influences that have kept me bound. Lead me on the path to true inner healing and deliverance. I surrender my emotions to You and ask for Your strength to seek therapy and counseling where needed. Connect me with the right people—those You have ordained to be instrumental in my breakthrough and healing journey.

Jesus, I declare that You are greater than my pain. I long to encounter You in the midst of my brokenness. Show me where You are in my pain, and minister Your healing to the deepest parts of my heart. Give me the discipline to dwell in Your Word, allowing it to cleanse and renew my mind. Reveal Yourself to me, Lord, and strengthen my faith to believe that You are the God who heals.

All this I pray in the mighty and holy name of Your Son, Jesus Christ.

Amen.

Prayer Prompts and Guidelines for Breaking Generational Curses, Demonic Vows, and Ungodly Soul Ties

Emotional healing is a deeply personal and spiritual journey. Whether it involves breaking generational patterns, releasing unhealthy ties, or renouncing harmful beliefs, prayer is a powerful tool to invite God's healing into these areas. The following prayer prompts are designed to guide you as you surrender these burdens to the Lord, focusing on generational curses, ungodly soul ties, and demonic vows that may be connected to your emotional wounds and struggles.

Before beginning, spend time in God's presence, asking the Holy Spirit to reveal areas needing healing. Pray for clarity regarding any demonic agreements, ungodly soul ties, or generational patterns that may be affecting your life. As insights arise, jot them down in your emotions journal for reflection and prayer. Trust that God will meet you in this sacred process, and personalize these prayers as needed.

Generational Curses

Definition:

Generational curses refer to the negative patterns, behaviors, or spiritual consequences of sin passed down through family lines. These patterns can manifest emotionally—such as anger, rejection, fear, or shame—creating cycles of dysfunction. The Bible references this concept in passages like Exodus 20:5-6 but also promises freedom through Christ in Galatians 3:13, who redeems us from every curse.

Prayer Prompt:

"Lord Jesus, thank You for Your sacrifice on the cross, which has redeemed me from every curse. Today, I bring before You the patterns of [name specific emotional struggles, e.g., fear, rejection, anger] in my family line. I renounce and break these generational curses in my bloodline in the mighty name of Jesus. Lord, I forgive my ancestors on both my mother's and father's side who unknowingly passed down these patterns. I also repent for any ways I have allowed these curses to take root in my life. Wash me with Your blood, Lord, and restore my family's legacy in alignment with Your will. I declare that these curses stop with me. Thank You, Jesus, for giving me a new identity as Your child. In Jesus' name, Amen."

Ungodly Soul Ties

Definition:

Ungodly soul ties are unhealthy emotional or spiritual attachments that hinder emotional freedom. While often associated with sexual relationships, soul ties can also form through manipulative, controlling, or abusive relationships. These ties can perpetuate cycles of emotional pain, dependency, or fear, blocking the wholeness God intends for us.

Prayer Prompt:

"Heavenly Father, I come before You in the name of Jesus, acknowledging that I have formed ungodly soul ties that are not aligned with Your will. I repent and ask for Your forgiveness for contributing to these bonds through sin, disobedience, or unhealthy attachments. In the name of Jesus, I renounce and break every ungodly soul tie formed with [name the person, relationship, or situation]. I release them into Your hands and sever every emotional and spiritual connection that hinders my freedom. By the authority of Jesus Christ, I cancel the power of these ties over my life. I forgive [name of person] for any hurt or harm they caused me, and I ask for Your healing to flow into those areas of my heart. Lord, renew my emotions, restore my identity in You, and help me to walk in the freedom and wholeness You've given me. Thank You, Jesus, for setting me free. In Jesus' name, Amen."

Demonic Vows

Definition:

Demonic vows are harmful agreements, often formed in moments of pain, anger, or despair, that contradict God's truth and allow the enemy access to influence our lives. These vows—such as "I'll never trust anyone again" or "I will always fail"—can create spiritual strongholds, shaping identity and perpetuating emotional wounds. **Proverbs 18:21** reminds us of the power of words, and breaking these vows is essential for reclaiming our identity in Christ.

Prayer Prompt:

"Heavenly Father, I come to You in the name of Jesus, acknowledging the power of Your truth over every lie. I recognize that in moments of pain, fear, or brokenness, I may have made vows or agreements that are not of You. I repent for speaking words or embracing beliefs that contradict Your promises. In the name of Jesus Christ, I renounce and break every demonic vow or agreement I have made, whether knowingly or unknowingly. I specifically break the vow that [state the vow or lie, e.g., 'I will always be alone']. By the power of the blood of Jesus, I cancel its hold over my life. I declare that my identity is

rooted in Your Word, which says that [insert relevant scripture, e.g., 'I am fearfully and wonderfully made' – Psalm 139:14]. Lord, replace every lie with Your truth and renew my mind daily. Thank You for setting me free from every chain and for restoring my heart, mind, and spirit to align with Your perfect will. I praise You for the freedom You have given me and trust in Your continual work of healing in my life. In Jesus' name, Amen."

As you pray through these prompts, trust that God is working in ways you may not yet see. Whether you are breaking generational patterns, severing unhealthy ties, or renouncing harmful vows, the Holy Spirit is with you every step of the way. Healing is a process, but freedom is a promise God delights in fulfilling. Keep seeking Him, and remember that His love is the ultimate source of restoration and wholeness.

For believers who feel these prayers are helpful but sense the need for deeper inner healing and deliverance, I encourage you to reach out to your local church leaders. Share your desire to pursue inner healing and deliverance, and inquire if they have a ministry dedicated to this area. If they don't, they may be able to direct you to another trusted ministry within the body of Christ. God often uses His church as a vessel for healing, and taking this step can be pivotal in your journey toward freedom and restoration.

REFLECTION QUESTIONS

1. Which truth about emotional healing—such as *"time does not heal all wounds"*—do you find most challenging to accept, and why?

2. How does understanding that healing is a journey, not a destination, change your perspective on your own healing process? What practical steps can you take to embrace this journey with patience and grace?

3. What are your thoughts on the idea that healing can open unexpected doors for growth? Have you experienced situations where addressing one wound led to uncovering another area that required healing? How did this affect your journey?

4. Are there emotional wounds or experiences in your life that you recognize as areas needing healing? How have these experiences shaped your thoughts, behaviors, relationships, or even your view of God?

5. Have you observed patterns of emotional abuse or neglect in your past? How have these patterns impacted your emotional health, self-esteem, relationships, or spiritual life?

6. Which aspect of the practical or spiritual paths to healing have you been neglecting, and how can you better integrate both into your journey? Which path feels most relevant to you right now?

7. How does the example of Jesus or other biblical figures like Joseph, Hannah, or David encourage you in your healing process? Reflect on how their stories of faith, perseverance, and restoration can inspire you to trust God in your pain.

8. What actions can you take to balance self-reflection with community support in your healing journey? Are there trusted individuals whom you can reach out to for prayer, accountability, or guidance?

9. Have you identified any generational patterns, ungodly soul ties, or demonic vows in your life? How can prayer and the spiritual tools in this chapter help you break free and embrace God's freedom?

10. What steps can you take today to align your healing journey with God's purpose for your life?

09

THE ART OF STEWARDING YOUR EMOTIONS

B ack in 2021, one of my childhood friends gave me a bonsai tree starter kit for my birthday. It was a thoughtful gardening gift, complete with everything I needed to grow bonsai trees like a pro: four seed packets for different tree varieties, burlap pots, a soil disc, bamboo markers, and a detailed instruction guide. My friend was practically glowing with excitement as he handed it to me. He couldn't stop raving about how much I'd love it.

To be honest, his excitement far outweighed mine. You see, I am *not* a plant lover—not even close. Gardening has never been my thing, especially in the middle of city life. While I admire the lush aesthetics of plants, my appreciation stops at decorating my home with artificial greenery. The idea of actually growing something, with all the care and patience involved? Hard pass. If my friend had given me a fully grown bonsai pruned to perfection, I would have been thrilled. But seeds? Seeds meant *work*—the kind that required planting, watering, waiting, and (gulp) patience.

This wasn't just a "you needed this" gift, as I described in a previous chapter. This was on another level. According to my friend, the whole point of the gift was the *process*. He wanted me to experience the lessons that come from cultivating life—lessons about care, consistency, and patience. But all I saw was a daunting task. Bonsai trees, I soon learned, are not your typical houseplants.

For the uninitiated, bonsai trees are miniature versions of full-sized trees, shaped and nurtured to resemble natural trees in the wild, only much smaller. The art of bonsai, with roots in ancient China and later refined in Japan, blends horticulture with aesthetics. Growing a bonsai tree from seed is not a quick project. Germination alone can take months, and it can take 3–5 years for seedlings to grow sturdy enough for shaping. Reaching full maturity? That can take 10–15 years. Yes, you read that right—*years*! Bonsai cultivation is a marathon, not a sprint. It's an exercise in patience, focus, and calm—a meditative practice for the truly dedicated.

And patience? That's never been my strong suit. In fact, it's been a lifelong struggle. So, you can imagine my enthusiasm for growing four bonsai trees simultaneously. But I decided to give it a try. I planted the seeds, took aesthetic photos for Instagram and Snapchat, and captioned them, "In my plant mom era." For the first few days, I felt the buzz of novelty, diligently following the instructions in the kit. Each morning, I checked the pots for signs of life.

Days turned into weeks, but nothing changed. The soil remained barren. Not a single leaf dared to sprout. My excitement fizzled as frustration took over. I wanted progress—*any* sign that my efforts weren't in vain—but the bonsai seeds demanded more patience than I could muster. One day, in a fit of frustration, I grabbed the pots, emptied them into the toilet, and flushed. That was the end of my brief stint as a plant mom.

Looking back, I laugh at the absurdity of it all. But the Lord revealed something deeper to me during a moment of reflection. He showed me that my inability to nurture those bonsai seeds mirrored my life as a steward at that time. It was a spiritual wake-up call, exposing how I had previously fallen short in stewardship as a Christian. Back then, I lacked the heart posture required to tend to what had been entrusted to me—be it plants, gifts, or even God's blessings.

This revelation was profound. As I reflected on my bonsai gift experience, God revealed a powerful parallel. In this scenario, He represented the gift giver, offering me something that went beyond my superficial desires for aesthetics or convenience. The bonsai kit symbolized the tools God provides to help us nurture and cultivate the gifts and resources He entrusts to us.

From the moment I received the gift, my initial reaction was frustration. I complained about how difficult, time-consuming, and challenging it would be to care for those plants. I grew impatient with the process, frustrated by the lack of immediate results, and ultimately discarded the gift entirely by flushing it away. I was more focused on curating an Instagram-worthy journey and glamorizing the experience for social media than on the behind-the-scenes work of nurturing, watering, and patiently waiting. My heart posture at that time was one of complaints, impatience, and ingratitude.

Looking back, this experience mirrored my life of stewardship during that season. Since then, God has taken me on a journey of transformation, teaching me the value and process of true stewardship. Over time, through discipline and the transformative work of the Holy Spirit, I grew into a better steward. God revealed to me the depth of what it means to steward well, showing me that stewardship is integral to spiritual maturity.

You may or may not be familiar with the concept of "stewardship," but here's the truth: your level of stewardship reflects your spiritual maturity. One of the markers of spiritual growth and personal development is how intentionally and faithfully you steward what God has entrusted to you. But what exactly does stewardship mean, and how does it apply to our lives as believers?

What is Stewardship?

Stewardship is the responsible management and care of resources, tasks, or relationships that have been entrusted to someone. It's about taking ownership of what has been placed in your care and making decisions that align with its intended purpose and value. From a biblical perspective, stewardship is the recognition that God is the ultimate owner of all things. We are not the owners—we are caretakers of His resources, whether they be material, spiritual, or relational. Biblical stewardship requires faithfulness, wisdom, and alignment with God's will.

To fully grasp what it means to be a good steward, we must first understand and accept the key biblical principles of stewardship:

1. **God as Owner**
   Stewardship begins with the understanding that God is the owner of *everything*. As 1 Corinthians 10:26 reminds us, "The earth is the Lord's, and the fullness thereof." We are caretakers entrusted with managing resources that ultimately belong to Him. Recognizing this truth is foundational to living as a good steward.

2. **Entrustment**
   God entrusts us with gifts, relationships, opportunities, and resources—not for our own glory, but for His. We are called to steward *everything* He places in our care, not just the parts that are easy or convenient.

3. **Accountability**
   Stewardship comes with accountability. Romans 14:12 reminds us, "So then each of us will give an account of himself to God." Similarly, 2 Corinthians 5:10 says, "For we must all appear before the judgment seat of Christ, so that each one may receive what is due for what he has done in the body, whether good or evil." We will one day stand before God to account for how we managed what He entrusted to us.

4. **Purposeful Use**
   Stewardship is not just about preservation—it's about fruitful multiplication. When God entrusts us with gifts and resources, He expects us to nurture, grow, and multiply them. Genesis 1:28 says, "Be fruitful and multiply and fill the earth and subdue it." God expects that we use His blessings to produce fruit that glorifies Him.

As believers, we are called to steward wisely and with gratitude. This requires a heart posture of humility, thanksgiving, and intentionality rather than frustration, entitlement, or complaining. Everything we have—our gifts, relationships, and opportunities—belongs to God, and we are merely caretakers. One day, we will give Him an account of how we managed what He entrusted to us.

Imagine if God had been the one to give me the bonsai kit. Can you picture Him asking me, "What did you do with the gift I gave you?" and me responding, "I flushed it down the toilet because it was too much work and took too long"? That would be unthinkable. Yet, isn't this exactly how many of us approach the gifts, relationships, and resources God has given us?

We complain about the process, grow frustrated with the slow results, and abandon what God has entrusted to us. Sometimes, we even discard these gifts altogether because we fail to see their value or purpose. Poor stewardship often stems from impatience, ingratitude, and a lack of understanding. And the consequences are visible: failed marriages, broken relationships, frustration in ministry, and unfulfilled purposes—all rooted in an unwillingness to steward well.

Stewardship is a serious matter. Without understanding and embracing it, many will grow weary in their walk with God. But when we learn the art of stewardship, we position ourselves to experience the fullness of His blessings, the growth of His gifts, and the advancement of His Kingdom.

The concept of stewardship is woven throughout the Bible, though it's easy to miss its lessons in the stories and teachings we read. One of the most vivid and relatable illustrations of stewardship is the *Parable of the Talents*. Jesus often taught in parables to reveal profound truths about the Kingdom of Heaven to those open to hearing while concealing them from those with hardened hearts. Parables were His way of illustrating divine mysteries in a manner both accessible and deeply spiritual.

The *Parable of the Talents*, found in Matthew 25:14–30, provides a powerful teaching on stewardship and accountability. In the story, a man prepares to go on a journey and entrusts his property to his servants. He gives one servant five talents, another two, and the last servant one, distributing them according to their abilities. The first two servants invest their talents, doubling what they were given. However, the third servant, motivated by fear, buries his talent in the ground, doing nothing with it.

When the man returns, he asks the servants to account for how they managed his property. The first two are rewarded for their faithfulness and productivity. The third servant, however, is reprimanded, and his single talent is taken away.

In this parable, the talents symbolize everything God entrusts to us—our gifts, resources, opportunities, and responsibilities. We are the servants, and God is the master who distributes these talents. Just as the servants were expected to use and multiply their talents, we are called to develop and actively steward what God has given us. The third servant's inaction, born out of fear, highlights the danger of passivity and unfruitfulness. God expects us to act in faith and obedience, trusting Him as we steward the resources He provides.

Just as the master in the parable returned to ask for an account, there will come a day when we must stand before God and give an account of how we managed what He entrusted to us.

Reflecting on Our Stewardship

The "talents" God entrusts to us take many forms. Below is an extensive—though not exhaustive—list of areas where we are called to steward well. As you read through it, reflect on each one and ask yourself, *Am I being a good steward in this area, or is this an area where my stewardship needs growth?*

- Time

- Finances

- Relationships (family, friends, community)

- Talents and skills

- Health (physical, mental, emotional)

- Spiritual gifts

- The Gospel (sharing and living out the Good News)

- Creation and the environment

- Opportunities

- Knowledge and education

- Influence and leadership

- Work and career

- Words and communication

- Technology and tools

- Creativity and ideas

- Rest and Sabbath

- Singleness

- Marriage

- Parenting and children

- Emotional wellbeing

- Physical resources (homes, cars, possessions)

- Seasons of life (youth, old age, transitions)

- Social media presence

- Ministry and service

- Community engagement

- Church and spiritual community

- Pain and suffering (how we process trials)

- Identity in Christ

- Boundaries

- Legacy (what we leave behind)

- Imagination and dreams

- Freedom (how we use our free will)

How did you feel as you went through that list? Were you reading confidently, or did you feel a nudge of conviction? The truth is that God has entrusted us with all these things, and stewardship extends into every area of life.

Emotional Stewardship: The Often-Overlooked Gift

One area of stewardship that many people overlook is the stewardship of their emotions. It's easy to focus on material possessions, relationships, or seasons of life, but emotions are also a profound gift from God. As mentioned in a previous chapter, emotions are part of what makes us reflect God's image. They help us carry out His purposes on earth, and we are called to steward them with wisdom and care.

Emotions are much like the talents in the *Parable of the Talents*. They are entrusted to us as powerful tools for connection, growth, and glorifying God. When stewarded well, emotions can deepen our relationships, enhance our understanding of God, and lead us to greater spiritual maturity.

What Is Emotional Stewardship?

Emotional stewardship is the intentional management, care, and use of your emotions as gifts from God. It involves acknowledging emotions as integral to your humanity and understanding their purpose in navigating life, relationships, and your connection to God. It's about aligning your emotions with His will, using them to glorify Him, build others up, and foster personal growth.

Emotions are not random or burdensome—they are purposeful. Joy reflects God's goodness. Grief draws us to His comfort. Even anger can inspire righteous action and reveal God's justice. Stewarding emotions well means being honest about what you feel, taking time to understand those feelings, and responding in ways that honor God. It's not about suppressing or being controlled by your emotions but aligning them with God's truth.

Emotions as Entrusted Talents

Your emotions are your talents. Just as the servants in the parable were called to multiply and invest their talents, we are called to channel our emotions into godly and productive actions. For instance:

- Let joy lead you into praise rather than into selfish pursuits.

- Let fear draw you into God's presence for empowerment rather than into stagnation or hiding.

One day, we will stand before God to give an account of how we've stewarded every area of our lives—including our emotions. Imagine God asking:

- "When I burdened your heart with compassion, what did you do with it?"

- "When you felt anger, did you seek My face or long for revenge?"

- "When you felt anxious, did you run to My peace or bow to fear?"

There will be a reckoning, and we will be accountable for how we managed the gift of emotions—a resource so intricately designed to help us love, grow, and glorify Him.

So, now that we understand we are called by God to steward our emotions, what does emotional stewardship actually look like? What does it mean to steward your emotions in the day-to-day, and what does it entail? Knowing you are called to steward your emotions is one thing, but the challenge many in the body of Christ face is not a lack of knowledge—it's the absence of practical discipleship that shows how to steward well.

Here are some key principles to help you master the art of stewarding your emotions, beginning with the importance of gratitude and thanksgiving.

Steward Thankfully

When considering biblical stewardship, it's important to remember that stewardship is as much about the *heart posture* as it is about actions. For example, when you're stewarding your time at work, your boss evaluates your performance based on measurable results: the tasks you've completed, the goals you've achieved, and your overall productivity. Your boss, however, cannot see your heart. They won't know if you spent the entire day grumbling internally about your workload or resenting the tasks you were given. As long as you smile at them and meet deadlines, they'll likely see you as a good steward.

But God operates differently. God sees beyond your external actions—He sees your heart. He knows whether your heart posture is one of gratitude, thanksgiving, and humility or one of frustration, entitlement, and complaint. Pretending to be a good steward outwardly while harboring ingratitude or disdain inwardly doesn't fool God. With Him, your heart posture matters as much as, if not more than, your actions.

Part of being a good steward is cultivating a heart of gratitude. For instance, if you're in a season of singleness, stewardship doesn't look like constantly complaining about being single and idly waiting for God to send you a spouse. That reflects poor stewardship. Instead, you could steward your singleness by embracing the opportunities it offers: going on missions for God, pursuing the dreams and passions He's placed in your heart, or dedicating time to grow closer to Him. A good steward asks, *God, what have You called me to do in this season?* And approaches it with gratitude rather than grumbling.

Ingratitude is a marker of poor stewardship, and a complaining heart is its fruit. Think about your own heart posture regarding your emotions. How often do you thank God for the way He's uniquely wired you? Do you thank Him for the gift of emotions—for making you sensitive and compassionate, for allowing you to feel deeply? How often do you express gratitude for the fact that your emotions reflect His image and are integral to your ability to live out His purpose?

Being a good steward of your emotions isn't just about controlling anger or managing feelings—it's about having a heart of thanksgiving. Many people complain about their emotions without even realizing it. They see emotions as burdens or signs of weakness, wishing they could suppress or ignore them. But that is not how God designed us to function, nor is it how we are called to steward our emotions. The first step in stewarding your emotions biblically is shifting your perspective to one of gratitude.

Rather than complaining about what God has given you, thank Him for entrusting you with His gifts. Thank Him for allowing you to feel. Thank Him for the joy of knowing what love feels like, for the blessing of experiencing happiness, and even for the difficult emotions—like grief or disappointment. Those "hard" emotions often lead us into deeper intimacy with God, where we encounter His comfort, restoration, and faithfulness.

Imagine a life without emotions. You wouldn't be able to celebrate your loved ones or mourn with them in their pain. You wouldn't feel the warmth of joy or the sting of sorrow. You would feel *nothing*. Emotions are integral to your humanity and are one of God's most profound gifts to us. Gratitude changes how you view them—it shifts your perspective from seeing emotions as burdens to recognizing them as the gifts they are.

As Philippians 2:14 reminds us, "Do everything without complaining and arguing." A complaining mouth reveals a heart lacking gratitude. Instead of grumbling about your emotions, take time to thank God for them. Thank Him that you're capable of feeling deeply, that you can rejoice, grieve, and love. Thank Him for creating you in His image, emotions, and all.

Gratitude is the foundation of good stewardship. It aligns your heart with God's will and reminds you that every good and perfect gift—including your emotions—comes from Him. Stewarding your emotions begins with thanksgiving. Let your gratitude remind you of their purpose: to glorify God, connect with others, and fully experience the life He has given you.

Steward Intentionally

The art of biblical emotional stewardship requires intentionality. Returning to the parable of the talents in Matthew 25:16, we see this intentionality reflected in the actions of the first two servants: *"He who had received the five talents went at once and traded with them, and he made five talents more."* Notice the phrase *"went at once and traded with them."* This was not a passive or hesitant action; it was deliberate and purposeful. The servant didn't sit idly, waiting for the profit to come to him. He actively sought out opportunities, negotiated, and worked until he doubled the talents entrusted to him.

In the same way, we are called to be active, intentional stewards—not passive ones. Stewarding intentionally means approaching your emotions with purpose and care. It involves acknowledging and naming your emotions instead of avoiding them, ignoring their purpose, or hoping they'll simply fade away. To steward your emotions well, you must engage with them intentionally, seeking to understand their purpose and significance in the moment.

A key aspect of intentional stewardship is identifying your emotions. This requires expanding your emotional vocabulary to articulate what you're feeling better. For instance, distinguishing *indifference* from *disappointment* enables you to engage more deeply with your emotional experiences. Naming your emotions brings clarity, but it's only the beginning.

Once you've identified what you're feeling, bring those emotions into God's presence. Pray intentionally, asking Him to reveal their purpose and guide your responses. Emotions are not random; they serve a purpose, often pointing to deeper truths about our hearts, circumstances, or relationships. Recognizing this allows you to steward them wisely and align your responses with God's will.

Recently, I experienced a complex mix of emotions that left me feeling confused and unsettled. I found myself feeling nostalgic, coupled with grief, whenever I reflected on getting older. I'd scroll through old photos from my college years, seeing a younger version of myself—energetic, vibrant, and still a size 2! Nostalgia would wash over me as I reminisced about those days, but it was quickly followed by grief over how much had changed.

I began to grieve the fact that I was no longer that 19-year-old girl. My desires, energy, and even my fashion sense had shifted drastically. I no longer had the stamina to pull all-nighters or the interest in partying and dancing the night away. The crop tops that once dominated my wardrobe no longer resonated with me. As I wrestled with these emotions, I felt guilt creeping in—a secondary emotion born out of thoughts like, "I shouldn't miss those days. God has brought me so far and delivered me from so much."

At first, I tried to ignore these emotions, pushing them aside in hopes they'd disappear. But God, in His grace, drew my attention to them. I brought my feelings into His presence, and with insight from the Holy Spirit, I began to understand what was happening. I realized I was struggling to fully embrace the current version of myself while clinging to the past version that made me feel fun, energetic, and vibrant.

In God's presence, I found the courage to name my emotions—nostalgia, grief, and guilt. Acknowledging them was freeing. Instead of denying or running from what I felt, I was honest with God about my internal struggle. This intentional act of naming and processing my emotions allowed me to find clarity and peace.

In that moment of honesty and vulnerability before God, I learned something about myself and something fundamental about Him. For myself, I realized that I struggle with embracing change. As spontaneous as I like to think I am, I prefer for the core aspects of my life to stay the same. Too much change can feel overwhelming.

As for God, I was reminded of one of His most profound attributes: *He does not change.* Change is inevitable in life—it's a constant reality on this earth. People often say, "The only thing constant is change," but that's not entirely true. Change is not the *only* constant—God is constant, too. He is unchanging, steadfast, and eternal. In that moment, God reminded me that He is *I AM.* He doesn't have an "old version" or a "new version" of Himself. He is the same yesterday, today, and forever.

In that sacred moment of prayer, God taught me an essential truth: to navigate the inevitable changes of life, my identity must be anchored in Christ and Christ alone—not in my current season, my personality, or even my relationships. Why? Because these things are fluid—they evolve and shift over time.

Take personality, for example. While I am still the bubbly, extroverted person I've always been, I've noticed a more reserved side emerging as I grow older. I've come to enjoy solitude and cherish my time alone with God. I'm also more discerning about what I share and with whom. The fashion sense that once defined me has shifted, and I no longer desire to wear the crop tops my 19-year-old self adored. These changes are not losses; they're signs of growth, wisdom, and transformation.

If my identity were rooted in my personality, fashion sense, or social circles, I would feel like I was losing myself every time God shifted something for my growth. I would resist the very transformation meant to make me more like Him. In clinging to the past, I would delay the blessings and new opportunities God is bringing into my life.

God reminded me that my identity is not found in the 19-year-old Ekemini, the 26-year-old Ekemini, or even the 50-year-old Ekemini I've yet to meet. My identity is in Him. I am made in the image of God, and so are you. Isn't that profound?

By bringing my emotions to God, I allowed Him to pour His truth, clarity, and peace into my heart. I entered His presence grieving and burdened with guilt, but I left feeling whole, secure, and at peace with the person I've become. This is what intentional stewardship of emotions looks like—praying about your emotions, asking God to reveal their purpose, and allowing Him to guide your response in alignment with His truth.

Intentional emotional stewardship doesn't stop at prayer; it extends to how you respond. While you may not always control how you feel, you can control how you choose to respond. Instead of reacting impulsively, take time to process your emotions and align your response with God's will. This practice requires patience, but it also creates opportunities to grow in the fruits of the Spirit.

For instance:

- When you take time to process your emotions thoughtfully, you develop the fruit of **self-control**.

- When you bring your emotions into God's presence and seek His truth, you develop the fruit of **peace**, as He brings clarity and reveals the purpose behind your emotions.

- When you face heavy grief and choose to name, process, and invite God into those emotions—rather than numbing them with alcohol, weed, or a counterfeit relationship—you cultivate the fruit of **long-suffering**.

Stewarding your emotions well requires a deliberate commitment to intentionality. This intentionality begins in the heart and is reflected in the actions you take—naming your emotions, processing them, inviting God into them, and responding with care rather than reacting impulsively.

Steward With Emotional Purity

Emotional purity is a crucial aspect of emotional stewardship. While discussions about purity often focus on sexual purity, that is only one dimension of the concept. Emotional purity is equally vital. To steward your emotions well, you must practice emotional purity intentionally and treat it as a priority.

So, what is emotional purity? Emotional purity refers to maintaining integrity, discernment, and boundaries in how we share and express our emotions, particularly in relationships. It means guarding our hearts by being mindful of the depth and timing of emotional connections, ensuring that our vulnerability aligns with wisdom and God's design for healthy relationships.

Think of emotional purity in the same way you think of your body as the temple of the Holy Spirit. As 1 Corinthians 6:19 reminds us, *"Your body is a temple of the Holy Spirit."* This means we are called to steward our physical bodies by guarding what goes into them, not just sexually but also in general—like being mindful of what we eat and consume. Similarly, what enters and exits your heart matters deeply to God. He calls us to steward our emotions and emotional well-being by maintaining emotional purity, guarding what we allow into our hearts and what we release from them.

Emotional purity requires intentionality and faithfulness in managing and expressing emotions. Scripture calls us to steward every area of our lives in ways that honor God and protect ourselves and others. When we fail to practice emotional purity, we risk unnecessary heartache, confusion, or entanglements that could lead to emotional turmoil. Emotional purity allows us to honor God by aligning our emotional connections with His will for relationships, prioritizing clarity and integrity over indulgence, and maintaining healthy boundaries that safeguard our spiritual and emotional health.

One of the most significant ways to maintain emotional purity is by avoiding premature intimacy. Premature intimacy occurs when people share too much personal information or engage in deep emotional vulnerability too quickly in a relationship. This lack of timing and discernment often creates the illusion of closeness but lacks the necessary foundation of trust and investment. In some cases, this can lead to what is known as false intimacy—a superficial sense of connection that appears genuine but lacks true depth.

Consider those love experiment shows where strangers declare things like, *"I feel like I've known you my whole life!"* after only a few days. While it may sound romantic, it's an example of premature intimacy—and it's dangerous. Premature intimacy is a hallmark of poor emotional stewardship. Genuine connection takes time, discernment, and intentional effort to build.

A few years ago, a friend invited me to hang out with her and some of her friends from church. I only knew my friend well; I was meeting the others for the first time. The one thing we all had in common was our shared love for Jesus, which made it easy to mingle and spark conversations.

During one of the conversations, someone said, "This is what I love about Christian circles. I just met you all, but I feel like we're besties already. We should totally have a sleepover!" Her words caught me off guard. While I appreciated her enthusiasm, her statement raised an alarm in my spirit.

I responded lightheartedly but firmly: "I know we all love Jesus, but no, we're not best friends yet, and we barely know each other. Let's take it slow before we start planning sleepovers!"

At that moment, I realized that emotional purity is necessary even in Christian relationships. There's a tendency in Christian communities to assume that shared faith automatically equates to deep emotional connection. While we are called to love one another and be friendly, deeper levels of emotional vulnerability require discernment and wisdom. True emotional intimacy should grow gradually, with the Holy Spirit guiding us as we discern when someone has earned a certain level of trust.

Emotional Purity in Action

What does emotional purity look like in practice? How do you steward your emotions in a way that maintains emotional purity? Here are some key principles and examples to help you avoid premature intimacy, unnecessary emotional turmoil, and the heartaches that come from blurred boundaries.

Avoiding Deep Emotional Sharing with the Wrong Person

Sharing intimate details about your life, struggles, or dreams with someone who has not earned that level of trust—such as a casual acquaintance or someone romantically available—can create unhealthy emotional bonds. Have you ever been in a situation where someone you barely know starts pouring out deeply personal and emotionally intimate details to you? How did it make you feel? It can be awkward, and in extreme cases, it may even feel like an emotional violation.

I've had such an experience myself. Years ago, a man I barely knew used a spiritually manipulative tactic, claiming that God told him I was his wife. He then proceeded to share extremely sensitive, deeply emotional parts of his life with me—information I had no business hearing from someone I'd just met. The conversation was deeply uncomfortable. I felt uneasy, burdened, and unsure how to respond. There was no mutual trust, respect, or established connection to create a safe space for such vulnerability. It felt like an emotional violation, which is exactly what it was.

This kind of premature emotional sharing created an unbalanced dynamic and a false sense of intimacy. It left me feeling burdened and obligated in ways I hadn't consented to, ultimately harming any possibility of a healthy relationship before it even began. Two violations happened in one meeting: first, his declaration of "God told me you're my wife," and second, the premature, deeply personal oversharing.

Vulnerability without boundaries can lead to one-sided dependency, misplaced trust, emotional entanglements, and even harm. Save deep emotional sharing for trusted friends, mentors, or those in a committed, God-honoring relationship. Not everyone needs to know the deepest parts of your life. Even when it comes to your dreams, it's essential to steward them wisely. If God places a project on your heart that is deeply personal and still in its incubation stage, sharing too much too soon can be dangerous. By placing something delicate in the wrong hands, you risk disappointment or emotional heartache if they don't steward that part of you well.

Just as God gives to us according to our abilities (as seen in the parable of the talents), we should also use wisdom and discernment in what we share with others based on their role in our lives and their emotional capacity. Be sensitive to the Holy Spirit in your conversations—sometimes He might nudge you with a quiet whisper: *"Don't share that with them"* or *"You've said too much, stop now."* Trust those nudges; they are for your protection.

Resisting Emotional Attachment Outside of Commitment

A significant part of emotional purity involves ensuring that the level of emotional attachment and intimacy in a relationship matches the level of commitment in that relationship. Allowing emotional intimacy to develop without a foundation of commitment can lead to unmet expectations, confusion, and heartache. This is how *situationships* are born.

A situationship is a romantic dynamic that lacks clarity, commitment, or defined purpose. It's characterized by emotional ambiguity, a lack of labels, inconsistent communication, and the absence of intentionality. While many people associate situationships with physical intimacy, they can also form through premature emotional attachment. Some people find themselves emotionally entangled in situationships without any physical intimacy involved—because emotional bonds can be just as binding as physical ones.

For example, when you tell someone, "I haven't told anyone this before," or "You're the only person who knows this about me," and they haven't clarified their romantic intentions or established a commitment, you're setting yourself up for an emotional situationship. You feel attached because you've emotionally bared yourself to this person but without the trust, commitment, or emotional safety that comes with a healthy, God-honoring relationship. You're left in a state of emotional ambiguity and confusion—feeling like you're in a relationship when, in reality, you're still single.

Situationships rarely evolve into committed relationships. They are often messy and painful, but they can be avoided by maintaining emotional purity and setting boundaries. Emotional intimacy should grow in alignment with the level of commitment in a relationship. For instance, engaging in late-night emotional conversations with someone of the opposite sex who isn't a committed partner can blur relational boundaries and open doors to temptation, misplaced feelings, and emotional ambiguity.

There's a common joke on social media about how boundaries seem to disappear, and conversations become flirty or overly intimate with friends of the opposite sex once the clock strikes midnight. While it's meant to be funny, there's a sobering truth to it. Engaging in those kinds of conversations can jeopardize emotional purity, leading to confusion and unguarded hearts. Set boundaries for emotional conversations, pray for wisdom and discernment, and consistently seek to honor God in your emotional stewardship. By doing so, you protect yourself and others from unnecessary heartache while cultivating relationships that are rooted in trust, clarity, and commitment.

Protecting Emotional Boundaries in Dating

While a dating relationship involves a level of commitment, it is not a covenant relationship. As such, it requires boundaries and emotional purity. Even in dating, wisdom and discernment are essential when deciding how deeply to share with your partner, particularly based on the stage of the relationship. The essence of godly, intentional dating is to evaluate the person and the relationship to discern whether you are emotionally, spiritually, and relationally compatible for marriage.

Dating is an evaluation process—a time to assess whether your values, purposes, and lives align for a lifelong commitment. Because of this, it's important to avoid blurring the discernment needed to make wise decisions. Emotional oversharing too early can complicate the process, clouding your judgment and creating bonds that are difficult to break if the relationship doesn't work out.

As you date, it's crucial to ensure that the emotional attachment you form matches the level of commitment and intimacy in the relationship. Take the necessary time to build trust and allow the relationship to grow organically. Manage the depth and pace of emotional intimacy to ensure the relationship develops healthily and aligns with God's design for love, respect, and mutual care.

Avoid diving into deep emotional wounds or personal traumas too soon. Instead, start by sharing lighter, meaningful aspects of your life, allowing vulnerability to grow naturally as trust is established over time. Emotional intimacy should not resemble the depth of a marriage bond when you are still in the early stages of dating.

Be upfront about your boundaries and what you are comfortable sharing or discussing at different stages of the relationship. Clear expectations help both partners navigate emotional intimacy responsibly. Additionally, be mindful of emotional dependency. While sharing emotions is an important aspect of a relationship, avoid relying solely on your partner for validation, comfort, or healing. Cultivate a support system that includes friends, mentors, and, most importantly, God, through personal prayer and reflection.

As you evaluate the relationship, guard against emotional manipulation by being aware of whether emotional sharing is being used to control or influence the other person unfairly. Pay attention to whether both you and your partner are practicing emotional honesty. Respect their boundaries as well, ensuring you're not crossing their emotional limits by oversharing or expecting emotional availability that hasn't been mutually established.

Ultimately, invite God into every stage of your relationship. Allow the Holy Spirit to guide you in guarding your heart and expressing your emotions. Pray for wisdom in pacing emotional intimacy, and seek God's discernment in navigating the relationship with clarity and purpose.

Lack of emotional purity in a dating relationship is not only a sign of poor emotional stewardship but can also lead to poor stewardship of the relationship itself. When emotional boundaries are respected, the relationship can grow with mutual respect, clarity, and wisdom. This fosters emotional and spiritual well-being for both partners, laying the foundation for a relationship built on trust and alignment with God's design.

These are just a few principles of emotional purity in action. Emotional purity is deeply connected to emotional stewardship because it embodies faithfulness, intentionality, and the establishment of healthy boundaries. It is about guarding your heart and mind by approaching emotional connections with wisdom and discernment. By practicing emotional purity, we honor God in our relationships, avoid unnecessary emotional turmoil, and protect ourselves from the heartache that comes from sharing the most vulnerable, intimate parts of ourselves with the wrong people or at the wrong time.

Steward With Relational Integrity

God is a triune God, existing as one in essence but in three distinct persons—a profound demonstration of relational unity and community. This highlights just how relational God is and serves as a reminder that biblical emotional stewardship also has a relational dimension. It involves loving your neighbor as yourself and stewarding their emotions alongside your own.

Jesus places great emphasis on this relational stewardship. In Mark 12:28–31, a scribe asks Him, *"Which commandment is the most important of all?"* Jesus replies that the greatest commandment is to *"love the Lord your God with all your heart and with all your soul and with all your mind and with all your strength."* Then He adds, *"The second is this: 'You shall love your neighbor as yourself.'"* For Jesus to elevate loving our neighbor as the second greatest commandment shows just how much importance He places on relational stewardship.

So, what does it mean to steward emotions with relational integrity? Stewarding with relational integrity involves two key responsibilities:

1. **Being mindful of how your emotions and words affect others.** This means honoring God and others by managing your emotions in ways that build trust, protect relationships, and reflect Christ's love.

2. **Protecting the emotions of others.** God calls us to care for and honor the emotions of those around us, just as we would want others to care for ours. This relational responsibility ties directly to loving your neighbor as yourself.

Gossip: The Silent Killer of Relational Integrity

One of the greatest threats to relational integrity is gossip. Gossip is a subtle, sneaky poison that destroys relationships, sows division, and causes emotional harm. While often normalized in our culture and even considered "fun," gossip undermines biblical emotional stewardship and relational integrity.

What is Gossip? According to Oxford Languages, gossip is *"a casual or unconstrained conversation or report about other people, typically involving details that are not confirmed as being true."* Gossip involves idle talk or rumors about someone's personal or private affairs.

In many circles, gossip has become so normalized that our consciences have become desensitized to it. We engage in it casually, often without realizing the harm it causes. Terms like "tea" or "gist" are used to make gossip seem harmless or even entertaining. But the truth is that gossip breaks trust, causes emotional wounds, and creates division in relationships.

Even within the church, gossip has found a foothold, often disguised as "concern" or framed as a prayer request. For instance, someone might confide in a trusted friend about something deeply personal, only for that friend to share it as a "prayer point" at the next prayer meeting—without the person's consent. This is a religiously cloaked form of gossip and can cause immense emotional harm.

Proverbs 16:28 warns us: *"A troublemaker plants seeds of strife; gossip separates the best of friends."* Gossip is divisive, sowing seeds of distrust and disunity. It is not merely casual conversation but a rebellion against God's design for unity and community. Gossip is antithetical to Christ's teachings and undermines the call to steward relationships with integrity.

Proverbs 26:20 adds, *"Fire goes out without wood, and quarrels disappear when gossip stops."* Gossip often fuels strife and conflict, making it a root cause of many relational breakdowns. Abstaining from gossip is essential for fostering trust and honoring relationships.

Handling Offense With Integrity

Stewarding emotions with relational integrity also means managing offense wisely. When someone hurts you, it's important to process your emotions in a way that honors God and protects the relationship. Venting carelessly to others or spreading gossip about the person who offended you only deepens the wound and creates barriers to reconciliation.

Matthew 18:15–16 offers a biblical approach to conflict resolution:

"If your brother sins against you, go and tell him his fault, between you and him alone. If he listens to you, you have gained your brother. But if he does not listen, take one or two others along with you, that every charge may be established by the evidence of two or three witnesses."

This passage outlines a clear and God-honoring process:

- First, address the issue one-on-one with the person who hurt you.

- If the conflict persists, involve one or two trusted, unbiased individuals to mediate and ensure fairness.

This approach preserves the dignity of both parties, protects emotions, and prevents gossip from spreading. Imagine the harm caused when an offense is handled poorly—venting to others, tarnishing someone's reputation, and creating emotional wounds that make reconciliation harder. This is why God calls us to handle conflict with love, wisdom, and integrity.

Practical Steps to Avoid Gossip

1. **Process Emotions With God First**: Before discussing your hurt with others, take it to God in prayer. Ask for clarity, peace, and wisdom in how to respond.

2. **Seek Trusted Confidants:** If you need to process your emotions with someone, choose a trusted confidant who can guide you with wisdom while honoring the person involved.

3. **Set a Standard in Conversations:** Politely withdraw or change the subject if a conversation veers into gossip. Avoid participating, even when it seems harmless.

4. **Honor Boundaries:** Protect the private details others have shared with you. Do not turn their vulnerability into idle chatter or "prayer points."

5. **Reflect Christ's Love:** Treat others as you would want to be treated. Protect their emotions and reputations as you would your own.

The Moral Responsibility of Relational Stewardship

Gossip isn't just a failure of emotional management—it's a failure of relational stewardship. Honoring God and others through relational integrity involves avoiding gossip, fostering healthy communication, and building trust.

Be intentional about how you manage your emotions, especially when hurt or offended. Choose empathy and constructive communication over unconstrained venting or character assassination. Refuse to build relationships on gossip or shared animosity. Instead, let your relationships be rooted in love, mutual respect, and a shared commitment to honor God.

Proverbs 18:8 reminds us: *"A gossip's words are like choice food that goes down to one's innermost being."* The words we speak can deeply impact others. Let's steward our relationships and emotions with care, ensuring they reflect Christ's love and bring glory to God.

Conclusion

Stewardship is not just a responsibility; it is a calling and a heart posture. To be a good steward, you must first recognize that God is the owner of all things. He has entrusted you with specific resources, gifts, abilities, and seasons—not for your benefit alone, but so you can manage them wisely and ultimately bring glory to Him.

Growing up, my mum often said, "I'm your mother, but I'm kind of like your nanny. You belong to God. He is your Father and Creator, and He has entrusted you into my care. My job is to raise you, nurture you, protect you, and love you. One day, I will stand before God and give an account of how I stewarded my calling of motherhood."

At the time, I thought she was being dramatic, calling herself our nanny. But as I've grown older, I've come to deeply understand her words. My mum wasn't downplaying her role as a mother—she was teaching me a lesson on stewardship. She was saying that my sister and I are gifts from God, entrusted to her care. While we belong to God, He called her to motherhood to reflect His love, nurture our growth, and guide us toward Him. And one day, she will stand before God to give an account of how she fulfilled that calling.

In the same way, one day, we will all stand before God and give an account of how we stewarded everything He entrusted to us.

- How are you stewarding your season? Whether it's a season of suffering, singleness, marriage, parenthood, or waiting, it matters to God.

- How are you stewarding your finances? Are you squandering resources or being stingy, or are you managing them with wisdom and generosity?

- What about the gospel? Are you stewarding the gospel of Jesus Christ well by sharing the Good News and living out the Great Commission (Matthew 28:16–20)?

Just as God calls us to steward these aspects of life, He also calls us to steward our emotions. And one day, we will give an account to Him for how we managed them.

- **Are you stewarding your emotions with gratitude?** Do you worship God and praise Him for the ability to feel, knowing your emotions are a gift that reflects His image?

- **Are you stewarding your emotions intentionally?** Are you naming them, processing them, and inviting God into your emotional experiences to shine the light of His truth?

- **Are you stewarding your emotions with emotional purity?** Are you guarding what enters and exits your heart and maintaining emotional boundaries?

- **Are you stewarding your emotions with relational integrity?** Are you protecting relationships through thoughtful words and actions that build trust and reflect Christ's love?

Conviction: God's Gift to Revive Your Heart

Perhaps this chapter has highlighted areas where you haven't stewarded your emotions well. This is not to cause shame or guilt. Instead, it may be the Holy Spirit tugging at your heart, revealing areas He wants to heal and revive. Conviction is a gift—a divine nudge that softens a hardened heart, sensitizes a dulled conscience, and draws us back to God.

God is extending an invitation to you: bring all of yourself to Him. Allow Him to fill you with His truth and mold you into the good steward He has called you to be.

The Journey of Stewardship

The path of biblical stewardship is not always easy. There will be days when naming your emotions or bringing them to God feels too painful. There will be moments when the lure of oversharing for a fleeting sense of intimacy feels tempting. Some days, finding something to thank God for may seem impossible. And there will be times when the urge to vent your frustrations or hurt will be overwhelming.

But remember this: God knows you completely. He has experienced anger, grief, disappointment, and jealousy. He sees the moments when your heart races, when you hold back tears, and when you feel utterly alone. He does not judge you for your emotions; instead, He embraces them as part of how He created you. He gave you the ability to feel so that you could build deeper intimacy with Him.

God doesn't expect you to steward your emotions perfectly on your own. That's why He gave you the Holy Spirit—to guide you, comfort you, and empower you. When you feel tempted to overshare or gossip, the Holy Spirit can help you develop the fruit of self-control. When fear, confusion, or anxiety weighs you down, the Holy Spirit can cultivate the fruit of peace within you.

Jesus is our ultimate example of stewardship. He stewarded His time on earth perfectly, fulfilling His assignment even to the point of death on the cross. He conquered it all so that you don't have to carry the weight alone. Surrender your emotions to Him, trusting that He can transform you into the good steward He has called you to be.

When the journey feels hard, remember His promise: *"My grace is sufficient for you, for my power is made perfect in weakness"* (2 Corinthians 12:9). His strength will sustain you, and His grace will equip you to steward your emotions and every aspect of your life well.

Prayer

Heavenly Father,

Thank You for the many gifts and resources You have entrusted to my care, including the precious gift of my emotions. Thank You for giving me the privilege and responsibility to steward these blessings on earth. Lord, I humbly admit that I have not always been a good steward. I confess that there have been times when my stewardship has fallen short of reflecting Your heart, especially in managing my emotions. I have not always been intentional or faithful with what You have entrusted to me.

Forgive me, Lord, for the ways I have mirrored the servant with one talent—failing to cultivate what You've placed in my hands. Forgive me for mismanaging my emotions and the other gifts You've given me. Forgive me for my pride and sense of entitlement over what ultimately belongs to You. Today, I surrender it all to You—my emotions, my relationships, and every resource You've placed in my care. Teach me, Lord, to steward well.

Fill me with Your Holy Spirit and reveal to me the areas where I have not been stewarding well. Help me to embrace and practice the principles of biblical emotional stewardship shared in this book. Deliver me from a heart of complaint, and instead, fill me with thanksgiving. Teach me to be more grateful, Lord, and to recognize Your hand in all areas of my life.

Help me to steward my emotions intentionally, naming them and bringing them into Your presence for wisdom and clarity. Send Your Holy Spirit to guide me through the deep emotions I sometimes avoid and grant me the courage to confront them with Your truth.

Lord, teach me to walk in emotional purity. Give me the wisdom and discernment to know when it is safe to share and when it is wiser to remain silent. Guide me in my relationships, and show me how to embody emotional purity in my daily interactions.

Lord, help me to stop gossiping. I know it grieves Your heart and sows seeds of division, disunity, and conflict. Strengthen me with the self-control to resist the temptation to gossip, and grant me boldness to live as a person of integrity, honoring You in how I speak and act. Help me to build trust in my relationships by protecting the emotions and reputations of others.

Above all, Lord, help me to honor You in everything I do—in how I feel, how I think, and how I choose to respond. Thank You for the assurance that You hear my prayers and the promise of Your guidance as I walk this journey of stewardship with You.

In Jesus' name,

Amen.

EXERCISE: EMOTIONAL STEWARDSHIP REFLECTION AND ACTION PLAN

Objective

This exercise is designed to help you evaluate how you currently steward your emotions and create an intentional plan to grow in emotional stewardship. It also enables you to apply the four principles of biblical emotional stewardship outlined in this chapter to your daily life and personal development. By becoming a better steward of your emotions, you not only honor God but also improve your emotional intelligence, strengthening your skills in the four pillars of emotional intelligence. Use your designated emotions journal to practice this exercise and document your observations, reflections, and progress.

Step 1: Reflect on Your Emotional Stewardship

Take time to thoughtfully answer these questions:

Recognize

- What emotions do I experience most often?

- Are there specific emotions I tend to avoid, suppress, or ignore—similar to how the servant in the parable buried the one talent?

- How do I typically respond to my emotions—constructively, impulsively, or passively?

Relational Impact

- How do my emotions affect my relationships with others?

- Have I ever hurt someone by not stewarding my emotions well (e.g., through gossip, outbursts, or withdrawal)?

- How do I process my emotions with God and invite Him into my emotional life?

Accountability

- In what areas do I need to grow to better steward my emotions?

- Who can I trust to help me grow and hold me accountable on this journey?

Step 2: Identify One Emotion to Steward Better

- Choose one emotion you feel needs better stewardship (e.g., anger, sadness, joy, or fear).

- Reflect on how you currently handle this emotion and its impact on your life and relationships.

- Be detailed—revisit specific memories or scenarios where you struggled to steward this emotion well.

Step 3: Create an Emotional Stewardship Plan

Develop a personalized plan for stewarding this emotion by following these steps:

Acknowledge the Emotion

- Write a prayer or statement recognizing this emotion as a gift from God.

  - Example: "Lord, I recognize that my anger is not inherently bad but a signal for justice or protection. Help me steward it well."

Set a Goal for Growth

- Define how you want to improve in stewarding this emotion.

  - Example: "When I feel anger, I will pause, pray, and respond calmly instead of lashing out."

Identify an Anchor Scripture

- Choose a Bible verse to guide and encourage you. Let it serve as a reminder and anchor in your journey.

  - Example: "Be quick to listen, slow to speak, and slow to become angry" (James 1:19).

Practical Action Steps

- List two or three specific actions you will take to better steward this emotion.

  - Examples:

    - Practice deep breathing or prayer when this emotion arises.

    - Journal triggers and ask God for insight on handling them.

    - Consult your therapist or counselor for additional strategies.

    - Share your progress and struggles with a trusted mentor or friend for accountability.

Step 4: Accountability Check

- Share your plan with a trusted friend, mentor, or small group for encouragement and accountability.

- Commit to reviewing your progress weekly or monthly, documenting these steps in your journal to track growth and for encouragement.

Step 5: Celebrate Progress

- Celebrate your growth, no matter how small. Write a note of gratitude to God for helping you grow in emotional stewardship.

- Reflect on your victories and thank Him for His grace in your journey.

- Write a letter to yourself as a reminder of how far you've come. These letters will encourage you in moments of struggle and serve as evidence of Christ's ongoing work in your life.

REFLECTION QUESTIONS

1. Have you ever received a gift that you didn't particularly like, appreciate, or know how to use? How did that influence the way you viewed the gift and how you chose to use—or not use—it?

2. Before reading this chapter, did you understand the concept of biblical stewardship? Did you see your emotions as something God has called you to steward? How has this chapter shaped or deepened your understanding of biblical emotional stewardship?

3. Of the four principles of emotional stewardship outlined in this chapter, which do you find most challenging to follow and uphold? Why do you think this is, and what steps can you take to grow in this area?

4. How often do you take time to thank God for the gift of your emotions? What practical steps can you take to cultivate a heart of gratitude for how He designed you to feel and connect with others?

5. Are there areas in your life where you may be oversharing or forming premature emotional bonds? What boundaries can you put in place to maintain emotional purity and protect your heart?

6. How mindful are you of the ways your emotions and words affect others? What intentional steps can you take to steward the emotions of those around you with care and integrity?

7. Have you ever found yourself engaging in or listening to gossip? How did it impact your relationships, and what strategies can you adopt to resist the temptation to gossip in the future?

8. Reflect on a recent conflict. Did you approach and resolve it in a way that honored God and protected the emotions of those involved? How can the principles outlined in Matthew 18:15–16 guide you in navigating future conflicts?

9. What season of life are you currently in—waiting, singleness, marriage, parenthood, suffering, influence, or another? How can you better steward your emotions in this season to glorify God and fulfill His purpose for you?

10. Jesus is the ultimate example of perfect stewardship. How does His life inspire you to steward your emotions and relationships more faithfully? What specific ways can you emulate His example in your daily life?

10

A LETTER FOR THE JOURNEY AHEAD

Life is like a music album—a collection of songs that weave together stories, emotions, and memories. Every album holds its own journey, a rhythm of highs and lows, harmonies and dissonance. When you press play on an album you've been eagerly anticipating, you're ready for an experience. You start at track one and let it carry you through, each song evoking something new within you.

But not every track is a favorite. Sometimes, within the first few seconds, you know a song isn't your vibe, and you skip ahead. Other times, you let it play, wondering if it will grow on you. Then, there are those tracks that strike a chord so deeply you replay them over and over, savoring every note, every lyric. It's a journey—sometimes thrilling, sometimes unexpected, sometimes reflective.

Life is much the same. It's a series of tracks; some we love and replay endlessly, and others we'd rather skip altogether. The moments of pure joy—like graduating, landing a dream job, or hearing "I love you" for the first time—are the tracks we replay in our minds, savoring their sweetness. These are the anthems that remind us of life's beauty and goodness.

But then there are the other tracks—the ones that feel too heavy to bear. Like the disappointment of a rejection email after pinning your hopes on that opportunity. Or the grief of losing someone you love, a friendship you cherished, or a relationship you thought would last forever. Or the anger that bubbles up when you're confronted with yet another injustice. These tracks are hard to sit with, and yet they are as much a part of the album as the joyful ones.

Our emotions are like the melodies that bind all these tracks together, invisible threads woven through every memory and experience. They are what make us human and what connects us to one another. They remind us that, no matter our differences, we all feel deeply. Joy and pain, love and fear, hope and despair—these emotions are life's universal language.

Maya Angelou once said, "People will forget what you said, people will forget what you did, but people will never forget how you made them feel." It's true. Our words and actions may fade, but the emotions we evoke in others remain. They are life's fingerprints on our hearts, reminders of where we've been, who we've become, and what we've overcome.

I think about my own tracks—the ones that brought joy and the ones that brought pain. I remember the heartbreak of my first breakup and the grief of losing friends who once felt like family. I remember the sting of unanswered prayers and the heavy weight of rejection after rejection. These were hard moments, ones I would have skipped if I could.

But I also remember the joy of new beginnings: the anticipation on my first date with my now-husband, the excitement when he proposed, and the gratitude when I landed a job I prayed for. I think of the laughter shared with friends who fill my life with light, the contentment of knowing God has surrounded me with His love through these people. These moments are proof that, even after the hardest tracks, there are still songs worth replaying.

There were times when I felt overwhelmed by the weight of certain struggles. But I'll never forget the day I was sitting in my college dorm, crying out to God, asking when and how He would heal my broken heart. It was then that He spoke to me through Ezekiel 36:26: "I will give you a new heart, and I will put a new spirit in you." I sat in silence, letting those words wash over me. Then I heard Him whisper, "I didn't say I would fix your heart. I said I would give you a new one."

That moment changed everything. God wasn't promising to glue the shattered pieces of my heart back together; He was promising something far greater—a new heart, one untouched by the pain of the past, capable of loving, trusting, and hoping again. A heart not defined by brokenness but by His promise of wholeness.

And He delivered. The wounds that once felt like permanent scars are now reminders of His healing power. Those memories of heartbreak, grief, and rejection have become landmarks of God's faithfulness. They are not just evidence of what I've endured but of how God has walked with me through it all, transforming my pain into purpose.

But then, there was the moment that changed everything. The passing of my father in 2021 shattered me in ways I didn't know was possible. It wasn't like any other pain I had felt before. Losing him was like losing a piece of the world I thought I understood. The journey to healing felt insurmountable—like trying to climb a mountain with no end in sight. And yet, just like every painful memory in my life, I can look back and see where God was in the midst of it all.

I will never forget the night before I learned of my father's passing. I was in my kitchen, and suddenly, the presence of the Holy Spirit filled the room. It wasn't just a feeling; it was a weight, almost tangible. I had never felt God's presence so strongly. It was as if He had stepped into my space, interrupting my mundane evening with His overwhelming nearness. I stopped everything, sensing that God had something to say.

As I began praying in the Spirit, His presence grew even closer, like a companion standing right beside me. Then, I heard Him whisper, "Come to me. Let me comfort you." I didn't understand why He was saying that—I didn't feel like I needed comforting. But still, I obeyed. I went upstairs, lay down in my bed, and simply soaked in His presence. I didn't speak; I didn't strive. I just rested, feeling as though God Himself was holding me. It was the safest, warmest, most loving embrace I had ever known. I fell asleep that night wrapped in His peace.

The next morning, I received the news: my father had passed away in his sleep. I was devastated. As tears poured down my face, I remembered the night before. And through the haze of grief, I whispered to God, "You knew."

God knew. He always knows. He is not bound by time as we are— He exists in the past, present, and future simultaneously. He knew the exact moment my father would pass. He knew how my heart would break and how the weight of grief would press down on me. He knew I would need His comfort before I even realized it myself. And so, He came to me ahead of time, preparing my heart in ways I could only recognize in hindsight. He grieved for me and with me before grief even reached my door.

That season was more painful than I can put into words. There were nights I cried until I had no tears left, days when the world felt unbearably heavy. And yet, God never left my side. He was there in the quiet of my sorrow, in the prayers of friends, in the healing words of my therapist, and in the moments of worship that lifted my spirit when I felt the heaviness. He didn't just stand with me in my grief—He stood in my future, holding my hand in the seasons of peace, joy, and restoration that were waiting for me, even though I couldn't see them yet.

This book is a testament to that healing journey. I couldn't have written these words if God hadn't walked me through the valleys of growth, awareness, and restoration. Friends, I want you to know this: *God knows.* He sees the wounds you try to hide, the betrayals that have scarred your heart, the tears you've cried in secret. He knows the weight of rejection, the ache of loneliness, the frustration of feeling unseen. He knows.

But here's the beauty: God doesn't just dwell in your pain. He is already present in your promise. He is weaving something beautiful out of what feels broken. He is aligning your steps with His purpose, guiding you on a path toward healing. All He asks is that you let Him in. Sit with your emotions—the overwhelming, uncomfortable, and even painful ones—and let Him meet you there. Don't run from them or bury them. When you do, you miss the chance to encounter God in ways you've never known. You miss the opportunity to see His heart, to feel His presence, and to experience His transformative power.

I encourage you to embrace your emotions, even the difficult ones. They are God's fingerprints on your soul, evidence that you are made in His image. They are not just a reflection of you—they are a glimpse of Him. They are a way to connect with His heart and to draw closer to Him. Your moments of heartbreak and suffering are opportunities for intimacy with the One who knows you fully and loves you deeply.

God often does His best work in our pain. It is in those moments of brokenness that His glory is revealed most profoundly. I think of Hosea, the prophet God instructed to marry Gomer, an unfaithful woman. Can you imagine the anguish Hosea must have felt? A man of God, asked to love someone who would break his heart time and time again. He must have felt betrayed, disrespected, and unappreciated—emotions that cut deep. Yet, God's instruction wasn't about punishing Hosea or subjecting him to purposeless suffering. It was about intimacy. It was about allowing Hosea to feel just a fraction of what God feels for us.

Through Hosea, God revealed His own heartbreak over Israel's unfaithfulness. In Hosea 2:13, God lamented, *"I will punish her for all those times when she burned incense to her images of Baal, when she put on her earrings and jewels and went out to look for her lovers but forgot all about Me," says the Lord.*

Imagine that—God felt forgotten. He felt abandoned. He felt grief. The anguish Hosea experienced in his marriage mirrored the emotions God felt for His people, His bride, who repeatedly turned away to chase after other gods. Hosea's suffering became a sacred connection to God's heart. Through the pain of betrayal and rejection, Hosea experienced a glimpse of the depth of God's relentless love for His people, even in their unfaithfulness.

God gave us emotions so we could understand a piece of His heart, connecting with Him in a way that transcends logic and reason. Just as Hosea's heartbreak drew him into deeper intimacy with God, our own emotions—both joyful and painful—invite us to know Him more deeply. They are a bridge, linking our finite experiences to the infinite love of our Creator.

Emotions are an invitation to connect with God, to feel with Him, and to see the world through His eyes. Without the difficult emotions, we wouldn't fully appreciate the beautiful ones. How could we know the sweetness of joy without tasting sorrow? How would we thank God for peace if we had never known chaos? The uncomfortable emotions give depth to the good ones and remind us that God is with us in all of it.

So, thank God for your emotions—the joyful and the challenging ones. They are evidence that you are alive, that you are human, and that you are deeply connected to the Creator who gave them to you. They are part of your journey, a journey that God is shaping into something beautiful, something whole, something that reflects His glory.

And now, if you've made it to this point—congratulations. You did it. You've reached the end of this book, and you didn't give up. You've journeyed through every page, every reflection, every truth. Pause for a moment. Breathe deeply. Let this accomplishment sink in. Celebrate yourself—not just for finishing a book but for embarking on a journey that requires courage, vulnerability, and faith. You've walked through the layers of your emotions, faced hard truths, wrestled with myths, and embraced revelations about who you are and how God designed you to feel.

This journey wasn't just about reading words on a page. It was about peeling back the layers of your soul and allowing God to meet you in the raw, unfiltered places. You didn't rush past the hard things. You lingered. You allowed yourself to feel, to process, and to open your heart to healing. That takes incredible courage. I want you to know this—I'm proud of you. Truly.

But here's the thing: this isn't really the end, is it? No, this is the beginning. This is the start of a new chapter in your life—the chapter where healing, transformation, and wholeness unfold. The chapter where confidence and emotional maturity become your reality. The chapter where your emotions align more beautifully with God's design. This is where the real journey begins, and I'm so excited for you.

Before you move forward, I want to leave you with a few words to carry with you:

First, consistency is key.

Consistency is the bridge between who you are now and who you are becoming. Be consistent in this journey. Take the time to work through the exercises, answer the reflection questions, and journal your thoughts. Let this process be intentional, even if it feels slow. Revisit the prayers in this book as often as you need. Pray them over your life and invite God into your journey every step of the way. Consistency turns intention into transformation. Every small step matters.

Second, resist the trap of isolation.

Growth and healing were never meant to happen in isolation. They are not solitary pursuits but are nurtured through connection and shared experiences. God created us for community. Relationship management, one of the pillars of emotional intelligence, cannot be cultivated alone. Pray for God to surround you with the right people—those who will walk with you, encourage you, and refine you. The enemy loves to use isolation to whisper lies, to convince you that you're better off alone. But don't believe it. You need people just as they need you. Let God lead you to a community that will nurture and challenge you in all the right ways.

Third, put God at the center.

There is no real emotional intelligence, no true healing or wholeness, without God. Even the most celebrated experts need Jesus, just as you and I do. Therapy is a gift. Professional counselors are a gift. Science and knowledge are gifts. But they are all tools that find their ultimate power when surrendered to the One who designed us. God has equipped you with everything you need, and He longs to walk this journey with you. Surrender the weight of transformation to Him. Let Him carry the burden, and let His truth guide every step.

Finally, remember that this journey is bigger than you.

It's not just about your healing—it's about the ripple effect your healing will have on others. If you manage your emotions now, your children will grow up in an emotionally safe environment. If you learn to forgive, your relationships will thrive with love and grace. The work you do today will impact your future, your relationships, and even generations to come. Your consistency and intentionality now will inspire others to embark on their own journeys.

Now, take a moment and imagine this:

Imagine a life where you have healthy boundaries and feel secure and authentic in your relationships—a life where you respond thoughtfully instead of impulsively and love freely without fear holding you back.

Imagine friendships built on genuine care, not gossip or animosity. A life where forgiveness flows easily, where grudges don't weigh you down. A life where your healing and growth inspire others to seek God and transform their lives.

This is the life God desires for you—a life marked by freedom, healing, and joy. It's a life where your emotions are no longer a burden but a gift—a life where you reflect His image in every interaction, every relationship, and every moment.

So, as you close this book, I encourage you to lean into this journey. Invite Jesus into every step. Trust Him to guide you, heal you, and transform you. Let go of the version of yourself that clung to dysfunction for survival. Embrace the version of you that God envisioned before He formed you in your mother's womb—the version that is fearfully and wonderfully made in His image.

Congratulations, my friend. You've begun something beautiful, and I can't wait to see what God will do in and through you.

Ekemini

FINAL REFLECTION

1. What is one concept, truth, or principle from this book that resonated most deeply with you? Why?

2. How has your understanding of emotions changed after reading this book? What new perspectives have you gained?

3. What does "being made in His image" mean to you now, especially in the context of your emotions?

4. Which chapter or section challenged you the most? How did you navigate through that challenge, and what did you learn from it?

5. Out of all the exercises and activities in this book, which did you enjoy most and why? Which was the most challenging and why?

6. What surprised you most about your emotions and how they connect to your faith journey? How did this surprise shape your understanding of yourself and God?

7. What is one emotional habit or pattern you're now inspired to change? Why is this change important to you?

8. Who in your life could benefit from what you've learned in this book? How can you share or model these insights with them?

9. As you close this chapter of your journey, what prayer, affirmation, or commitment will you carry with you to stay consistent and intentional in your growth?

10. How will you celebrate the emotional and spiritual growth you've experienced while reading this book? What does celebrating your progress look like for you?

ACKNOWLEDGMENTS

This book is a testament to the fact that no one accomplishes a vision alone. Writing and publishing this book was a journey full of moving parts, layers, and steps, and I am deeply grateful to everyone who supported me along the way.

First and foremost, I want to thank God, the giver of grace, wisdom, and revelation. Lord, this book exists because of You. Thank You for entrusting me with the privilege of stewarding the truths You poured into my heart. I'm not naturally a writer, but Your Holy Spirit guided me every step of the way—from structuring the chapters to providing examples that would resonate with readers. Thank You for being my source of strength and creativity, for giving me the capacity to complete this assignment, and for carrying me through when I felt overwhelmed. Every insight, every word, and every page is Your work through me. I'm merely the vessel You chose to use to bring this to life. Thank You, Lord, for the love and restoration that flows through Your Word. I owe everything I am to You, and I will always love You.

To my beloved husband, Tobi, I don't even know where to begin. Thank you for being my anchor, my encourager, and my greatest supporter. Your unwavering love, provision, and sacrifices made this journey possible. Thank you for believing in me, even in moments when I struggled to believe in myself. You're truly a gift from God, and I do not take you for granted. Thank you for working so hard to provide for our family, for giving me the space and time to fully focus on this book, and for stepping in when I needed you most. I'm grateful for every late night you spent reading my chapters and offering thoughtful feedback, for the way you see me through God's eyes, and for speaking life into my purpose. The grace and speed I experienced in writing this book were because of how well you stewarded this assignment alongside me. You truly are my best friend and my greatest blessing. I love you, baby.

To my incredible mother, Mama Uddie, I love you more than words can say. You are my forever hype woman, my prayer warrior, and my source of endless encouragement. Thank you for always believing in me and reminding me of God's promises over my life. You've been a pillar of support from the beginning, always cheering me on and pushing me to pursue my God-given dreams. Your love, prayers, and wisdom have been my foundation, and I'm forever grateful for you. I love you, Mama.

To my family and friends, thank you for being my tribe. Your love, encouragement, and support carried me through this journey. Thank you for celebrating every step—big or small—and for always believing in me. To my dear friend Anne-Loïs, thank you for being my accountability partner during those "Productivity Saturdays." Your feedback, encouragement, and excitement for this book meant the world to me. You're a true friend, and I'm grateful for you.

To the incredible professionals who helped bring this book to life— thank you for taking my vision and executing it so beautifully. Katherine, your meticulous editing and invaluable insights greatly enhanced the quality of my manuscript. Anze, your breathtaking cover design perfectly captured the heart of this book, and I am truly grateful for how you brought my vision to life. HMD Publishing, thank you for the stunning interior design and layout; your attention to detail made this book visually gorgeous. To the authors and ministers who graciously answered my many questions as a first-time author, thank you for your wisdom and generosity. You know who you are, and I am deeply appreciative.

Finally, to you—the reader—thank you for investing in this book and in your journey of transformation. I am deeply honored that you chose to hold this work in your hands. My prayer for you is that God will complete the good work He has started in your life and that this book will be a tool that draws you closer to Him.

With love and gratitude,
Ekemini

NOTES

Chapter One: What is Emotional Intelligence?

Google AI. (n.d.). *Definition of emotional intelligence*. Retrieved October 2024, from https://www.google.com

Galatians 5:22-23

Job 4:7-8

Chapter Two: Understanding Emotions

Gura, L. (n.d.). *Understanding emotions part 1* [Video]. YouTube. https://youtu.be/0j7dwG1cXc4

Psalm 23:4 (ESV)

Green, J. (2012). *The fault in our stars*. Dutton Books.

Philippians 4:8 (ESV)

Chapter Three: Debunking the Myths

Ephesians 4:26-27 (ESV)

Psalm 34:18 (NLT)

Chapter Four: Primary and Secondary Emotions

Genesis 4:1-16

Genesis 4:3-5 (NLT)

Genesis 4:8 (NLT)

Genesis 4:6-7 (NLT)

Chapter Five: Emotions: God's Gift to Us

Acts 2:38 (ESV)

1 Corinthians 12

1 John 4:18 (ESV)

Isaiah 61:3 (NKJV)

Romans 12:6-8

Philippians 4:7 (NKJV)

Psalm 42:11 (NIV)

Luke 6:45 (NIV)

Revelation 21:4 (NIV)

John 16:8 (ESV)

2 Corinthians 7:10 (NIV)

Chapter Six: The Most Emotionally Intelligent Man

John 8:58 (ESV)

Exodus 3:14

John 10:30 (ESV)

John 6:35 (ESV)

Matthew 4:3 (ESV)

Jeremiah 1:5 (ESV)

Matthew 26:39 (ESV)

Genesis 16:13 (NLT)

John 11:35 (ESV)

Mark 5:25-34 (ESV)

John 4:1-26

Luke 13:10-17

Matthew 9:10-13 (NIV)

Mark 2:1-12 (NIV)

John 17:20-23

John 13:1-17 (NIV)

Luke 22:24-27 (NIV)

John 21:15-17 (NIV)

Luke 23:34 (ESV)

Matthew 18:21-22 (ESV)

Mark 1:35 (NIV)

Luke 5:15-16 (NIV)

Mark 1:37-38 (NIV)

John 6:14-15

Luke 6:12-13

Mark 9:2-8

Matthew 26:36-39

Mark 3:31-35 (NIV)

John 5:1-15

Matthew 16:23 (ESV)

John 2:13-17 (NIV)

Mark 6:1-13

Matthew 10:14 (NIV)

Chapter Seven: Emotional Idolatry: Life After Eden

Genesis 1:26 (ESV)

Genesis 1:27 (ESV)

Genesis 2:18 (ESV)

Genesis 2:23 (NLT)

Genesis 2:25 (NLT)

Genesis 2:16-17 (NLT)

Genesis 3:1 (NLT)

Genesis 3:4-5 (NLT)

Genesis 3:6 (ESV)

Genesis 3:7 (NLT)

Genesis 3:10 (CSB)

Genesis 37

2 Samuel 11

John 18:10

Genesis 4:7 (NLT)

Proverbs 4:23 (NLT)

Proverbs 23:7 (NKJV)

2 Corinthians 10:5 (ESV)

Philippians 4:13 (NKJV)

Proverbs 18:21 (NKJV)

Matthew 6:14-15 (ESV)

Psalm 139:14 (ESV)

Jeremiah 29:11 (ESV)

Ecclesiastes 5:3 (NLT)

Genesis 37:5-10

Genesis 41

Daniel 2

Daniel 4

Matthew 1:20

Matthew 2:13

Matthew 13:25 (NKJV)

Psalm 4:8 (NLT)

Isaiah 54:17 (NKJV)

2 Timothy 1:7 (NKJV)

1 Corinthians 6:19-20

Ephesians 6:12 (KJV)

Furtick, S. (2018, August 6). *Need meters* [Video]. YouTube. Elevation Church. https://www.youtube.com/watch?v=xDlwuDRLVoE

Psalm 7:11 (NKJV)

Ephesians 4:26-27 (ESV)

1 Samuel 18:10

2 Timothy 1:7 (NLT)

Chapter Eight: Emotional Healing

Romans 7:22-24 (NLT)

Jeremiah 1:4-5 (NLT)

Jeremiah 1:6 (NLT)

Jeremiah 1:7-8 (NLT)

Psalm 147:3 (NKJV)

Matthew 11:28 (NLT)

National Domestic Violence Hotline. (n.d.). *What is emotional abuse?* The Hotline. Retrieved December 2024, from https://www.thehotline.org/resources/what-is-emotional-abuse/

Healthdirect Australia. (n.d.). *Emotional abuse.* Retrieved December 2024, from https://www.healthdirect.gov.au/emotional-abuse#what-is

Isaiah 61:1-3

Romans 12:2

Luke 10:19

Ephesians 6:12

Luke 23:34 (ESV)

Exodus 20:5-6

Galatians 3:13

Proverbs 18:21

Chapter Nine: The Art of Stewarding Your Emotions

1 Corinthians 10:26 (ESV)

Romans 14:12 (ESV)

2 Corinthians 5:10 (ESV)

Genesis 1:28 (ESV)

Matthew 25:14-30

Philippians 2:14 (NLT)

Matthew 25:16 (ESV)

1 Corinthians 6:19 (ESV)

Mark 12:28-31 (ESV)

Oxford Languages. (n.d.). *Definition of gossip*. Retrieved December 2024, from https://www.google.com

Proverbs 16:28 (NLT)

Proverbs 26:20 (NLT)

Matthew 18:15-16 (ESV)

Proverbs 18:8 (CSB)

Matthew 28:16-20

2 Corinthians 12:9 (ESV)

James 1:19 (NIV)

Chapter Ten: A Letter for the Journey Ahead

Goodreads. (n.d.). Maya Angelou quotes. Retrieved December 2024, from https://www.goodreads.com/quotes/1274-people-will-forget-what-you-said-people-will-forget-what

Ezekiel 36:26 (NLT)

Hosea 2:13 (NLT)

ABOUT THE AUTHOR

Ekemini Ogunsola is a disciple, author, podcaster, passionate communicator, and faith-based emotional intelligence coach. She is the creator and host of *The Yellow Podcast*, where she delves into topics on personal development, faith, and emotional wellness.

With a bachelor's degree in Communication and Social Influence, Ekemini brings a strong background in strategic communications and extensive expertise in emotional intelligence. Through her coaching practice, she empowers individuals to navigate conflict, set boundaries, improve relationships, and experience emotional healing using practical strategies grounded in biblical wisdom.

Ekemini serves in the prayer ministry, small group ministry, and inner healing and deliverance ministry at her local church, helping others break free from emotional bondage and embrace their God-given purpose. She lives in Philadelphia with her husband, Tobi, and enjoys hosting game nights, taking long walks, and engaging in meaningful conversations.

You can connect with Ekemini on Instagram @kemxvi.